How To Survive Teaching Health

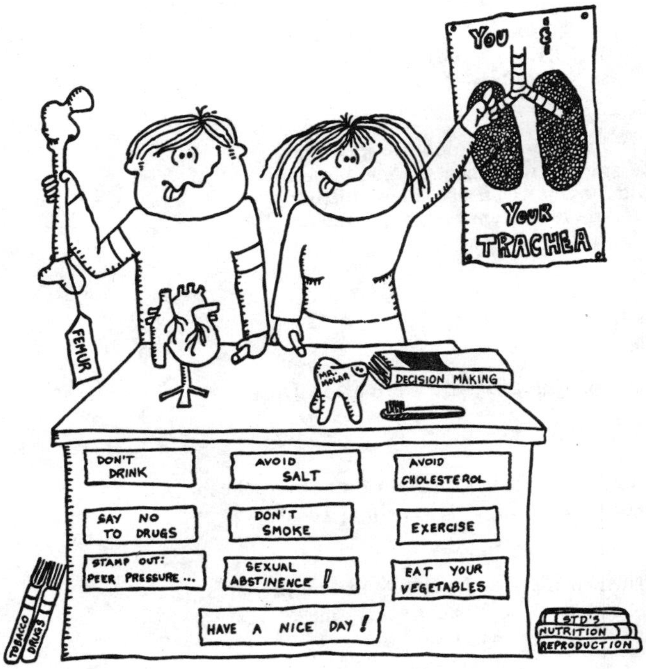

Games, Activities, and Worksheets for Grades 4-12

Illustrated by
Patricia Rizzo Toner

Kenneth G. Tillman, PH.D.
Patricia Rizzo Toner, M.ED.

PARKER PUBLISHING COMPANY
West Nyack, New York 10995

Library of Congress Cataloging-in-Publication Data

Tillman, Kenneth G.
How to survive teaching health: games, activities, and worksheets for grades 4–12 / Kenneth G. Tillman, Patricia Rizzo Toner.
p. cm.
ISBN 0-13-425174-1
1. Health education (Elementary) 2. Health education (Secondary)
3. Activity programs in education. 4. Educational games.
I. Toner, Patricia Rizzo, 1952– . II. Title.
LB1587.A3T55 1990
613′.0712—dc20
89-49290
CIP

10 9 8 7 6 5 4 3

ISBN 0-13-425174-1

PARKER PUBLISHING COMPANY
BUSINESS & PROFESSIONAL DIVISION
A division of Simon & Schuster
West Nyack, New York 10995

PRINTED IN THE UNITED STATES OF AMERICA

Dedication

I wish to dedicate this book to Rotary International for its leadership, and to Rotarians throughout the world for their involvement in improving the health, safety, and well-being of children. This interest has been highlighted by the Rotary PolioPlus program, which is designed to eradicate polio, as well as measles, diphtheria, tetanus, whooping cough, and tuberculosis. Rotary has pledged money, and even more importantly, person-power to achieve this goal. Too often, people in the industrialized countries forget that these diseases still kill over three million children annually and cripple an equal number. Rotary is to be commended for being the first private, voluntary organization, with its scope and influence, to enter into the war for child survival. As an indication of the commitment of Rotarians, the original pledge of $120 million given in 1985 on the occasion of the 40th anniversary of the United Nations had by 1989 resulted in contributions and pledges of over $230 million. Rotary has provided an important impetus to the immunization programs of organizations such as the World Health Organization (WHO), the Pan American Health Organization (PAHO), and the United Nations International Children's Emergency Fund (UNICEF).

Kenneth G. Tillman

I wish to dedicate this book to Dr. Patricia Morris, Dr. Lillian Wright ("Tiger Lil"), and to Dr. Ken Tillman, three of many professors at Trenton State College who gave me the support and encouragement needed to pursue a career in HPE.

Patricia Rizzo Toner

Acknowledgments

To Dee Tillman for typing the manuscript and providing continual support as the book evolved from a concept through countless hours of research, writing, and rewriting.

To Jeanne Cortina and Stephanie Schmitter for their support and willingness to pitch in when needed during the writing process.

To the graduate students of Trenton State College, who have shown time and time again that health teachers are creative.

To the Health and Physical Education staff of the Council Rock School District, who developed some of the activities and successfully used them in their classes:

Bill Mauro, Dist. Coord.	Linda Goldman	Judy Byrne
Wendy Armour	Barbara Synder	Steve Harnish
Larry Jerrom	Mike Flaherty	Bill Hoffman
Joan Levin Scott	Jim Dunn	Ed McHugh
Dr. Konnie McCaffree	Errol Faunce	Theresa Kulpinski
Cynthia Romanowski	John Gerney	Steve Androstus
Russ VanCamp	Jim Muldowney	Bill Watts
Rich White	Yvonne Puryear	Larry Hess
Marian Milliken	Sandi Wiggins	
Colleen Bradley	Marilyn Gerney	

To Council Rock students Stacy Kennedy and Andrea Bezark for the use of their "Health Rap."

About The Authors

Kenneth G. Tillman, Ph.D., is currently professor of Health, Physical Education and Recreation and Director of International Education at Trenton State College, Trenton, NJ. He has held several administrative, coaching, and teaching positions. He is co-author, with Ms. Toner, of two highly popular physical education books: *What Are We Doing in Gym Today?* and *You'll Never Guess What We Did in Gym Today!* He has also authored a physical education administration book and two wrestling books, as well as numerous articles and chapters in other books. He has written physical education curricula for several schools and served as a consultant for curriculum development.

Patricia Rizzo Toner, M.Ed., has taught Health and Physical Education in the Council Rock School District, Holland, PA, for over 16 years and she has also coached gymnastics and field hockey. She is the co-author with Dr. Tillman of two books: *What Are We Doing in Gym Today?* and *You'll Never Guess What We Did in Gym Today!* Besides her work as a teacher, Pat is also a freelance cartoonist. A member of the American Alliance of Health, Physical Education, Recreation and Dance, Pat received the Hammond Service Award, the Marianna G. Packer Book Award and was named to Who's Who among Students in American Colleges and Universities, as well as Who's Who in American Education.

About This Resource

Every teacher can use a new idea. *How to Survive Teaching Health* brings you not one, but hundreds of ideas you can use to make your health classes come alive. These activities have all been enthusiastically received by students of all ages.

How to Survive Teaching Health is for busy teachers who are looking for ways to keep their health classes exciting. It places in your hands a comprehensive collection of over 200 high-interest health education activities, all organized for easy use. Following Unit 1, which contains games and techniques you can adapt to any subject or use as-is, you'll find a multitude of ready-to-use materials and activities specifically designed to teach about:

- Coping with change
- Physical fitness
- Nutrition
- Grooming
- Consumer health
- Human growth and development
- Substance abuse prevention
- Body systems
- Diseases and disorders
- Safety and accident prevention
- Environmental health
- Health-related careers

You may wish to "pick and choose" activities from the 13 units in this book, or follow them more systematically. Among other features, you'll find more than 80 pages that are fully reproducible for easy incorporation into your lesson plans. Activities employ board games, TV game show-type competitions, peer teaching, booklet writing, surveying, model making, simulations, videotaping and many other lively techniques you can use on an individual, group, or whole-class basis. The approach throughout is upbeat, with lighthearted cartoons to entertain you and an emphasis on helping students to make healthy choices for themselves and their families.

Motivating students in a required health class isn't always easy, but with this book you'll have a whole new "bag of tricks" to keep students interested and learning. We hope it will help you not only to survive, but to *love* teaching health!

Kenneth G. Tillman

Patricia Rizzo Toner

Contents

UNIT 1

LIGHTS, CAMERA, ACTION!

Games & Activities Adaptable To Any Unit

This unit provides examples of games and activities that are easily synchronized with health topics. Remember that each game and activity can be redesigned for any health topic that is being covered. Use the examples, make some modifications, and the students will look forward to your next creative activity.

Board games are particularly easy to create. Using a ditto master or photocopied sheets of paper, a simple board game can be constructed for any unit. First, draw a pathway of blocks or circles on the ditto or master sheet. Fill in the pathway with appropriate instructions. Perhaps add a few cartoons, and you are ready to go. Run off enough copies so that groups of four to five can play. When finished, the sheets can be discarded. (Instructions for a more permanent set-up are also provided.)

The following activity demonstrates a sample game called Disease Detectors, which can be used to review knowledge of present-day diseases and disorders as well as diseases that "plagued" our ancestors. Keep in mind that games can be changed to fit any unit or grade level. Feel free to modify them to suit your particular needs.

Activity 1. Disease Detectors (Constructing a Board Game)

Concept/Description: While attempting to answer questions dealing with knowledge of disease cause and prevention, players will reinforce their knowledge, as well as accumulate points towards winning the game.

Game Objective: To be the player with the most points after all players have finished.

Materials Needed:

For each group of 4–5:

- 1 dittoed game board
- 1 die (can be purchased at a toy store, 5&10, etc.)
- 1 pencil per person
- 1 set of question cards
- 1 set of chance cards
- 1 sheet of notebook paper
- 1 large shipping envelope to hold materials
- 1 answer key (follows the section on directions)

Note that materials can be as simple or as elaborate as you care to make them. For instance, you could laminate the game sheets and cards to reuse them or use index cards in different sizes or colors to distinguish chance cards from question cards. Bingo chips with letters, numbers, or symbols written on them with a permanent marker pen can be used as playing pieces.

Directions: Each group of 4–5 students is given a packet (envelope) containing a die, game sheet, chance cards, and question cards.

1. Place all chance cards and question cards face down in their respective piles.
2. Appoint one member per group as the scorekeeper. This person places each player's name at the top of a sheet of notebook paper and places a total of 50 points under each name. The scorekeeper will keep track of all points for all players. (See Figure 1-1.)

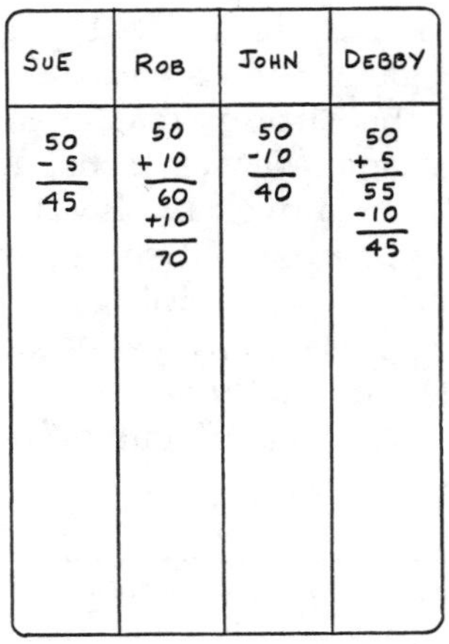

SUE
ROB
JOHN
DEBBY
50
- 5
45
50
+ 10
60
+10
70
50
-10
40
50
+ 5
55
-10
45

Fig. 1-1. Scorekeeping for Disease Detectors.

3. Each player chooses a simple symbol, letter, or number that he or she will pencil in at the starting block. Bingo chips may also be used as previously described, but we've found it easier to have students roll the die and lightly pencil in their symbol on the appropriate block. (This eliminates hitting the game board and sending the pieces flying:) After each roll of the die, students would gently erase their previous mark.
4. The teacher (or an appointed student) is the answer keeper and should sit in an easily accessible spot.
5. As play proceeds, the scorekeeper for each group adds and subtracts points as indicated by the cards or the game board. NOTE: Points received from other players must be subtracted from one score and added to the recipient's. For example, if Sue lands on a space that instructs her to "Give All Players 5 Points," the scorekeeper must subtract 5 times the number of players in the group from Sue's score. Then the scorekeeper adds 5 points to all other scores.
   If, however, Rob lands on "Lose 15 Points," then 15 points are subtracted from his score and given to an "imaginary bank." Since the "bank" total isn't tabulated, nothing occurs. In other words, the "bank" has unlimited funds—A problem we'd all like to encounter!

Disease Detectors Rules for Play

1. Roll the die and move the number of spaces indicated.
2. Land on XXX and you must Start Over. You do not receive an additional 50 points, however.
3. Land on the happy face and you may Roll Again.
4. If you land in the hospital, you must roll a 1, 3, or 5 to get out—unless you hold the "Get out of Hospital Free" card. Turn that card in on your next turn and roll as before.
5. Land on (?) and you must choose a question card (small card). Read your card silently and check the answer with the answer keeper (who will have the key). Go by the number on the card.
6. If the answer is correct, the scorekeeper will add 10 points to your score; if incorrect, 10 points will be subtracted.
7. At any time, you may forfeit *one* turn, take a Chance Card (large card) and follow the directions. This may be done by each player only *once* per game.
8. If you are the *first* player to finish the game, add 20 points to your score, but you must continue to collect or pay points when indicated.
9. The winner is the player with the *most* points after *all* the players have finished.

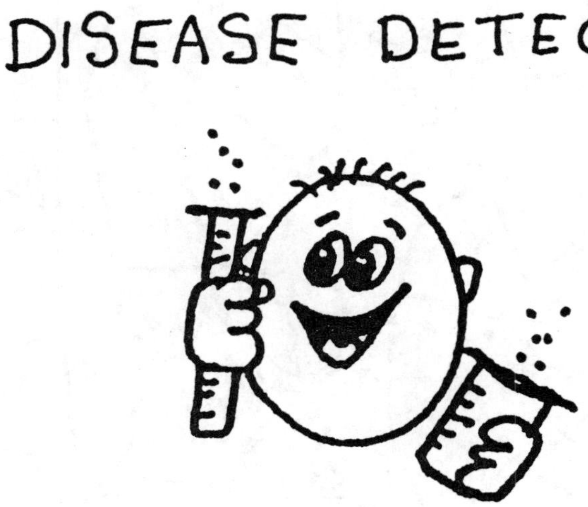

Disease Detectors Game Board

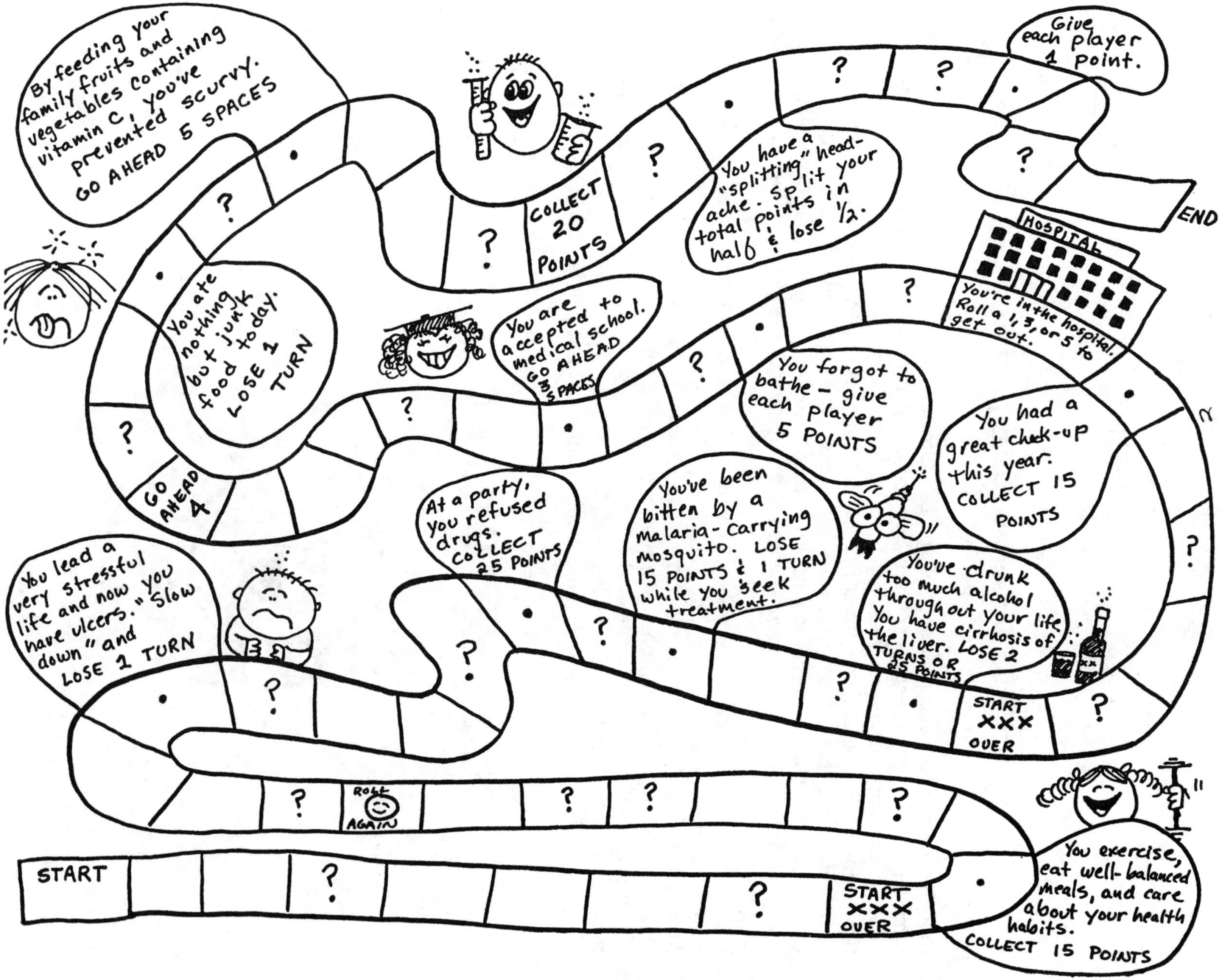

Disease Detectors Question Cards

James just moved to Philadelphia. It's 1793 and a mosquito has bitten him . . .

1

Robert hasn't eaten in weeks. His stomach is swollen and his skin is rough . . .

2

Christopher's gums are bleeding. He's been given a lemon to help . . .

3

Sarah doesn't get enough sunlight or vitamin D. Now her bones are weak . . .

4

William has been bitten by an infected flea . . .

5

Stephen just drank contaminated water . . .

6

Mary's been bitten by a mosquito. Her liver is failing and she has a high fever . . .

7

Shakeel lives in the far east. His heart is failing and he needs vitamin B . . .

8

Jane has a fungus infection. Her feet burn and itch . . .

9

Jean has <u>one</u> of many infections <u>caused</u> by a virus . . .

10

Susan stepped on a nail. Her neck muscles are stiff . . .

11

Charles has severe stomach pains because he worries a lot . . .

12

Disease Detectors Question Cards

Diane sneezes when she's around cat hair, dust, pollen, etc. . . .

(13)

Richard's arteries are clogged with fatty deposits . . .

(14)

Abby has severe lung irritation and sometimes coughs, wheezes, and has shortness of breath

(15)

Joseph has an inflamed and swollen liver from using a contaminated needle . . .

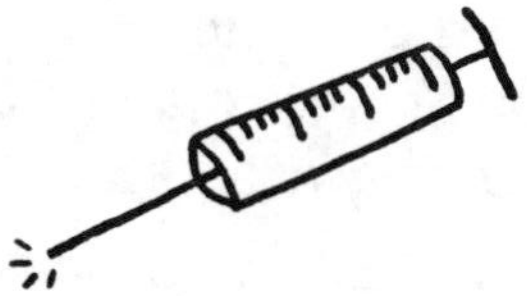

(16)

Dexter has constant high blood pressure . . .

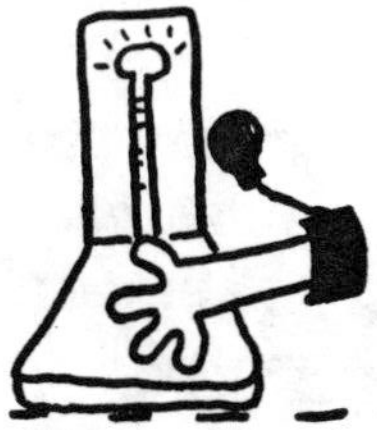

(17)

Thomas has an inflammation of the membranes around the brain and spinal cord . . .

(18)

Margaret has a very contagious eye infection also called "pink eye" . . .

(19)

Wesley has a fever, sore throat, nausea, chills and is weak. His problem is also called the "kissing disease" . . .

(20)

Mrs. Brown has a disease characterized by the abnormal growth and spread of cells . . .

(21)

Ronald has a genetic disease in which his blood doesn't clot properly . . .

(22)

Mr. Smith has cancer of the white blood cells . . .

(23)

Henry has a deadly disease which is also called A.I.D.S. . . .

(24)

Disease Detectors Question Cards

Mr. Johnson has suffered from a blood vessel clot in his brain . . .

25

Sharon's disease causes a build-up of thick mucus in the lungs and affects the sweat and other glands.

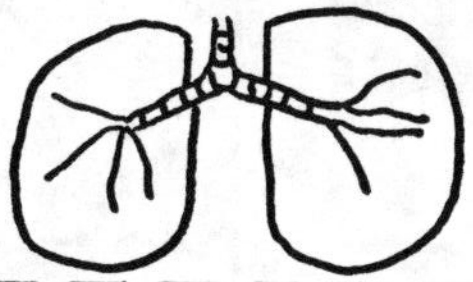

26

Colleen has an infection of the tonsils and has severe throat pain . . .

27

Mrs. Jones has a disease that causes a gradual weakening and atrophy of some muscles . . .

28

FREE CARD

ADVANCE 10 SPACES

OR COLLECT

10 POINTS

29

GET OUT

OF HOSPITAL

FREE

SAVE THIS CARD, YOU MAY NEED IT OR

TURN IN FOR 15 POINTS

30

Disease Detectors Chance Cards

CHANCE

COLLECT 10 POINTS
FROM EACH PLAYER

CHANCE

COLLECT 30 POINTS
FROM THE BANK

CHANCE

PAY 5 POINTS TO EACH
PLAYER

CHANCE

START OVER
OR
LOSE ½ OF YOUR POINTS

CHANCE

ROLL THE DIE.
COLLECT 10 TIMES THE
AMOUNT SHOWN ON
THE DIE.

CHANCE

DOUBLE YOUR MONEY
OR POINTS

CHANCE

START OVER

CHANCE

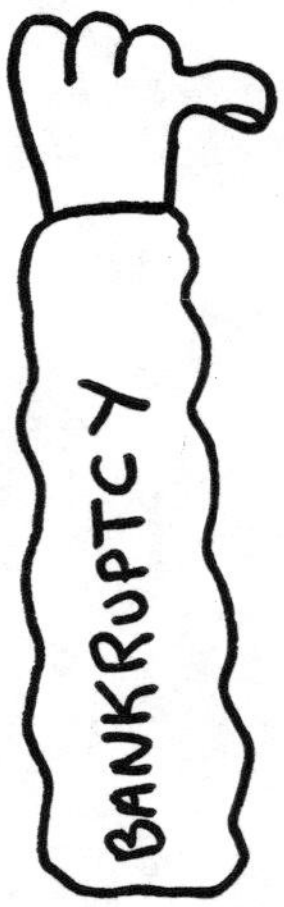

LOSE ALL YOUR MONEY

Answer Key:

1. Yellow Fever
2. Malnutrition, Famine, Starvation
3. Scurvy
4. Rickets
5. Plague
6. Cholera
7. Malaria
8. Beri-Beri
9. Athlete's Foot
10. Cold, Flu, Chicken Pox, Measles
11. Tetanus
12. Ulcer
13. Allergies
14. Atherosclerosis
15. Asthma
16. Hepatitis
17. Hypertension
18. Meningitis
19. Conjunctivitis
20. Mononucleosis
21. Cancer
22. Hemophilia
23. Leukemia
24. Acquired Immune Deficiency Syndrome
25. Stroke
26. Cystic Fibrosis
27. Tonsillitis
28. Muscular Dystrophy
29. (FREE CARD)
30. (GET OUT OF HOSPITAL FREE CARD)

Activity 2. Jeopardy (Group and Individual)

The idea behind this old favorite, adapted from the TV game, is to look at or listen to the answers and try to come up with the questions. Use it in the classroom as a test review or just to reinforce knowledge of material. Although it can be played many ways, we have included two fairly simple methods. The first is for large group play, and the second is an individual or small group (2–3) game.

Group Jeopardy:

Concept/Description: Students will use their familiarity with the TV game of *Jeopardy* to review information learned in class or from out of class assignments.

Game Objective: To score the most points by successfully coming up with questions to fit given answers.

Materials Needed:

Question/Answer key
Chalkboard
Chalk
Eraser

Directions:

1. Draw the categories and point values on the board for all to see (Figure 1-2).
2. Divide the class into two groups and allow each group to choose a spokesperson who will confer with the group and give the "answer" in question form. (Usually, 15 seconds is the time allotted to answer.)

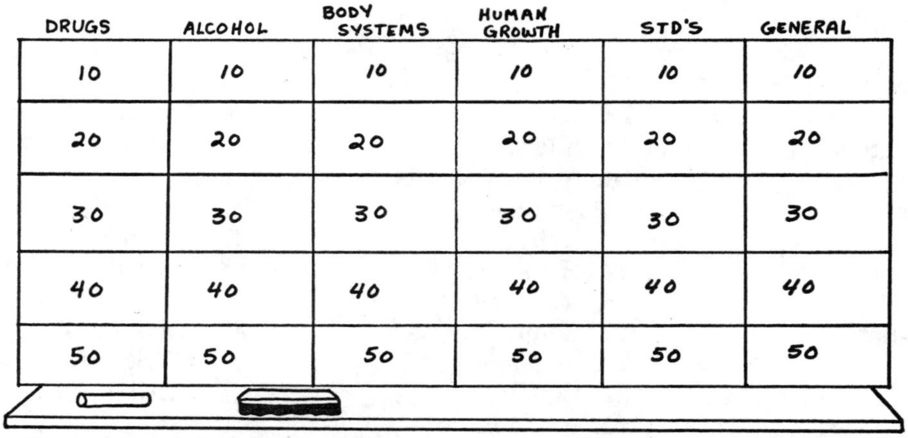

Fig. 1-2. Jeopardy chalkboard set-up.

3. Play proceeds as follows: Group A chooses a category and a point value (higher point values are the more difficult questions). For example, Group A may choose "Alcohol for 30." From the answer key, the teacher would read, "The organ responsible for oxidizing alcohol." The group confers and the spokesperson says, "What is the liver?" The teacher informs group members that they are correct and awards Team A 30 points while erasing that category and point value from the grid. It is now Group B's turn.
4. If Group B is incorrect on its turn, the point total is deducted from B's score (some scores go into negative numbers), but the category remains open. Play goes to Group A, and members of Group A may choose that same question or a new one.
5. To keep both groups interested and involved, alternate play from Group A to B regardless of correct or incorrect answers.
6. Continue play until all categories are used.
7. Remember, answers must be in question form to count. (For younger grades, you may wish to modify the format.)

NOTE: It is desirable to make several copies of the answer key and cross off categories on your sheet, as well as on the board. This makes for easy reference and avoids discrepancies.

Individual Jeopardy:

Game Objective: To score the most points by successfully coming up with questions to fit given answers.

Materials Needed:

Pens or pencils
Game sheets
Answer key

Directions:

1. Give each person or small group of 2–3 a Systems Jeopardy game sheet.

2. On the teacher's signal, the individuals or groups attempt to fill in the blocks with the correct questions. (You may wish to allow the use of notes.)
3. If you do not wish to make this competitive, simply collect the finished sheets and total the points for each category.
4. To make this a competitive game, you may wish to do the following:
   (a) Set a time limit by putting times on the board with bonus point values. For example, if the paper is finished between 1:15 and 1:30 and *all* answers are correct, the winners get 10 bonus points; if finished between 1:30–1:45, the winners get 8 points, etc. If answers are incorrect, they must keep trying until all are correct. NOTE: Be sure to have an answer key readily available.
   (b) Rather than a time limit, give the first paper turned in with *all* answers correct 20 points. The second gets 15 points; the third gets 10 points, etc. Anyone who finishes with all correct answers gets 5 points.

Activity 3. Tic-Tac-Toe

Concept/Description: A common childhood activity is used as the format for reinforcing health concepts and facts. Any level of difficulty can be incorporated into this activity.

Game Objective: To win the most rounds of Tic-Tac-Toe by answering questions correctly and placing "X" 's and "O" 's strategically.

Materials Needed:

Questions (See sample questions.)
Chalkboard
Chalk
Eraser

Directions

1. Draw a large Tic-Tac-Toe grid on the board. Place an "X" to one side of the grid and an "O" to the other (Figure **1-3**).

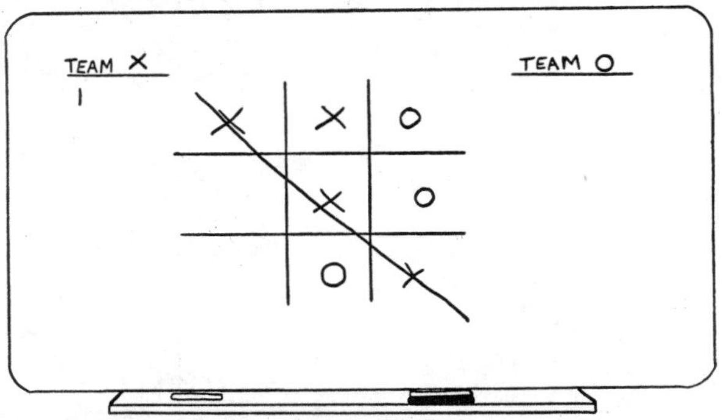

Fig. 1-3. Set-up for Tic-Tac-Toe.

Group Jeopardy Answer Key
(for Junior and Senior High Grades)

		DRUGS	ALCOHOL	BODY SYSTEMS	HUMAN GROWTH	STD'S	GENERAL
10 pts.	Q	What are stimulants?	What is a depressant?	What is the circulatory system?	What is a sperm cell?	What are sexually transmitted diseases?	What are flashbacks?
	A	Drugs that speed up the body.	The type of drug alcohol is.	System that carries O_2 and food to cells	Male sex cell.	What STD stands for.	Hallucinations years after an hallucinogenic drug has been taken.
20 pts.	Q	What are narcotics?	What is cirrhosis?	What are the kidneys?	What is menstruation?	What is abstinence?	What is heroin?
	A	Drugs derived from the opium poppy	Disease of the liver due to alcohol.	Organs in the excretory system that filter the blood.	Occurs when an egg isn't fertilized.	Most certain way not to contract an STD.	A derivative of morphine thought to cure morphine addiction.
30 pts.	Q	What is alcohol?	What is the liver?	What are the mouth, esophagus, stomach, small and large intestines?	What are the Fallopian tubes?	What is a virus?	What are the ELISA and the Western Blot tests?
	A	Most abused drug in the U.S.A.	The organ that oxidizes alcohol.	5 major organs of digestion.	Where fertilization occurs.	Type of pathogen that AIDS is.	2 tests for the presence of the AIDS virus.
40 pts.	Q	What is phencyclidine?	What is Alcoholics Anonymous? (AA)	What is the nervous system?	What is breech birth?	What is hepatitis?	What is a Caesarian section?
	A	Angel dust or PCP's proper name.	An organization that helps alcoholics recover.	System that controls all others.	Baby born feet or buttocks first.	A liver infection often NOT acquired sexually.	Baby born by surgical incision in the uterus.
50 pts.	Q	What is psilocybin?	What are absorption, distribution, oxidation, and elimination?	What is the endocrine system?	What is a hysterectomy?	What is candidiasis?	What is the gall bladder?
	A	Mushrooms that are chewed to produce hallucinations.	The 4 processes alcohol goes through in the body.	System of glands that produce hormones.	Surgical removal of the uterus.	A common vaginal yeast infection.	Organ that stores bile produced by the liver.

Name ______________________ Date ______________ (1-7)

Systems Jeopardy

Directions: Shown below are ANSWERS.
Place the proper question in the box above the answer.

	DIGESTIVE	CIRCULATORY	NERVOUS	RESPIRATORY	ENDO/EXC
10 pts.	?				
	A Churns and mixes food with acids.	The number of chambers in the human heart.	The name for a nerve cell.	The name for the wind pipe.	The organs that filter the blood.
20 pts.	?				
	A A tube from the mouth to the stomach.	The heart's *upper* chambers.	The three major organs of the nervous system.	The two main organs of breathing.	The hormone produced by the pancreas.
30 pts.	?				
	A The gastric juice secreted by the mouth.	The heart's *lower* chambers.	A type of nerve that orders movement.	The two gases exchanged while breathing.	The two glands that give an "energy boost" during emergencies.
40 pts.	?				
	A The five major organs of this system.	The three types of blood cells.	The three parts of the brain.	The name of the air sacs in the lungs.	The organ that holds and stores urine.
50 pts.	?				
	A The finger-like tubes in the small intestines.	The clear fluid blood cells float in.	The difference between nerve cells and other kinds of cells.	The flap of skin over the trachea that keeps out food.	The organs that produce estrogen and egg cells.

Systems Jeopardy Answer Key

		DIGESTIVE	CIRCULATORY	NERVOUS	RESPIRATORY	ENDO/EXC
10 pts.		What is the stomach?	What is four?	What is a neuron?	What is the trachea?	What are the kidneys?
	A	Churns and mixes food with acids.	The number of chambers in the human heart.	The name for a nerve cell.	The name for the wind pipe.	The organs that filter the blood.
20 pts.		What is the esophagus?	What are the atria?	What are the brain, spinal cord and nerves?	What are the lungs?	What is insulin?
	A	A tube from the mouth to the stomach.	The heart's *upper* chambers.	The three major organs of the nervous system.	The two main organs of breathing.	The hormone produced by the pancreas.
30 pts.		What is saliva?	What are the ventricles?	What is a motor nerve?	What are CO_2 and O_2?	What are the adrenal glands?
	A	The gastric juice secreted by the mouth.	The heart's *lower* chambers.	A type of nerve that orders movement.	The two gases exchanged while breathing.	The two glands that give an "energy boost" during emergencies.
40 pts.		What are the mouth, esophagus, stomach, small & large intestines?	What are red, white, and platelets?	What are the cerebrum, cerebellum and medulla?	What are the alveoli?	What is the bladder?
	A	The five major organs of this system.	The three types of blood cells.	The three parts of the brain.	The name of the air sacs in the lungs.	The organ that holds and stores urine.
50 pts.		What are the villi?	What is plasma?	What is "they cannot repair themselves when damaged"?	What is the epiglottis?	What are the ovaries?
	A	The finger-like tubes in the small intestines.	The clear fluid blood cells float in.	The difference between nerve cells and other kinds of cells.	The flap of skin over the trachea that keeps out food.	The organs that produce estrogen and egg cells.

2. Divide the class into two teams, X and O. Further divide each team into four equal groups numbered 1–4.
3. Ask Group #1 of team X (X1) a question. If, after conferring with the other members of X1, the group answers correctly, one member of X1 draws an "X" on the Tic-Tac-Toe grid in any position the group wants.
4. Play proceeds to Group #1 of O team (O1). If correct, a group member draws an "O" on the grid. Group X2 goes next, then O2, and so on.
5. If a question is answered incorrectly by either group, the other group must then attempt to answer the same question. This is considered a bonus because, whether correct or incorrect, the second group still gets their next move.
6. Play continues until one team has Tic-Tac-Toe (three "X" 's or three "O" 's horizontally, vertically, or diagonally) or until a stalemate occurs.
7. After Tic-Tac-Toe, the winning team receives a slash mark for winning the round, and a new round begins. Be sure to alternate which team starts each round.

   NOTE: This activity is a great way to reinforce playground rules, classroom rules, safety in the lunchroom, hallways, etc. You could also hold up various signs or symbols such as a stop sign, railroad crossing sign, poison symbol, etc., and ask students what they mean or say.

Sample Questions (for an Elementary Safety Unit):

1. What should you always do before crossing a street? (Look both ways.)
2. If a stranger offers you candy, what should you do? (Say "No," run away, tell an adult.)
3. What should you do if your clothing catches on fire? (Stop, drop, and roll.)
4. How should you carry scissors? (With the point facing downward.)
5. What is the proper behavior for a fire drill? (Walk quietly and in a straight line to the playground area.)

Activity 4. Blackjack

Concept/Description: The game of Blackjack is played with questions on selected health topics used as a basis for receiving cards.

Game Objective: To win the most games of Blackjack by forcing an opponent to go over 21, or by getting 21.

Materials Needed:

A deck of cards (extra large decks work well)
Chalkboard
Chalk
Questions (See sample questions.)
Eraser
Something to make cards visible to the class (chalkboard, ledge, music stand, easel, etc.)

Directions:

1. Divide the class into Groups A and B.
2. Further divide the groups into equal parts numbered 1–4.
3. Shuffle the cards and give each group one card, face up.
4. Team A, group #1 (A1), goes first, followed by B1, then A2, and so on.
5. Ask A1 a question. Group members have 10 seconds to confer with the other members of A1 and then give their answer. If the answer is correct, they get another card face up.
6. Once a team has *two* cards face up, it may begin to pass cards to the opponent's team on its turn in an effort to throw the opponent over 21. The team may also keep the cards and attempt to reach 21 itself.
7. If a group goes over 21, the opposing team gets a slash mark for winning the round, and the next round begins.
8. If a team reaches 21, it automatically wins the round and receives 2 slash marks. If 21 is reached with just 2 cards, the team receives 3 slash marks (Figure 1-4).
9. The team with the most slash marks (points) at the end of the game is the winner. Be sure to alternate which team starts each round.

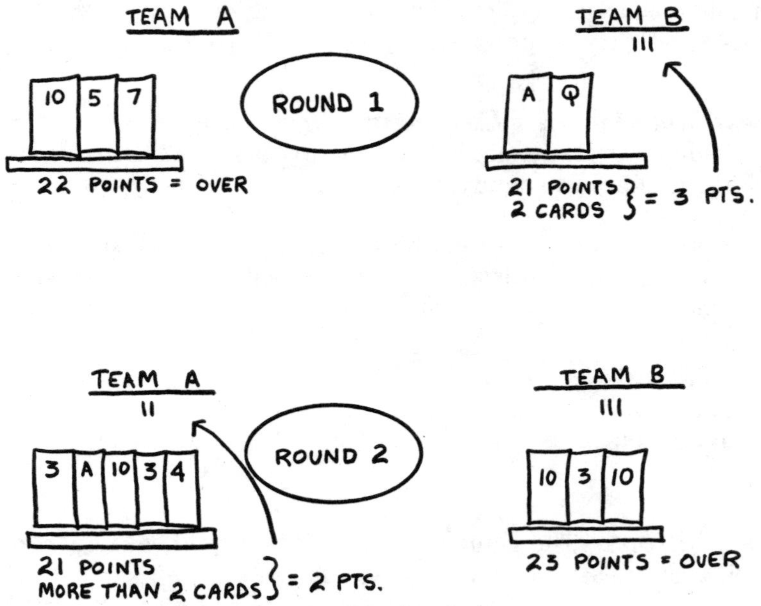

Fig. 1-4. Team scoring for Blackjack.

Sample Questions (for a Junior/Senior High Unit on Substance Abuse):

1. Name the drug category that speeds up the body systems. (Stimulants)
2. Name the drug category that slows down the body systems. (Depressants)
3. Name the drug that comes from the Indian hemp plant and is smoked or eaten. (Marijuana)
4. What drug is most abused in the U.S.? (Alcohol)
5. What drug is an animal tranquilizer that was taken off the market because it caused undesirable side effects in animals? (PCP, angel dust, phencyclidine)
6. Name the organ responsible for oxidizing alcohol. (Liver)

7. Name the four processes alcohol goes through in the human body. (Absorption, distribution, oxidation, elimination)
8. Name a place that an alcoholic can go to get help with his or her disease. (Alcoholics Anonymous)
9. Name a place a teenager who has a relationship with an alcoholic can go for assistance. (Alateen)
10. What is the name of the expensive stimulant that has caused some people to die by causing heart problems? (Cocaine)

Activity 5. Trash Can Basketball

Concept/Description: A physical skill—shooting a basket—is incorporated into a game in which students give their answers to health-related questions. Combining a mental and physical task serves to focus the students on health-related issues.

Game Objective: To score the most points by answering questions correctly and making "baskets."

Materials Needed:

Questions (See sample questions.)
Chalkboard
Eraser
Trash can or container
3 small foam balls or 3 paper wads

Directions:

1. Set the trash can or container about 10 feet from the balls or paper wads.
2. Divide the class into two equal teams, A and B.
3. Ask one group a health-related question. One person is to answer. (Set up a rotation so a different team member answers each time.)
4. If the answer is correct, the team receives 1 point, *plus* the person who answered gets a shot at the basket. If the shot goes in, the team receives an additional point.
5. Play then proceeds to the opponents.
6. Continue until time is up. The team with the most points is the winner.
NOTE: If a team answers correctly but misses the shot, it still receives the point for answering correctly. If team answers incorrectly, it does not attempt a shot.

Fig. 1-5. Set-up for Trash Can Basketball.

Variations:

1. Use questions with one-, two-, and three-part answers. If they are answered correctly, the person receives 1 point *plus* 1, 2, or 3 shots. If, for example, a three-part answer is required and the student can only answer two parts, you may treat it as an incorrect answer. With younger children, you may wish to give partial credit and allow them a shot.
2. A team member must shoot a basket before the team is permitted to answer a question.
3. Give two points for answering the question if the basket is made.

Sample Questions (for Various Ages and Topics):

One-Part Questions:

1. Name the bone that protects the brain. (Skull)
2. How many bones are in the human body? (About 206)
3. Which female reproductive organ produces egg cells? (The ovaries)
4. What hormone is produced by the ovaries? (Estrogen)
5. When a fertilized egg cell splits in two, what occurs? (Identical twins)

Two-Part Questions:

1. Name two drugs that are depressants. (Alcohol, barbiturates, heroin, etc.)
2. Name two hallucinogens. (PCP, LSD, DMT, psilocybin, etc.)
3. Name two eating disorders. (Anorexia nervosa and bulimia)
4. Name two diseases of the circulatory system. (Atherosclerosis, hemophilia, hypertension, leukemia, etc.)
5. Name two diseases of the digestive system. (Colitis, ulcer, colon cancer, etc.)

Three-Part Questions:

1. Name the three types of blood cells. (Red, white, and platelets)
2. Name the three parts of the brain. (Cerebellum, cerebrum, and medulla oblongata.
3. Name the three things you must do to safely lose weight. (Eat less, maintain a balanced diet, and exercise)

4. Name three health-related professionals. (Surgeon, nurse, doctor, podiatrist, ophthalmologist, etc.)
5. Name three sexually transmitted diseases. (chlamydia, pelvic inflammatory disease, syphilis, gonorrhea, herpes, etc.)

Activity 6. Family Feud

Concept/Description: Using the TV *Family Feud* game-show format, the students are challenged to give the best answers to a series of health questions relating to topics covered in class.

Game Objective: To have two "families" compete in answering health questions. The family with the most points at the end of all the rounds is the successful family.

Materials Needed:

Stapler (staples removed)
Chalkboard
Chalk
Eraser
Answer key (See sample questions.)

Directions:

1. Draw the game board on the chalkboard as shown in Figure 1-6.

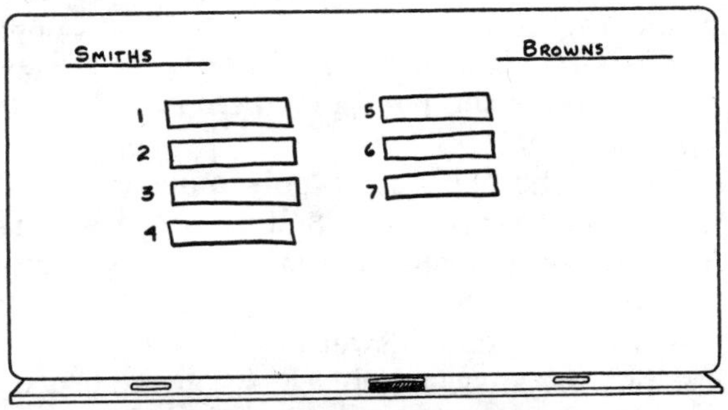

Fig. 1-6. Family Feud Set-Up for a Seven-Answer Question.

2. Divide the class into two "families"—they love to choose their own family name. Further divide the "families" into groups of four representing the four family members.
3. Ask each family to send forward one member of Group #1.
4. The two students stand facing the teacher's desk with their arms at their sides.
5. Place the *empty* stapler an equal distance from the two opponents. (The stapler is used as a "buzzer.") The first player with a hand on the stapler gets to answer

the question. Remind students to use the flat part of their palm with their fingers fully extended to avoid pinching their fingers.

6. Ask a question preceded by the statement, "I surveyed a studio audience and got their best response to this. . . ." For example, name a reason why someone may abuse drugs. (By the way, the teacher is the studio audience and can award points to the various responses before the game starts. Try to have the points total 100 for each round if possible, so each participant will have an opportunity to make the same contribution to his/her family.)
7. After the question is asked, the first to hit the stapler gets to answer the question. If the answer is the #1 answer on your list, that family gains control of the question.
8. If the answer is *not* #1 *or* if it is not on your list, the opponent gets a chance to answer.
9. If the opponent's answer is worth more points (higher on your list), the opponent's team then takes control of the question.
10. Once control has been established, the family decides whether to Play or Pass.
    (a) If Play is chosen, the team must successfully guess *all* the answers before getting 3 Strikes (or incorrect guesses). In rotation, the playing family's groups (1–4) continue to make a guess until all blocks are filled in (matching your answer key) or until 3 Strikes are recorded. If *all* are guessed, that family is awarded the sum of all the points (usually 100). If 3 Strikes are recorded, the opposing family gets to confer and come up with *one* answer that it believes will fill in a block correctly. If the answer is correct, the opposing family steals the points for that round. If incorrect, the original family keeps the points.
    (b) If Pass is chosen, the opposing family must try to come up with all the correct answers before it registers 3 Strikes. (Passing is an assumption that the other team will not be able to answer and that your team will be able to steal the points.)
11. After each guess, refer to your answer key. If the guess is #3 on your key and worth 29 points, put the answer in block #3 on the board and "29" next to the block. This indicates that the team got the third best answer and now has 29 points. For each incorrect answer, place an X (strike) on the board. After a few minutes, the board may appear as shown in Figure 1-7.
    NOTE: To keep the game more interesting and more of a challenge, it is best to make up questions with 6 or more answers.
12. After Round 1 is completed and points are totaled and awarded to one of the teams, a member from group #2 of each family comes to the front to try to gain control of the next question.
13. Play continues until time is up or until a set number of questions have been asked. The family with the most points is the winner.

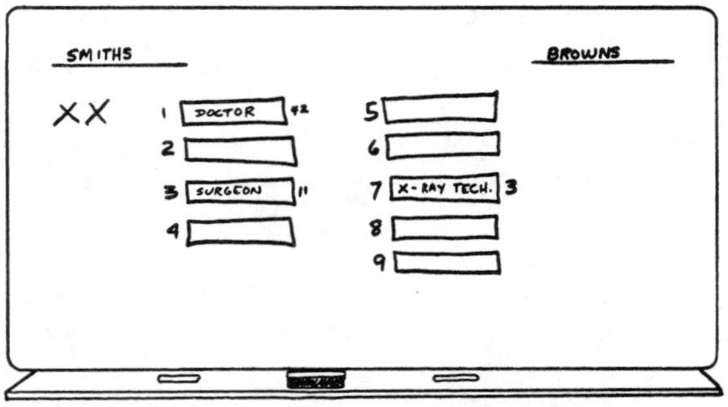

Fig. 1-7. This board shows the Smiths with 2 strikes and 3 correct answers so far.

Sample Questions:

NOTE: Questions should be based on what you personally have covered in class. These are examples of questions for various grade levels.

Name a digestive organ:
1. Stomach 28
2. Large intestine 20
3. Small intestine 17
4. Esophagus 11
5. Mouth 9
6. Liver 8
7. Pancreas 7

Name a reason why someone may abuse drugs:
1. Conformity 30
2. Fun 22
3. Curiosity 16
4. Boredom 12
5. Rebellion 8
6. Escape 7
7. Availability 5

Name a first-aid emergency:
1. Someone not breathing 29
2. Bleeding 20
3. Drowning 14
4. Poisoning 12
5. Fracture 10
6. Shock 7
7. Electric shock 4
8. Burns 3
9. Suffocation 1

Name a health-related career:
1. Doctor (Physician) 42
2. Nurse 22
3. Surgeon 11
4. Dentist 9
5. Podiatrist 6
6. Psychologist 4
7. X-ray technician 3
8. Gynecologist 2
9. Dermatologist 1

Name a food in the Fruits and Vegetables food group:
1. Apple 39
2. Banana 18
3. Corn 15
4. Grapes 8
5. Oranges 7
6. Lettuce 5
7. Tomatoes 4
8. Potatoes 3
9. Carrots 1

Activity 7. Truth or Deception

Concept/Description: Students' knowledge of health topics are tested using a game format.

Game Objective: To be the first team to get Tic-Tac-Toe by identifying whether answers to health questions are correct or incorrect.

Materials Needed:

9 chairs
Chalkboard
Chalk
Eraser
Questions (See sample questions.)

Directions:

1. Place 9 chairs in front of the chalkboard in 3 × 3 rows. Have the chairs face *away* from the board and toward the class. Place a Tic-Tac-Toe grid on the chalkboard, above the chairs (Figure 1-8).
2. Choose 9 students and have them sit in the 9 chairs. Each chair corresponds to a position on the Tic-Tac-Toe grid.

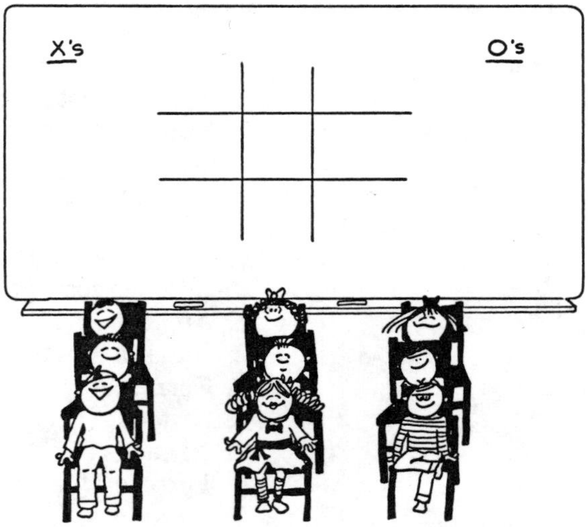

Fig. 1-8. Set-up for Truth or Deception.

3. Choose a scorekeeper who will write an X for one team and O for the other on the board.
4. Divide the class into X and O teams.
5. Start the game with either the X or O team. The teams alternate and a team member chooses a "health expert," who is one of the students sitting in one of the chairs. (The teacher can select the students who will choose the health

expert or set up a rotational system so that each team member gets to choose.) The teacher asks a question of the chosen expert, who then attempts to answer it. Experts should fake an answer if they don't know the correct answer.

6. The person who chose the expert then agrees or disagrees with the star's answer.
7. If the person who agreed or disagreed is Correct, he or she puts the respective symbol (X in this case) on the board that corresponds to the star's position in the 3 × 3 grid of chairs.
8. If Incorrect, nothing is put up since the team must earn the spot themselves.
9. Alternate by asking O and then X a question until one team gets Tic-Tac-Toe.
10. The first team to get Tic-Tac-Toe wins the round. If there is no winner, then the team with the most "X"s or "O"s wins the round.
11. After 3 rounds, switch the stars.

Sample Questions to Truth or Deception:

1. What connects muscles to bones? (Tendons)
2. What are the tough cords that connect bones to bones called? (Ligaments)
3. What is the muscle that straightens your arm called? (Triceps)
4. What is the watery fluid in the front of the eye called? (Aqueous fluid)
5. Which system breaks down food so it can be used for energy? (Digestive)
6. What is the first aid for a bruise? (Ice, compression, elevation)
7. What are the tiny finger-like projections in the intestines called? (Villi)
8. Respiration is another name for what body function? (Breathing)
9. What is the outer covering of the lungs called? (Pleura)
10. What are the lower heart chambers called? (Ventricles)

Activity 8. Blackboard Baseball

Concept/Description: Students' knowledge of health topics can be measured by their success in scoring runs in a game with a baseball format. They are given questions that differ in difficulty to determine a single, double, triple or home run.

Game Objective: To score the most runs in a simulated baseball game by correctly answering health questions of different degrees of difficulty.

Materials Needed:

Chalkboard
Chalk
Eraser
Question cards

Directions:

1. Divide the class into two equal teams (Phillies and Mets, for example). Further divide each team into four equal groups numbered 1–4, representing batters 1, 2, 3 and 4.
2. Draw a baseball diamond on the chalkboard as shown in Figure 1-9.

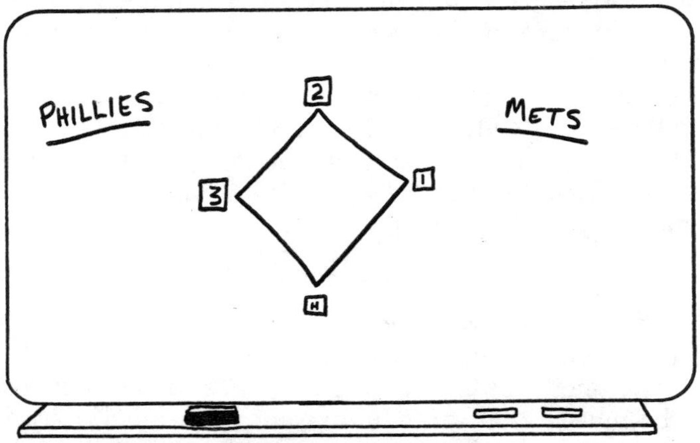

Fig. 1-9. Blackboard Baseball set-up.

3. Questions are categorized as single, double, triple, and home run, ranging from simple to very difficult questions.
4. Start with Group #1 members of the Phillies, for example. Ask them to choose a single, double, triple, or home run question. The teacher reads the question from the category they've chosen. The group (with *no* help from the other groups), confers for 10 seconds and gives its answer.
5. If correct, an "X" is placed by first base for a single question, by second for a double question, and by third base for a triple question. If a home run question is answered correctly, the team gets a run.
6. If Group #1 of the Phillies is correct, move to Group #2 of the Phillies and so on until a question is missed which is an Out. Since there is only *One Out per Side*, erase the base runners. The play then goes to the Mets.
7. To keep the game simple, move *all* players the same number of bases. For example, if there is a player on second (Figure 1-10) and the next group gets a "single" question correct, erase the "X" on second base and move the runner one base to third. Then, place an "X" on first base. (Figure 1-11). If the next group chooses and correctly answers a "double" question, X3 is moved to second, X2 to third, X1 goes home, and a run is recorded (Figure 1-12).
8. If you run out of a category of questions (some teams like to try to use up all the singles), then play with only the remaining categories.
9. Place all incorrectly answered questions back in the pile for future use, and place the correctly answered questions aside.

Sample Questions:

"Single" Questions for a Unit on the Senses:

1. Name the receptor for the sense of taste. (Taste buds)
2. Which sense does the auditory nerve deal with? (Hearing)
3. Which sense does the optic nerve deal with? (Vision, sight)

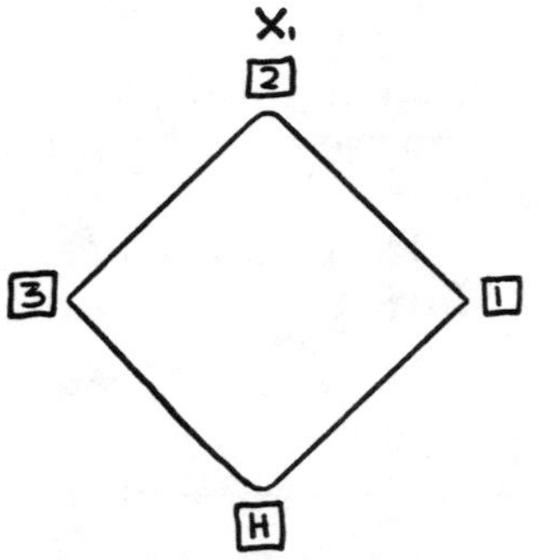

Fig. 1-10. Runner on second.

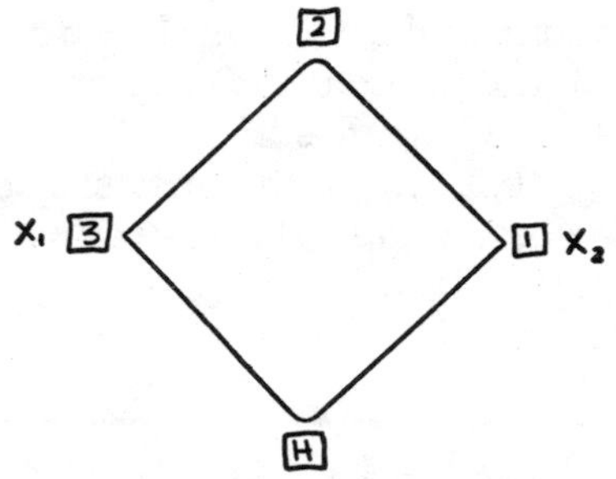

Fig. 1-11. Runners on first and third.

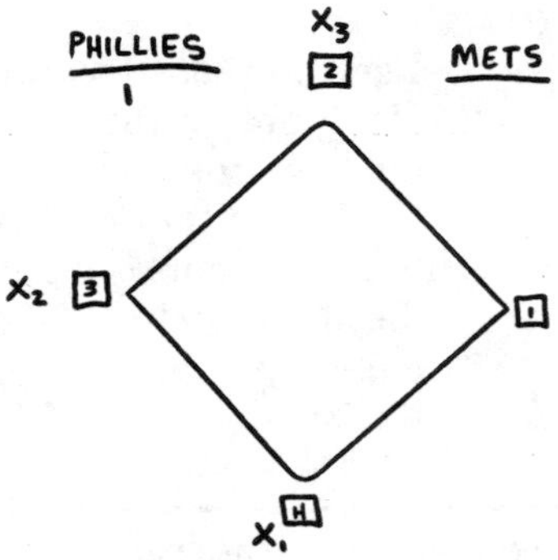

Fig. 1-12. Runners on second and third, with one run being scored.

4. What is the receptor for the sense of touch? (Skin)
5. Where is the olfactory nerve located? (Nose)

"Double" Questions for the Same Unit:

1. Name the largest organ in the human body. (Skin)
2. Which part of the eye is eye color? (Iris)
3. What is the unit called that measures sound intensity? (Decibel)
4. What is the hole in the center of the eye that lets in light called? (Pupil)
5. Where are the 3 bones of the ear located? (Middle ear)
6. What helps to cleanse the eyes? (Tears)
7. Which part of the ear contains over 2000 wax glands? (Ear canal)
8. Where is "bitter" tasted on the tongue? (Back of the tongue)

"Triple" Questions:

1. What is the name of the membrane stretched at the end of the ear canal? (Ear drum or tympanic membrane)
2. Name the watery fluid in the front of the eye. (Aqueous humor)
3. Name the snail-shaped part of the inner ear. (Cochlea)
4. What do the ears control besides hearing? (Balance)
5. Which of these is filled with fluid: Semi-circular canals, outer ear, or inner? (Semi-circular canals)
6. Which part of the eye focuses light on the retina? (Lens)

"Home Run" Questions:

1. Where are the rods and cones found? (Retina)
2. What are the four basic tastes? (Salt, sweet, sour, bitter)
3. Name the three ear bones. (Hammer, anvil, stirrup)
4. Name the five basic skin sensations. (Touch, pain, pressure, heat, cold)
5. What is another name for the whites of the eye *and* spell it. (Sclera)

Variations:

1. Let one team bat until three outs are made.
2. Have only difficult questions and give four clues to the question. If the player answers the question with the first clue, it is a home run, with the second clue a triple, etc. Four attempts are permitted.
3. Same format as #2 except that any wrong answer is an out. The player can ask for another clue if she/he doesn't know the answer with the first, second, or third clue.

Activity 9. Password

Concept/Description: Two teams compete to see who can score the most points. Teammates give one member of their team clues to assist the member in coming up with the correct answer. The purpose is to have students share as much descriptive information as possible about a health term or topic.

Game Objective: To be the first team to guess the password by putting together the various clues.

Materials Needed:

2 chairs
Chalkboard
Chalk
Eraser
Password sheet

Directions:

1. Place two chairs in front of the class with the backs facing the chalkboard (Figure 1-13).
2. Divide the class into two equal teams, and have one person from each team sit in the chair, facing his or her team.

Fig. 1-13. Set-up for Password.

3. Alternate the team that starts each round since this makes an important difference in the game.
4. Be sure that the two students in the chairs face their classmates before the teacher writes the first word on the board.
5. Starting with Team A, for example, say "10 points." Students from Team A raise their hand to give *one-word clues*. The person in the chair chooses one person, hears the clue, and takes a guess at the password. If correct, the team is awarded 10 points; if incorrect, play goes to Team B for 9 points. If Team B's answer is incorrect, play goes back to Team A for 8 points, and so forth, until the word is guessed or until there are no more points.
6. After a word is guessed, have two new people sit in the chairs. Write a new word on the board, and start again.

NOTE: Only *one-word* clues may be given, and *no* part of the word may be used in the clue. For example, if the password is heart attack, neither "heart" nor "attack" may be used as a clue.

Sample Passwords (for a Unit on Diseases and Disorders):

Contagious	Malnutrition	Ulcer
Beri-Beri	Hemophilia	STDs
Leukemia	Muscular Dystrophy	Scurvy
Emphysema	Communicable	Lung Cancer
Multiple Sclerosis	Rickets	Meningitis
Infection	Cystic Fibrosis	

Activity 10. Picture Stories (I See What You Mean . . .)

Concept/Description: To combine drawings that relate to health topics with stories about the drawings at each child's level of ability.

Objective: To draw an outline of a picture relating to a health topic that is being studied and then to write a story about the picture following the outline.

Materials Needed:

Paper
Pens or pencils
Information on various units

Directions: Using a pencil, lightly sketch an outline of a picture that deals with the information being studied. (For example, a unit on the skeletal system may have a drawing of the humerus.) Then, using pertinent information, write a story along the outline of the drawing that describes the picture (Figure 1-14).

Fig. 1-14. Sample picture story.

The age of the student will determine the complexity of the picture story that is used. This is a perfect way to correlate health education and art instruction.

Activity 11. Puzzle Sheets (A Puzzling Activity!)

Concept/Description: Children love puzzles! Several different types of puzzles with tips on how to set them up are described.

Objective: To provide puzzles that will excite and challenge students while teaching health information.

Materials Needed:

Dittoed puzzle sheets: Reproductive System Crossword Puzzle; Seek and Find
Writing implements

Directions: There are many types of puzzles that can be constructed and placed on dittos to pass out to students. A fun approach is to have groups of 3–4 students make up their own puzzle sheets and then pass them out for other groups to solve. Here are some types of puzzles you may wish to include on your sheets:

A. Crossword Puzzles:

The fastest and easiest way to construct a crossword puzzle is to use graph paper and write words on some topic that will intersect and form a crossword puzzle as is shown at the top of Figure 1-15. Next draw the appropriate boxes, and then come up with the questions such as those shown at the bottom of Figure 1-16. Transfer the questions and blank grid to dittos and reproduce (see accompanying page). Adding sketches or using colored dittos make these sheets even more appealing.

Fig. 1-15. Sample crossword answer key.

B. Seek and Find:

Figure the number of words you'd like to use (usually 15–20 is adequate) and jot them down. Make a grid as illustrated on the accompanying worksheet, and fill in your words vertically, horizontally, and diagonally with a ball point pen. Using a felt-tipped pen, circle the words lightly on your ditto so that you will automatically have an answer key. Then, fill in the blank spaces with any letters, using a ball point pen once again.

To add excitement to this type of puzzle, have groups of 3–4 work on a Seek and Find and race them against time. For example, if they finish in 15 minutes, they receive 10 extra credit points; in 20 minutes, 5 points, etc. Anyone who finishes at all receives 1 point.

C. Add and Subtract the Letters:

Choose a word that deals with the unit being studied. By adding and subtracting letters devise a puzzle that will work out to the desired vocabulary word. Students can also devise these and try them out on classmates.

Sample Add-and-Subtract Puzzles:

1. ABCDEFGO – ABDEFG + NOSE – OE + UMMM – MM + EAR – A = ______________
(consumer)
2. BAD – B + OVER – O + BAT – BA + WISE – W = ______________
(advertise)
3. SQUAT – ST + CRACKER – CR + YOU – OU = ______________
(quackery)
4. CANDY – DY + COUCH – OUCH + EARRING – ARING = ______________
(cancer)
5. ACTION – ATION + YOU – YO + REST – ST = ______________
(cure)

Name ______________ Date ______________ (1-9)

Reproductive System Crossword Puzzle

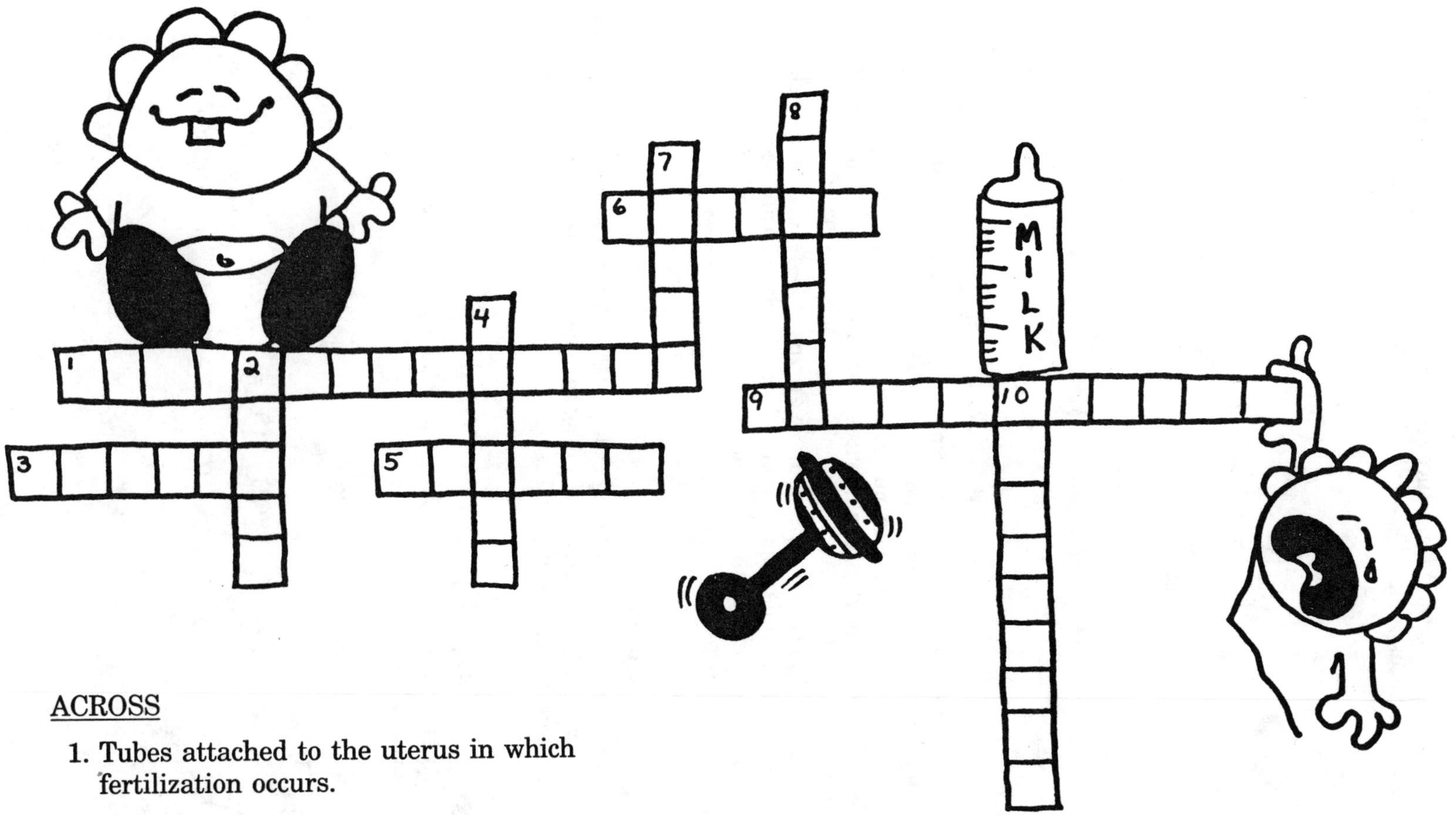

ACROSS

1. Tubes attached to the uterus in which fertilization occurs.
3. The birth canal.
5. Opening to the uterus and a common site of cancer.
6. Male organs that produce sperm and testosterone.
9. Tube that carries sperm *from* the testes.

DOWN

2. Female organ that produces egg cells and estrogen.

DOWN, cont.

4. Organ that houses the fetus during pregnancy.
7. Male organ of intercourse.
8. Tube that carries semen and urine in males and urine in females.
10. When two egg cells are fertilized by two sperm cells, ______________ twins occur.

Name ______________________________ Date ____________________ (1-10)

Seek and Find

A	R	E	D	L	U	M	N	S	S	E	N	O	M	R	O	H	C	T	R
C	B	X	S	E	L	C	I	R	T	N	E	V	C	H	T	I	I	E	N
E	X	C	R	E	T	O	R	Y	T	H	C	S	R	I	S	N	R	L	E
N	P	I	T	U	I	T	A	R	Y	G	L	A	N	D	A	S	C	Q	U
D	U	N	A	E	H	T	A	I	L	N	E	M	A	B	A	T	U	A	R
O	M	M	N	S	A	E	I	L	F	I	S	E	Y	E	N	E	L	A	O
C	Y	T	S	G	H	V	G	B	O	N	E	E	R	H	U	I	A	R	N
R	S	O	U	C	U	M	U	L	E	D	L	C	T	N	N	R	T	H	H
I	S	L	A	N	E	R	D	A	O	S	N	A	O	S	I	H	I	T	A
N	T	U	B	H	M	E	E	D	M	A	S	I	U	Y	E	A	O	E	M
E	O	L	I	U	E	N	G	D	P	E	T	L	M	E	V	T	N	R	U
H	E	U	I	N	T	R	S	E	U	S	I	O	T	O	P	H	A	U	S
E	A	R	R	S	O	M	S	R	E	N	T	S	E	A	V	E	C	N	C
O	T	W	H	W	E	A	I	G	O	N	V	S	G	T	A	A	E	L	L
A	L	E	T	D	O	N	I	S	I	L	O	O	E	S	S	T	R	A	E
B	U	H	T	I	E	D	R	A	D	I	O	R	Y	H	T	A	U	Y	S
K	I	D	N	E	Y	S	R	E	O	M	E	E	U	S	E	M	W	L	F
C	N	H	A	N	D	B	T	T	S	G	N	U	L	C	H	I	C	A	L

Kidneys
Bladder
Urine
Adrenals
Ovary
Testes
Pancreas
Thyroid
Hormones

Endocrine
Excretory
Insulin
Growth
Pituitary gland
Urethra
Waste
Neuron
Brain

Muscles
Lungs
Heart
Ventricles
Atrium
Circulation
Digestion

D. Unscramble the Words:

This type of puzzle is often used, but to add a twist, have each group of 3–4 scramble a set of ten related words. On a given signal, have the group pass on its sheet to another group. See which group can unscramble its list the fastest. (Be sure to emphasize correct spelling, for much frustration results in trying to unscramble misspelled words.)

Sample Unscrambles:

1. inrfsiedhp .... friendship
2. tadnig .... dating
3. nftaiautoin .... infatuation
4. eolv .... love
5. arrmigae .... marriage
6. rumattiy .... maturity
7. auesxltiy .... sexuality
8. ivodrce .... divorce
9. csedaolcene .... adolescence
10. tegaengmne .... engagement

Activity 12. Dough Art

Concept/Description: Children make dough and use this medium to simulate various health-related objects which can be preserved. This process can be used to help students visualize health concepts and for review purposes.

Objective: To make a variety of objects out of dough, which relate to the health unit being studied.

Materials Needed:

Mixing bowls
Flour
Salt
Water
Baking facilities
Cookie sheets
Paints, brushes, etc.

Directions: A favorite activity for those who like to get their hands into whatever they are doing is dough art. To make a batch of dough, mix the following ingredients in a large bowl:

4 cups unsifted flour
1 cup salt
1½ cups water

Knead for 5–10 minutes (very important!). Then shape the dough into various forms that depict a health concept that is being studied. Bake at 350° F for about 15 minutes; and allow to cool. The forms should now be ready for painting. This activity can be used in a number of ways. For example, students can make model cells, or they can design a system. Different groups can be responsible for different organs in this study.

Have students use cookie cutters, spoons, plastic knives, *plus* their own dough art tool ideas.

Once the dough is dry, it can be painted and shellacked or sprayed with acrylic spray coating to preserve it. The hardened dough can also be glued to cardboard and labeled.

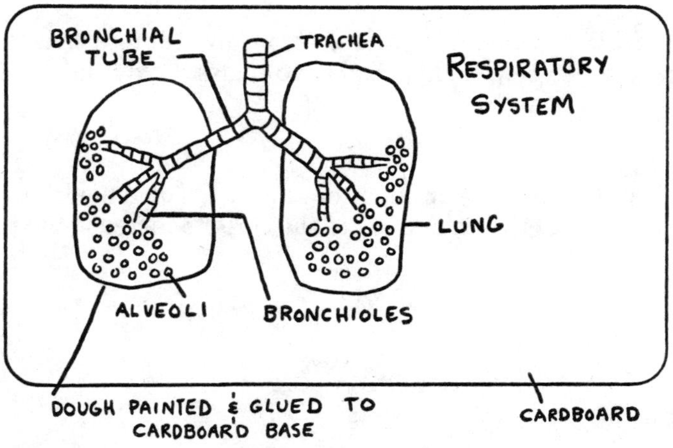

Fig. 1-16. Sample dough-art project.

Activity 13. Health Newspaper (Extra! Extra! Read All about It!)

Concept/Description: Students write a newspaper geared to health in general or to a particular facet of health that is being studied. Every part of a regular newspaper can be written with a health emphasis.

Objective: To write a newspaper that will cover the health topics covered in class in an entertaining manner.

Materials Needed:

Dittos
Writing instruments

Directions: An activity that is simple, yet very effective, is the production of a health newspaper, either on a particular unit or on a group of units.

Students can create puzzles, poems, stories, drawings, want ads, etc. These can be transferred to dittos, after your inspection, and reproduced for class members or, money permitting, to the student body and parents.

A trip to the library or use of health books and pamphlets can provide a source of information. The real excitement comes when students see their ideas in print—and be sure to allow them to sign their names to their work.

Depending on the age group with which you are working, you may wish to include health advice columns, fashions, sports information, travel, collaged photos (these reproduce very well on a photocopying machine), or even obituaries (deaths due to various poor health practices). Be sure to keep each column geared towards health, fitness, etc.

Activity 14. Plays and Skits (To Be or Not to Be . . .)

Concept/Description: Students immerse themselves into a health topic by being given the opportunity to develop a skit or play to highlight the health topics or issues being studied.

Objective: To have students design a skit or play based on a health topic that is being studied and present it to the other members of the class to increase the pertinence of the topic.

Directions: These activities always manage to add a little humor to your lessons. Allowing small groups the freedom to design their own skit, play, or rap provides a very enjoyable learning experience. Given certain guidelines, you'll find students often respond with original and clever ideas, representing their needs and interests.

Setting the following guidelines can eliminate many problems:

1. The skit must include *all* members of the group.
2. A written dialogue must be carefully and completely written and submitted. (A sample rap done by two 8th grade girls for a unit on consumer health-grooming is included below.)
3. All props must first be cleared with the instructor before being used. (This is to avoid having mom's wedding dress cut into pieces to be used as an arm sling.)
4. The skit must be from 3–5 minutes in length.
5. The skit must include at least *2 facts* about the topic assigned. (Example: A skit on first aid might explain the Heimlich maneuver and treating shock.)

Sample "Health Rap":

One day in gym I got hit with a ball.
I fell right back and smashed my head into a wall.
I went to the nurse, she looked real placid.
She said, "All you need is some acetylsalicylic acid!"
While I was there, she checked my head for lice.
She said, "Sit down, dearie, let me give you some advice!"
"Your hair is really dirty and rather sick looking.
You could use all that grease for baking and cooking.
And speaking of dirt, just look at your face!
It looks like pepperoni all over the place.
Benzoyl peroxide is what you need.
5–10% ought to clear your face with speed.
Halitosis is the way I'd describe your breath.
If someone were to smell it, they'd be facing death!
Your apocrine gland odor is really bad, too.
That's why people keep a safe distance from you.
Buy a lotion anti-perspirant, you can find it in a mall.
And it's so much better than an aerosol."
The nurse gave me ice and sent me on my way.
And as I walked out the door she said, "Have a nice day!"

UNIT 2

DEALING WITH FEELINGS

Activities for Coping with Change

Students of all ages feel stress. Stress occurs in school as well as at home. The activities in this chapter are designed to help students face stressful situations. More importantly, the activities are fashioned to develop coping skills that will become part of a student's life.

It is important that students learn to understand themselves. This is an objective of units that zero in on stress and coping skills. Students find that other people have similar concerns and pressures. By getting a grasp of their own feelings and attitudes, they will realize that they are not unique. Using a game and activity format makes learning about themselves less threatening and makes it easier for them to share personal thoughts and ideas. Games in this chapter carefully refrain from forcing students to express feelings and yet establish an environment where they will feel comfortable when sharing information about themselves.

Realistic goal-setting is another important skill for students to develop if stress is to be handled positively. Activities in this unit help students realize that stress is normal. They will have the opportunity, through simulations and activities, to learn healthy ways to handle stress that is part of their lives.

Frequently, students have a distorted view of what other families are like and the problems that confront individuals as well as families. These activities are planned to provide a realistic view of life and to confront issues that cause students stress as their personal situations undergo change.

Activity 1. Scavenger Hunt (Getting to Know Class Members)

Concept/Description: Often the start of school (for any grade) is somewhat stressful. Getting to know each other can lessen the stress.

Objective: To find people in the class who fit the characteristics described on the Scavenger Hunt Sheet by talking to them.

Materials:

Pen or pencil
Scavenger Hunt Worksheet

Directions:

1. At the start of the school year, semester, etc., instruct students to take their sheet and circulate through the room trying to find people to fit the categories found on the Scavenger Hunt Worksheet.
2. When they find a person, they should ask his or her name, talk a moment, and jot the name down. (Be sure to join in the activity, also.)
3. After a specified time, have students return to their seats. Carry on a class discussion, asking who the students found that fit each category. Both you and your students will get to know a little about each other in an enjoyable, comfortable way.

Activity 2. A Picture Is Worth A Thousand Words (A Pictorial Autobiography)

Concept/Description: By concentrating on their interests and values, students will learn more about themselves and their feelings.

Objective: To construct an autobiography using both pictures and words.

Materials:

Scissors
Glue or paste
Construction paper
Old magazines
Markers, pens

Directions:

1. Have students write a brief autobiography by cutting out magazine pictures describing the things they value. Suggest that they construct their story as if they were meeting someone for the first time.
2. Have them fill in the story by using words combined with pictures when possible.
3. Display the stories in your classroom.

Variation:

Draw pictures in place of magazine cut-outs.

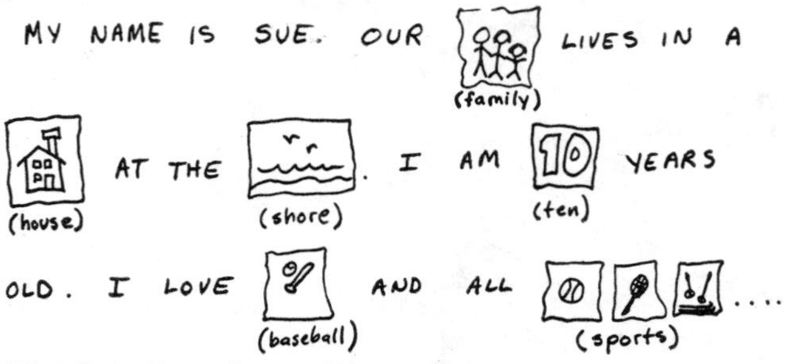

Fig. 2-1. Sample autobiography.

Name ________________________________ ________ Date ____________________ (2-1)

Scavenger Hunt

Find someone who:

1. Likes to ski (snow or water) ______________________________
2. Has travelled across the U.S. ______________________________
3. Was born in another state ______________________________
4. Has more than 3 siblings ______________________________
5. Has been to Florida ______________________________
6. Has been to a rock concert ______________________________
7. Likes to cook ______________________________
8. Likes to jog ______________________________
9. Likes school ______________________________
10. Plays an instrument ______________________________
11. Likes the cafeteria food ______________________________
12. Received *two* A's on his or her last report card ______________________________
13. Gets along well with his or her parents ______________________________
14. Has played 18 holes of golf ______________________________
15. Has a brother or sister under 3 ______________________________

Activity 3. How Do I See Myself? (Describing Yourself)

Concept/Description: By concentrating on certain characteristics, it is possible to learn what you are like.

Objective: To rank order a group of qualities that describes you.

Materials:

"How Do I See Myself?" Worksheet (See p. 2-2)
Pen or pencil

Directions:

1. Read each quality listed on the worksheet and determine how each applies to you.
2. Write the qualities that you feel apply and do not apply to you on the worksheet. (The left side of the continuum is for qualities that are highly descriptive of you, and the right side is for qualities that you feel do not apply.) Include all the qualities that are listed.

Activity 4. Lend Me Your Coat! (A Personal Coat of Arms)

Concept/Description: By visually depicting values and interests, students can learn more about themselves.

Objective: To construct a Coat of Arms by cutting out pictures, drawing pictures, or using photos to describe yourself.

Materials:

My Personal Coat of Arms Worksheet (See p. 2-3)
Magazines
Photos
Scissors
Glue or paste
Construction paper

Directions:

1. Have students determine the size of My Personal Coat of Arms Worksheet. (Use the worksheet or use cardboard, posterboard, etc.)
2. Cut out magazine pictures, use photos, or draw things in the shield that show your values, interests, or beliefs.
3. Display the Coat of Arms in the classroom.

Name ______________________________ Date ________________

How Do I See Myself?

Directions: Read each quality listed on the worksheet and decide how each applies to you. Write the qualities you feel apply to you the best at the left, and those which apply to you least at the right.

Name ______________________ Date ______________ (2-3)

My Personal Coat of Arms

Directions: Cut out magazine pictures, use photos, or draw things in the shield that show your values, interests, or beliefs.

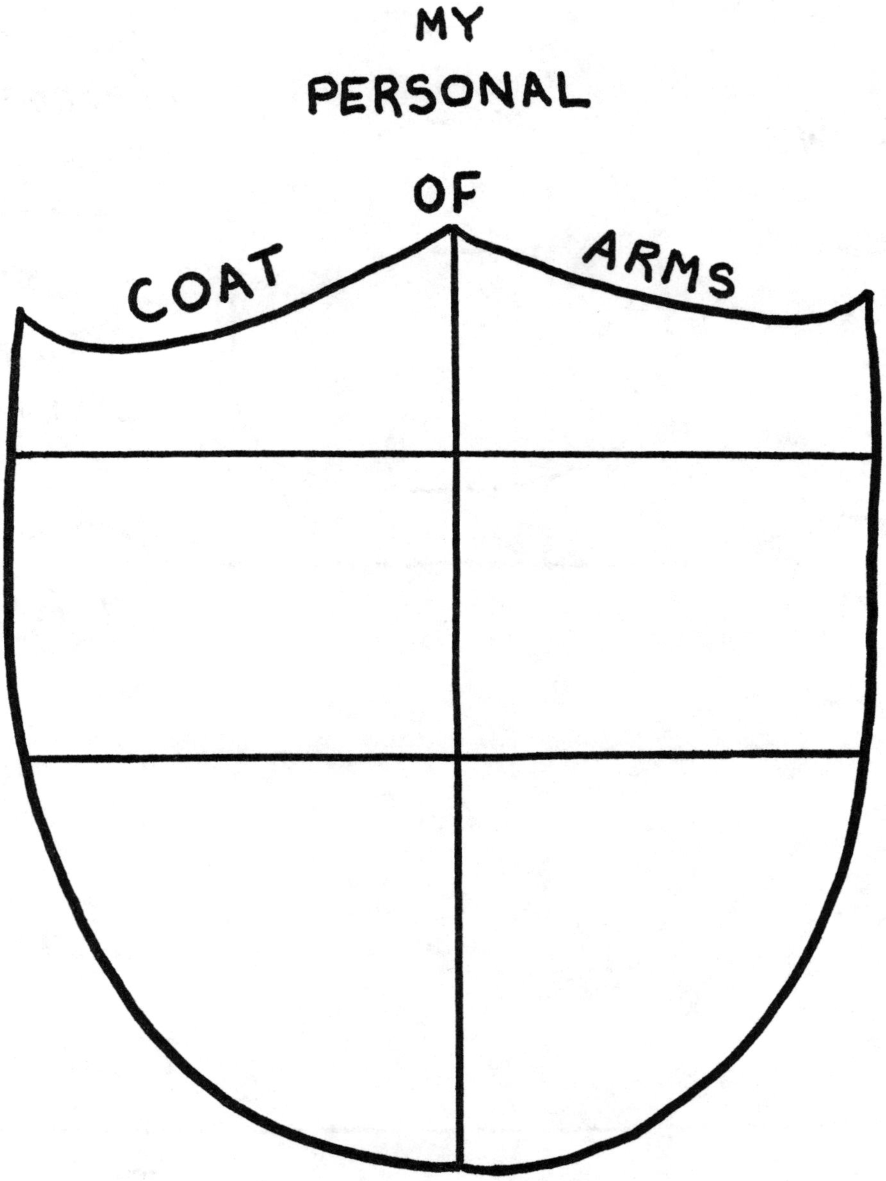

Variation:

Have students put their names on the back of their Coat of Arms, and have class members try to guess to whom each Coat of Arms belongs based on what they know of each other.

Activity 5. Here's My Card (A Personal "Business Card")

Concept/Description: Business cards tell us about the person who gives them out. "Student business cards" will help students know themselves.

Objective: To have students write down their positive qualities in business card format.

Materials:

Pieces of oaktag, construction paper, etc.
Crayons, markers
Pens, pencils
Scissors

Directions:

1. Have students design a "business card" describing their positive qualities.
2. Have them list what they have to offer and include any sketches, cartoons, etc., they wish.
3. Cards can be made any size you or your students choose. Allow for individual creativity.
4. Display the cards on a bulletin board.

Fig. 2-2. Sample "business card"

Activity 6. The Sound of Music (Theme Song)

Concept/Description: Songs are capable of expressing a person's feelings and values.

Objective: To have students choose songs that express their feelings, thoughts, beliefs, and values.

Materials:

Songs students choose
Paper and pen or pencil

Directions:

1. Have students choose a song that expresses their ideals, beliefs, feelings, etc.—in other words, their "theme song."
2. Have them write down the words to the song. (Many tapes, albums, and CD's have the words printed on the jackets.)
3. Have them present the songs in a one-page essay or as an oral report explaining why this song means something to them.

   NOTE: If the song is personal, the students may feel uncomfortable doing an oral report; therefore, make it optional.

Activity 7. Plus and Minus (Strengths and Weaknesses)

Concept/Description: Understanding that we all have strengths and weaknesses is important so that while we emphasize our positive points and work on our weaknesses, we realize that we are not alone in the attempt.

Objective: To recognize specific strengths and weaknesses and ways to work on these weaknesses.

Materials:

My Strengths and Weaknesses Worksheet (See p. 2-4)
Pen or pencil

Directions:

1. Have students fill out the worksheet.
2. Have a class discussion pointing out that everyone has strong points as well as areas that need improvement.
   NOTE: Since discussing their personal feelings makes some students uncomfortable, be sure to "relax" the atmosphere by allowing students to volunteer their answers.

Activity 8. A Sticky Situation (Positive Points)

Concept/Description: We all have positive points, and often we don't realize what they are.

Name ________________________________ Date ________________ (2-4)

My Strengths and Weaknesses

1. I feel proud when ____________ says I ________________________________

   ____.

2. I feel left out and lonely when ________________________________

   doesn't ask me ____.

3. I feel happy when ____.

4. I get angry when ____

   corrects me on ____.

5. ____________________ usually make me feel ____________________

   ____.

6. It's disappointing when ____.

7. No matter how hard I try, I never ________________________________

   ____.

8. The only thing I really enjoy is ________________________________

   ____

9. My strengths / My weaknesses

My strengths	My weaknesses
____________________	____________________
____________________	____________________
____________________	____________________
____________________	____________________
____________________	____________________
____________________	____________________

10. Pick *one* weakness and tell what you could do to improve yourself.

    ____

    ____

    ____

    ____

Objective: To learn our positive qualities from other people's observations of us.

Materials:

Blank labels or stickers (large enough to write on)
Pens or pencils
5 × 7 cards

Directions:

1. Divide class into groups of 4–6 and sit in a circle. Give each person a 5 × 7 card and one sticker for each person in the group.
2. Have students write their name in the upper corner of the 5 × 7 card and on each sticker (as small as possible).
3. Pass your card to the right. When you get someone's card, take a sticker, and write 3 positive qualities about that person (for example, 1. great athlete, 2. caring, and 3. funny). Then paste the sticker onto his or her card.
4. Continue passing the cards around and filling in stickers until you get your card back.
5. Discuss how it made you feel to hear positive things from others. Discuss why some people look for the negative qualities in others to make themselves look better or because they are jealous (Figure 2-3).

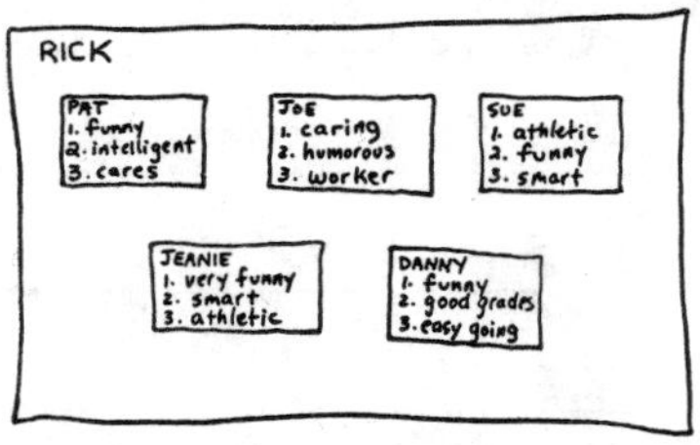

Fig. 2-3. Sample sticker card

Activity 9. "I'm Impressed!" (First Impressions)

Concept/Description: We cannot judge people by their outward appearances alone, and we must first get to know them before making a positive or negative opinion about them.

Objective: To assist students in understanding that it is important to know a person before making judgments.

Materials:

Construction paper
Glue
Cut-out pictures from magazines or newspapers

Directions:

1. Leaf through magazines or newspapers and cut out pictures of people that may or may not be known to your students.
2. Paste each picture onto a piece of construction paper and number each. On the back, jot down who the person is and the reason for their being in a magazine. For example, you may have a picture of John Doe, who was arrested for burglary.
3. Show each picture to the class and ask each member to briefly jot down their first impression of the person shown.
4. Later, go back to each card and ask various students for their first impressions. Then explain what you know of the person and see if their impressions were wrong. (Often, students will mistake convicts for reputable businessmen, etc.)
5. Discuss how first impressions can be misleading. Could first impressions be important when applying for a job, meeting new people, etc? How or why?

Variation:

Another idea, which is more costly, but permanent, is to make slides of the various pictures.

Activity 10. What, Me Worry? (Everyday Pressures)

Concept/Description: The better you know yourself, the better you'll be able to cope with pressure.

Objective: To list some of the pressures and worries we face.

Materials:

Paper
Pens or pencils
Chalkboard
Chalk, eraser

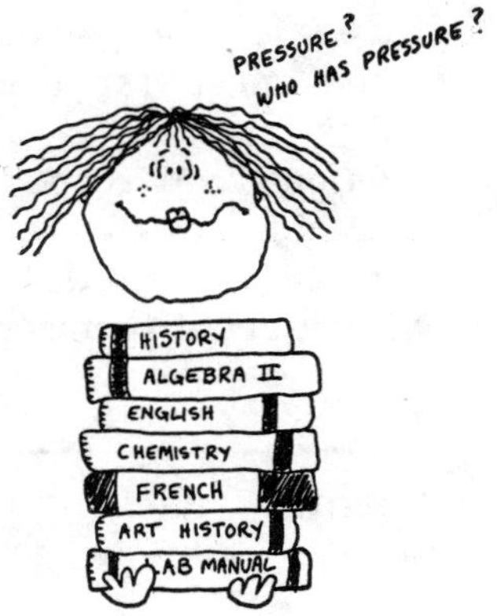

Directions:

1. Have students list all the pressures they personally face (grades, friends, parents, weight, acne, money, etc.)
2. After a designated time, ask members to volunteer some items of their list. Write their responses on the board.

3. Discuss these pressures. Are their parents facing the same kinds of pressures? What pressures might adults encounter?
4. What positive things do some people do when the pressures get too great? (Ask for help, talk to a friend, write down their feelings, talk to a counselor, parent or teacher, etc.)
5. What negative things do they do? (Suicide, run away, drugs, alcohol, lash out at others, etc.)

Activity 11. Cooperation Station (Getting Along Together)

Concept/Description: Examining group dynamics while carrying out a cooperative task helps students to understand themselves and the processes involved in cooperating.

Objective: To complete a group task and determine the group's level of cooperation.

Materials:

3 empty coffee cans per group
2 2″ × 4″ boards approximately 5 feet long per group
4 cones
Stop watch or wall clock

Directions:

1. Divide the class into 2 or 3 groups and give them the following task: Groups must get all members of their group from point A to B (using cones, mark off a distance of 10–15 yards), using only the equipment given, and may not touch the ground beneath them (whoever touches must start over).
2. Time each group.
3. Discuss how each group functioned and cooperated. Who became the leader in each group? How was leadership decided? Was there agreement or disagreement? Were anyone's ideas blocked or put down? Did everyone get a chance to give ideas? What did they learn about themselves?

Activity 12. Party Time (A Seating Chart)

Concept/Description: Establishing a seating chart of people you like and dislike will assist you in getting a better grasp of your values.

Objective: To set up a party seating chart for 9 people and yourself.

Materials:

Party Time Seating Chart (See p. 2-5)
Pens or pencils
Follow-Up Questions Worksheet (See p. 2-6)

Directions:

1. Give each student a Party Time Seating Chart and a follow-up ditto.
2. Tell the students that they are expected to host a party for 9 other people. They can choose any 6 people in the world that they admire or like (living or dead), but must also choose 3 people that they do not like.
   NOTE: Be sure that they use initials or symbols and do not announce their dislikes to the class.
3. Ask them to seat the 9 people and themselves at the table and to include the reasons why they invited each person and why they seated them where they did.
4. Ask them to then complete the Follow-Up Questions Worksheet.
5. Discuss.

Activity 13. What Do You Want? (Understanding Goals)

Concept/Description: By recognizing our goals, we can work towards those goals and thereby reduce some stress.

Objective: To list goals and time frames.

Materials:

Goals Worksheet (See p. 2-7)
Pens or pencils

Directions:

1. Have students list both their long-term and short-term goals on the worksheet.
2. List ways to accomplish these goals.
3. Compare goals and discuss what may happen to people who set their goals too high.
4. What may happen to people who have no goals or who set their goals too low?
5. How can knowing your goals help you? Can goals change with time?

Name ______________________ Date ______________ (2-5)

Party Time Seating Chart

Directions: You are hosting a party for nine other people. You may choose any six people in the world (living or dead) whom you like or admire, but must also choose three people you do not like (use code to signify these people and *do not* share your dislikes with the class). Now you must seat these people and yourself at the table. Explain why you invited each person and why you seated them as you did. When you have finished, complete the follow-up sheet.

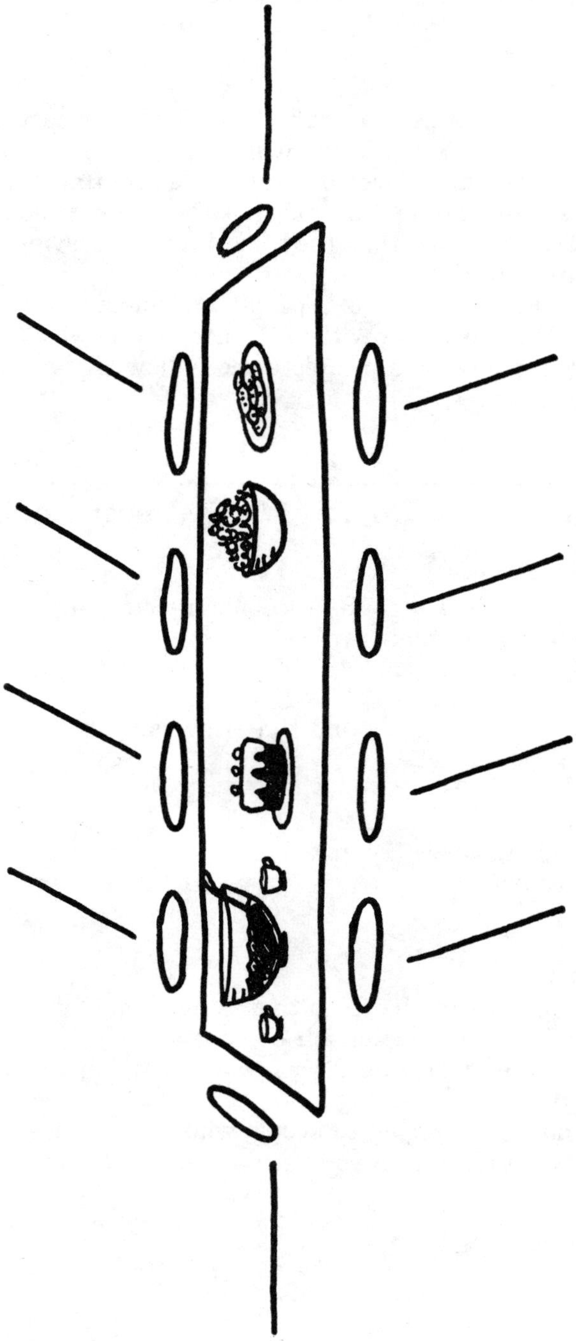

Name ______________________________ Date ____________ (2-6)

Follow-Up Questions to Party Time Seating Chart

	Circle One	
1. Did you seat a person with whom you enjoy talking on your right?	YES	NO
2. Is the person on your left someone you like or admire?	YES	NO
3. Did you invite friends?	YES	NO
4. Did you invite someone who is or was a famous person?	YES	NO
5. Did you try to position the outgoing guests with shy guests?	YES	NO

6. Do you think you are a considerate host or hostess based on questions 1–5? Why or why not?

____

____

____

7. List some things you could do to make sure that the party will be a successful one.

____

____

____

____

Name ______________________ Date ____________ (2-7)

Goals

What I want to accomplish:	What I can do to help myself reach this goal:
1. In the next two days:	1. ______
	2. ______
	3. ______
2. By *next* Friday:	1. ______
	2. ______
	3. ______
3. By Christmas vacation:	1. ______
	2. ______
	3. ______
4. By summer vacation:	1. ______
	2. ______
	3. ______
5. By the end of high school:	1. ______
	2. ______
	3. ______

Activity 14. Help! (Finding Sources of Help)

Concept/Description: There are many social services in the school and in the community that are available to help with problems.

Objective: To find sources of help in the school and community for various problems.

Materials:

Finding Help in School and Community Worksheet (See pp. 2-8, 2-9)
Local phone books
Pens or pencils

Directions:

1. Give each student (or small group) a worksheet and a phone book (many phone companies will donate them free of charge for school activities).
2. Have students read each worksheet situation and then look in the phone book for an agency or organization that could be called for help. Jot down the name, address, and phone number.
3. Discuss the school professionals available, such as psychologist, counselor, principal, nurse, etc.

Activity 15. The Perfect Family (TV Families)

Concept/Description: It is important to understand that all families have problems and difficulties that can usually be worked out with love and understanding. TV is sometimes unrealistic in its portrayal of family life.

Objective: To determine how realistically family life is portrayed on TV.

Materials:

Chalkboard
Chalk
Eraser

Directions:

1. Ask students to consider the TV families on shows that they can recall (present or past). Jot down their responses on the board. (*cont. on p. 60*)

Name ____________________ Date ____________ (2-8)

Finding Help in School and Community

List sources, both school and community, where these people could find help. Include both the name of the organization and phone number.

Problem	*Possible services that are available and phone number*
Susan has trouble controlling her temper. She has a young child. She is afraid she will harm her daughter when she gets frustrated.	1. ______ 2. ______ 3. ______
Tom's parents used to have cocktails before dinner. Now Tom's dad seems to always have a drink in his hand. His dad seems to always argue with Tom, and the fighting is getting worse.	1. ______ 2. ______ 3. ______
Cathy was working later than expected. On the way to her car, someone began to follow her. The parking lot was not well lighted, and she was raped.	1. ______ 2. ______ 3. ______
Tom and Jan have been having sexual intercourse for several weeks. Jan's period is two weeks late, and she suspects she might be pregnant. Tom and Jan decide they want to get help instead of waiting.	1. ______ 2. ______ 3. ______
Bill sees no point in living. His mother died several years ago, and he and his father don't get along now. His married sisters are wrapped up in their families. He has no desire to live and feels he may just as well commit suicide.	1. ______ 2. ______ 3. ______
Julie is married to Bill, who seems very nice and is well liked by his friends. When Julie and Bill are alone, Bill often loses his temper and beats Julie.	1. ______ 2. ______ 3. ______
John has noticed that he has a discharge and a burning sensation when he urinates. He has had sexual intercourse and wonders if he could have a sexually transmitted disease (STD).	1. ______ 2. ______ 3. ______

Problem	*Possible services that are available and phone number*
Jenny's mother has a new boy friend. She spends all her time with him and resents it when Jenny comes home from school or work. Jenny is 17 and suggests to her mother that she will move out if she's not wanted.	1. __________ 2. __________ 3. __________
Mark comes home from school each day to find his dad in the midst of a poker game. The games have been lasting into the night, and the stakes have gotten quite high. Mark's dad has been losing, and he no longer is concerned about the family's money needs. All he wants to do is try to win back all the money he has lost.	1. __________ 2. __________ 3. __________
Janet is a 14-year-old who has been unhappy at home. Her parents won't give her as much freedom as she wants, and she's tired of doing what they tell her to do. They are fed up with her and have told her to go find some place else to live where she can do what she wants.	1. __________ 2. __________ 3. __________
Beth feels that one of her teachers has been picking on her constantly. No matter what she does in that class, she is always in the wrong.	1. __________ 2. __________ 3. __________
Since getting cut from the team, my older brother and his friends spend a lot of time after school getting high. I'm afraid he will hurt himself or become addicted to one of the drugs. How do I stop him from taking them?	1. __________ 2. __________ 3. __________
My father and I had a big fight the other day. He threatened to kill me if I stepped into the house again. I'm staying with a friend for now, but his parents are separated and I can't stay there for long. I have no place to go.	1. __________ 2. __________ 3. __________
I'm running away from home. Why not? Everything at home is a bust. I sure don't see any way it's going to get better, and I'm not sticking around to see it get worse. School has been one hassle after another. I've had it.	1. __________ 2. __________ 3. __________

2. Ask them which shows try to portray the "perfect family"? Place a star next to each one.
3. What traits do these so called "perfect" families have?
4. How realistic are these families?
5. What are real families like? (Consider good and bad traits.)
6. Discuss that most families have some problems and ways to lessen those problems through communication, love, and understanding.

Activity 16. Getting to Know You (Interviewing Parents)

Concept/Description: Students sometimes have erroneous ideas about their parents' views.

Objective: To compare parents' views with what students think their views are.

Materials:

What I Think Worksheet (See p. 2-10)
Parent Interview Worksheet (See p. 2-11)
Pens or pencils

Directions:

1. Have students fill out the What I Think Worksheet based on what they feel one or both (2 sheets) of their parents or guardians will say.
2. For extra credit, have students take the Parent Interview Worksheet home and ask the questions listed.
3. Have students discuss what they thought their parents would say *with* what their parents actually said.
4. Have students bring both sheets to class and discuss what they learned about their parents.

Activity 17. A Matter of Opinion (Individual Differences)

Concept/Description: In the struggle for independence, there may be many ways in which you disagree with your parents but, more importantly, there may also be many ways in which you agree.

Objective: To recognize that individual differences in opinion between children and parents are a normal part of the struggle for independence.

Materials:

A Matter of Opinion Worksheet (See p. 2-12)
Pens or pencils

Directions:

1. Have students fill out Matter of Opinion Worksheet.
2. After all sheets are completed, ask students:
   (a) In what areas did you agree with your parents? Did anyone agree in all areas? Why might that be rare?
   (b) Why might you disagree in certain areas? Give examples.
   (c) Why is it important to recognize individual differences not only between you and your parents but between you and others?

Activity 18. Who's the Boss? (Birth Order)

Concept/Description: Birth order itself does not determine a child's personality, but it may influence how he or she interprets his/her place in the family.

Objective: To list advantages and disadvantages of various birth-order positions and to draw conclusions based on these lists.

Materials:

Paper
Pens or pencils

Directions:

1. Divide the class into the following groups:
   (a) Only children
   (b) First born
   (c) Second born
   (d) Middle of three
   (e) Youngest
   (f) Twins (if any)
   (g) Middle child—large family
2. Appoint a secretary and a spokesperson for each group. The secretary will jot down the group's opinions and the spokesperson will report back to the class.
3. Ask the groups to write down all the advantages and disadvantages of their birth position.

Name ______________________ Date ______________ (2-10)

What I Think

*Answer as you think your parent or guardian would answer.

1. The most important thing that I accomplished in my life was ______________________

2. When I was 15, I wanted to grow up to be ______________________

3. My biggest disagreement with my parents as a teenager was over ______________________

4. My favorite activity or hobby is ______________________

5. My biggest worry is ______________________

6. One thing my parents always told me to do was ______________________

7. My parents disciplined me by ______________________

8. What I want most from my children is ______________________

*These answers are what I think my (check one) would say.

mom ______

dad ______

guardian ______

other ______

Name ____________________ Date ____________ (2-11)

Parent Interview

*Ask your parents these questions for extra credit.

1. The most important thing that I accomplished in my life was ____________________

2. When I was 15, I wanted to grow up to be ____________________

3. My biggest disagreement with my parents as a teenager was over ____________________

4. My favorite activity or hobby is ____________________

5. My biggest worry is ____________________

6. One thing my parents always told me to do was ____________________

7. My parents disciplined me by ____________________

8. What I want most from my children is ____________________

*These answers are what my (check one) says.

mom ______

dad ______

guardian ______

other ______

Name ______________________ Date ______________ (2-12)

A Matter of Opinion

Topic	Your feelings or choices	Your parents' feelings or choices
1. Entertainment?		
2. TV shows you like?		
3. Sports?		
4. Books?		
5. Attitudes toward spending money?		
6. Favorite foods?		
7. Type of jokes or humorous situations?		
8. Religious beliefs?		
9. Attitudes toward others?		

4. After all groups have completed the task and reported back to the class, discuss whether their interpretations of their place in the family can affect their relationships with others.

Activity 19. Get a Job (Family Responsibilities)

Concept/Description: Family members have responsibilities that vary with age and role in the family.

Objective: To have students write out the responsibilities of each family member and make an objective analysis of the division of responsibilities.

Materials:

Paper
Pens or pencils

Directions:

1. Have students write each family member's name at the top of a column.
2. Under each name list all of that person's responsibilities, such as paying bills, taking out the garbage, setting the table, etc.
3. At the conclusion, have students write their analysis of the division of jobs.
4. Discuss their findings and whether or not they feel it is fair.
   NOTE: Plan on hearing about how "easy" their brothers and sisters have it while they are being "tortured."
5. Ask if they realized just how numerous their parents' responsibilities were?

Activity 20. Mom Likes Me Best (How My Parents Feel)

Concept/Description: Students will learn more about themselves by finding out the opinions of their parents.

Objective: To encourage family involvement in discovering strengths, weaknesses, and in building self-esteem.

Materials:

Parents' Questionnaire (See p. 2-13)
Pens or pencils

Directions:

1. Ask students to take the Parent Questionnaire home to be completed (for extra credit).
2. Discuss their findings and whether or not they were surprised by any answers.

Activity 21. Splitting Headache (Understanding Divorce)

Concept/Description: In a divorce situation, all involved experience some degree of hurt or frustration.

Objective: To help students understand and discuss some of the feelings divorce may bring about.

Materials:

Kinds of Wants Worksheet (See p. 2-14)
Pens or pencils
Chalkboard
Chalk, eraser

Directions:

1. Give students a 5–10 minute time limit to finish the statement "I want . . ." on the worksheet. Allow them to write as many things as they want in that time period.
2. Go over the categories on the worksheet and ask students to place each "want" in one of the categories shown.
3. Ask which category has the most? Why?
4. Ask what they do when they don't get what they want? (e.g., cry, throw a fit, sulk, etc.)
5. Are certain needs more important than others? Which ones?
6. In a divorce situation, is anyone getting what he or she really wants? Discuss.
7. What types of frustrations might the following person(s) experience in a divorce situation?
   (a) Children
   (b) Parent who is left behind
   (c) Parent who leaves
   (d) Families
   (e) Stepparents
   (f) Stepchildren
   (g) Others

Name ______________________ Date ______________ (2-13)

Parents' Questionnaire

1. My son's (daughter's) greatest assets are ____.

2. His (her) other strengths are ____.

3. One thing I would *never* change about my child is ____.

4. I would like to see my son or daughter ____.

5. I feel pleased when my child ____.

6. I am disappointed when my child ____.

7. One thing I really enjoy about my son (daughter) is ____.

8. One thing I'd like to say to my child is: ____.

Other comments:

Name ______________________________ Date ______________ (2-14)

Kinds of Wants

Directions: First, list as many wants as you can in the spaces below.

I want . . .

____________	____________	____________
____________	____________	____________
____________	____________	____________
____________	____________	____________
____________	____________	____________
____________	____________	____________
____________	____________	____________
____________	____________	____________

There are different categories of needs. After you have listed your wants, try to categorize them according to the divisions listed below. Write the letter of each category next to your want. You may have more than one category for each one.

This "want" shows a need for:

A = Achievement and recognition

E = Education

L = Love and friendship

W = Work

D = Life-and-death situation

T = Travel

H = Good health

M = Material possessions

O = Other

UNIT 3

PHYSICAL PFFFT . . . NESS

Activities to Encourage Physical Fitness

The activities in this unit are designed to assist children in understanding why fitness is important. As teachers are covering physical fitness principles, they can use these activities to assist their students in obtaining an understanding of why they should exercise, the changes that take place in their bodies when they exercise, and how they can become physically fit.

Activity 1. A Nice Beat (Taking a Pulse After Exercise)

Concept/Description: A person's cardiorespiratory fitness is determined by the efficiency of the heart in pumping blood to all parts of the body. The heart can be trained to supply more blood per stroke by exercising it through aerobic activities.

Objective: To be able to raise the heart rate through aerobic activities and count the number of heart beats per minute.

Materials:

Stopwatch (A wristwatch with a second hand can also be used.)
Exercise and Recovery Heart Rate Worksheet (See p. 3-1)
Pencil for each student

Directions:

1. Show each student how to find his or her resting pulse. Have the students count their pulse for one minute and then record the number of beats on their cards (Or use 30 seconds to count and multiply by 2).
2. Have the students use different aerobic exercises, such as fast walking, jogging, or running in place for different periods of time. (See the sheet). Then have students check pulse rates and record them.
3. Variation for young children: Check pulse in terms of slow beats and fast beats to teach this activity concept.

Activity 2. Right On Target (Charting Heart Rate)

Concept/Description: A person's heart rate will return to its resting rate sooner in a heart that has been exercised than in one that has not been exercised.

Objective: To determine the length of time it takes the heart beat to return to its starting point.

Materials:

Wall clock or watch with second hand
Exercise and Recovery Heart Rate Worksheet (See p. 3-1)
A pencil for each student

Directions:

1. Have students record their resting heart rate.
2. Use an aerobic exercise to raise their pulse rate, staying within safe limits.
3. Have each student check his/her pulse periodically until reaching his/her exercise heart rate. This is determined by subtracting the student's age from 220 and multiplying this figure by 60% (or 0.6).
4. Have students check their heart rate every two minutes after reaching their target exercise rate. Record the heart rate to see how long it takes to return to the resting rate.
5. Variation for young children: Have the children feel that difference in the speed of their heart beat immediately following exercise and in various time increments following exercise.

Activity 3. Slow It Down! (Slowing the Resting Heart Rate)

Concept/Description: If the heart is exercised on a regular basis with sufficient intensity, it will have a slower resting beat.

Objective: To show students how they can use an aerobic program to attain a slow resting heart rate.

Materials:

Watch
Recording card (Figure 3-1)
Pencils

Name ______________________________ Date ______________ (3-1)

Exercise and Recovery Heart Rate Worksheet

My age ____________

Find your target exercise heart rate by subtracting your age from 220 and multiplying the result by 60% (or .6).

My target exercise heart rate is ____________.

My resting heart rate is ____________.

Type of exercise ______________________________

Heart rate following different exercise time periods	Heart rate after completing exercise
1 minute ____________	2 minutes ____________
2 minutes ____________	4 minutes ____________
3 minutes ____________	6 minutes ____________
4 minutes ____________	8 minutes ____________
5 minutes ____________	10 minutes ____________
6 minutes ____________	12 minutes ____________
7 minutes ____________	14 minutes ____________
(activity 1)	(activity 2)

Directions:

1. Record resting heart rate at beginning of the physical fitness unit.
2. Gradually improve the cardiorespiratory fitness level of the students until they can sustain their exercise heart rate for 20 to 30 minutes. Do this three times per week.
3. Have the students check their resting heart rate on a weekly basis to monitor changes that occur. Emphasize that each person is different so that students should not compare their rates with each other but see what happens to themselves.

Name ______________________

Date	Resting Heart Rate

Fig. 3-1. Personal Heart Rate Recording Card

Activity 4. Have a Heart (Differences in Resting Heart Rates)

Concept/Description: Due to age, sex, personal characteristics, and exercise habits, people have different resting heart rates.

Objective: To help students understand some of the reasons for differences in heart rates and realize that exercise habits have an impact on the efficiency of the heart.

Materials:

Watch
Heart Rate Variations Worksheet (See p. 3-2)
Pencils

Directions:

1. The students will take their recording cards home and take the resting heart rate of at least six people.
2. Students will record the heart rate of their parents or guardians and at least one older adult.
3. Students will record the heart rate of one person who exercises on a regular basis.
4. The class will compare the different resting heart rates that they recorded and discuss some of the reasons why resting heart rates vary. Do not use names.

Activity 5. Pinch an Inch (Triceps Pinch to Determine Body Fat) (Activity for older students)

Concept/Description: Excess fat is one of the major deterrents of a satisfactory level of physical fitness, even for youth. Students should be knowledgeable about body fat and its impact on physical fitness.

Objective: To assist students in understanding that excess fat accumulates in various parts of the body. (It should also be emphasized that some fat is critical for health.)

Materials:

Ruler for every two students

Directions:

1. Show the students how to pinch the triceps fat between the thumb and forefinger. Have them pinch the triceps at the midpoint between the shoulder and elbow on the back of the arm (Figure 3-2).
2. Pair up the students
3. Have students measure the thickness of triceps fat on their partner and record their findings.
4. Have students research different ways that body fat can be measured and find out which way is most accurate. Also have them find out the recommended body fat levels for a physically fit person.

Fig. 3-2. Triceps pinch

Name ______________________________ Date ________________ (3-2)

Heart Rate Variations

1. Name ______________________________ Age ______ Resting pulse ______

   Exercise ______________________________ Minutes/week ______

2. Name ______________________________ Age ______ Resting pulse ______

   Exercise ______________________________ Minutes/week ______

3. Name ______________________________ Age ______ Resting pulse ______

   Exercise ______________________________ Minutes/week ______

4. Name ______________________________ Age ______ Resting pulse ______

   Exercise ______________________________ Minutes/week ______

5. Name ______________________________ Age ______ Resting pulse ______

   Exercise ______________________________ Minutes/week ______

6. Name ______________________________ Age ______ Resting pulse ______

   Exercise ______________________________ Minutes/week ______

7. Name ______________________________ Age ______ Resting pulse ______

   Exercise ______________________________ Minutes/week ______

8. Name ______________________________ Age ______ Resting pulse ______

   Exercise ______________________________ Minutes/week ______

Notes:

Activity 6. A Charming Couple (Exercise and Diet)

Concept/Description: Body fat is influenced by both exercise and diet.

Objective: Students will understand the relationship between exercise and diet in controlling body fatness.

Materials:

Caloric chart of commonly consumed foods
Chart showing caloric expenditure during daily activities
(See pp. 78-83)

Directions:

1. Have the class select, with their teacher's assistance, food from the caloric chart that would typically be consumed by a student their age during one week.
2. With their teacher's help, have the students design a week of activity for someone their own age and compute the total caloric expenditure for that week.
3. Have each student show how he or she would recommend that the person whose activity schedule and food consumption had been selected by the class could best lose one pound in a week (3500 calories).
4. Compare the students' recommendations to see how caloric expenditures were increased and/or caloric consumption decreased. Use the activity to show how both of these factors must be considered in controlling body fat.

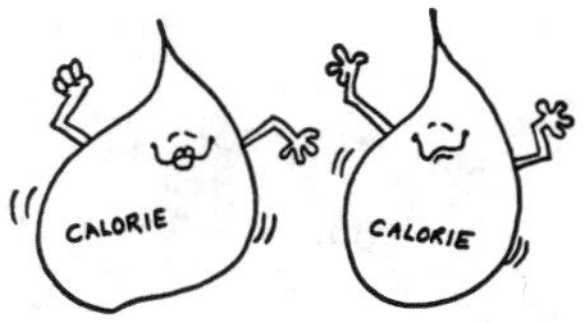

Activity 7. Count on It! (Calorie Counting)

Concept/Description: Exercise is an important factor in controlling a person's weight.

Objective: The students will understand how playing physical games is important in preventing them from becoming fat.

Materials:

Equipment for any team game
Chart showing calorie expenditures during various activities (See pp. 78-83)

NUTRITION TABLE OF COMMON FOODS

Food	Amount	Calories
Almonds, whole	12 to 14	85
Apple	1 medium	70
Apple juice	½ cup	60
Applesauce:		
unsweetened	½ cup	50
sweetened	½ cup	115
Apricots:		
canned in syrup	½ cup	110
dried	5 halves	50
fresh	3 medium	50
Apricot nectar	½ cup	70
Asparagus	4 medium stalks	10
Avocado	½ 10-ounce avocado	185
Bacon:		
crisp, fried	2 slices	90
Canadian, uncooked	3 ounces	185
Banana	1 medium	100
Bagel	1 medium (2 ounces)	160
Beans, cooked:		
green, fresh or frozen	½ cup	15
limas, fresh or frozen	½ cup	95
wax, fresh, frozen	½ cup	45
Beans, kidney, canned	1 cup	230
Beef, broiled meat only,		
ground, lean	3 ounces	185
round, lean	3 ounces	160
sirloin, lean	3 ounces	185
Beets, fresh	2 (½ cup dried)	25
Biscuits:		
baking powder	1 (2-inch diameter)	90
refrigerator	1 biscuit	
Blueberries, fresh or frozen, unsweetened	½ cup	40
Bologna (all-meat)	1 ounce	80
Bouillon cubes	1 cube	5
Breads, one ounce slices		
French or Italian	1 slice	65
rye	1 slice	60
white	1 slice	70
white, raisin	1 slice	65
whole wheat	1 slice	65
Bread crumbs, dry	¼ cup	100
Broccoli, fresh or frozen, cooked	1 cup	20
Brussel sprouts, fresh or frozen, cooked	1 cup	55
Butter	1 tablespoon	100
Cabbage, fresh:		
boiled	½ cup	15
raw	½ cup (shredded)	10
Cakes:		
angel food	1/12 of 10-inch cake	135
chiffon	1/16 of 10-inch cake	215
chocolate cake, fudge frosting	1/16 of a 9-inch layer cake	235

*mg = milligrams

Source: Abstracted from publications issued by U.S. Department of Agriculture and Data submitted by Food Manufacturers.

Food	Amount	Calories
cupcake, plain	1 medium	90
yellow cake, fudge frosting	1/16 of a 9-inch layer cake	275
Candy:		
caramel, plain	1 piece	40
chocolate, milk	1 ounce	145
gum drop	1 small	10
sour ball	1 large	35
peanut brittle	1 ounce	120
Canteloupe	½ (5-inch diameter)	60
Carrots:		
cooked	½ cup sliced	20
raw	1 5½" × 1" carrot	20
Catsup	1 tablespoon	15
Cauiflower, cooked	½ cup	15
Celery, raw	1 large stalk	15
Cereals, ready-to-eat:		
all-bran flakes	1 ounce	70
corn flakes	1 ounce	110
puffed rice, wheat	1 ounce	110
rice krispies	1 ounce	110
raisin bran	1 ounce	105
shredded wheat	1 ounce	110
Cheese:		
American, processed	1 ounce	105
Cheddar	1 ounce	115
cheese spread	1 ounce	80
cottage, creamed	⅓ cup	85
cream	2 tablespoons (1 ounce)	105
Mozzarella, whole milk	1 ounce	90
Parmesan or Romano, grated	2 tablespoons	50
Ricotta, partially skimmed milk	⅓ cup	85
Roquefort or bleu	1 ounce	105
Swiss, processed or natural	1 ounce	105
Cherries:		
canned in syrup	½ cup	115
fresh, sweet	½ cup	40
Chicken, fryers, uncooked:		
breast, with skin	1 whole (¾ pound)	295
leg and thigh, with skin	1 small (½ pound)	190
light meat, without skin	4 ounces	115
dark meat, without skin	4 ounces	130
Chocolate:		
milk	1 ounce	145
semi-sweet	1 ounce	145
Chocolate pudding	½ cup	175
Cod, uncooked	4 ounces	90
Cola drinks	8 ounces	90
Collards, cooked	½ cup	25
Cookies:		
chocolate chip	1 (1-inch diameter)	50
fig bar	1 square	50
gingersnap	1 small (2-inch diameter)	30
oatmeal	1 large (3-inch diameter)	65
sandwich, creme	1 cookie	50
vanilla wafer	1 cookie	20

*mg = milligrams

Food	Amount	Calories
Corn, cooked:		
canned, whole kernel	½ cup	85
fresh or frozen	1 ear (5-inches long)	70
Cornmeal, uncooked	1 cup	500
Crackers:		
graham	4 (2½-inch diameter)	110
oyster	10 crackers	45
rye wafer	2 wafers	45
saltine	4 squares	50
Cranberries, raw	1 cup	45
Cranberry sauce	2 tablespoons	40
Cream:		
half-and-half	1 tablespoon	20
heavy	1 tablespoon	55
	1 cup	840
light	1 tablespoon	30
	1 cup	505
sour	1 tablespoon	25
Cream of Wheat, dry	1 ounce	100
Cucumber, raw	1 medium (10 ounces)	43
Danish pastry, plain	4 ½-inch piece	275
Doughnut, cake-type	1 medium	125
Egg, raw	1 medium	70
Eggplant, cooked	1 cup, diced	40
Flounder, raw	4 ounces	90
Flour:		
all-purpose	1 cup	420
whole-wheat	1 cup	400
Frankfurter, all-meat	1.6 ounce frankfurter	135
Fruit cocktail, canned	½ cup	95
Gelatin dessert	½ cup	70
Gelatin, unflavored, dry	1 envelope	25
Grapefruit	½ medium	45
Grapefruit juice	½ cup	50
Grape juice	½ cup	85
Grapes	20 grapes	50
Gravy, canned beef	2 tablespoons	15
Haddock, uncooked	4 ounces	90
Halibut, uncooked	4 ounces	115
Ham, boiled	1 ounce	70
Honey	1 tablespoon	65
Ice cream, vanilla	1 cup (10% butterfat)	255
Ice milk, vanilla	1 cup	200
Jam or jelly	1 tablespoon	55
Lamb chop, lean, cooked	4 ounces (with bone)	140
Lemon or lime juice	¼ cup	15
Lentils, dried, raw	2½ tablespoons	85
Lettuce, raw	1 cup, chopped	10
Liver, uncooked:		
beef or calf	4 ounces	155
chicken	4 ounces	145
Lobster, cooked meat	3 ounces	80
Macaroni and cheese	1 cup	430
Macaroni, uncooked	1 ounce (½ cup cooked)	105
Margarine	1 tablespoon	100
Marshmallows, plain	1 average	25

*mg = milligrams

Food	Amount	Calories
Matzoh, plain	1 regular	120
Milk:		
buttermilk	1 cup	90
condensed, sweetened	½ cup	490
evaporated, undiluted	½ cup	175
low fat, 1% fat	1 cup	105
skimmed	1 cup	90
whole, 3.5% fat	1 cup	160
Milk, dry, non-fat instant	⅓ cup (makes 1 cup liquid)	80
Molasses, light	1 tablespoon	50
Muffins:		
corn	1 (2⅜-inch diameter)	125
bran	1 (3-inch diameter)	105
English	1 (3½-inch diameter)	140
Mushrooms:		
canned	1 cup (solids and liquid)	40
fresh	1 pound	125
Noodles, uncooked	1 ounce (½ cup cooked)	110
Oatmeal, uncooked	1 ounce (¾ cup cooked)	105
Oils, vegetable:		
corn, cottonseed, olive, soybean, etc.	1 tablespoon	125
Olives, green, pitted	4 medium	20
Onion, raw	1 medium	40
Orange	1 medium	65
Orange juice, fresh, frozen, canned	½ cup	55
Pancakes, from mix	2 (4-inch diameter)	120
Parsley, raw	5 tablespoons, chopped	5
Pea, green:		
canned	½ cup	60
frozen	½ cup	60
Pea, split dry	½ cup	345
Peach nectar	½ cup	60
Peaches:		
canned, syrup pack	½ cup halves with syrup	100
fresh	1 medium	35
Peanuts, roasted	8 to 10	55
Peanut Butter	1 tablespoon	95
Pears:		
canned, syrup pack	½ cup halves with syrup	100
fresh	1 medium	100
Pecans	9 medium halves	70
Peppers, green	1 medium	15
Pickle, dill	1 (4″ × 1¾″ pickle)	15
Pie crust, made with vegetable shortening:		
homemade, single crust	1 9-inch shell	900
Pies:		
apple, double crust	⅙ of 9-inch pie	405
cherry, double crust	⅙ of 9-inch pie	410
custard	⅙ of 9-inch pie	330
lemon meringue	⅙ of 9-inch pie	355
pecan	⅙ of 9-inch pie	575
Pineapple, canned:		
slices, syrup-pack	2 slices	90
slices, juice-pack	2 slices	65
Pineapple juice	½ cup	65
Pizza, cheese	⅛ of 14-inch pie	185

*mg = milligrams

Food	Amount	Calories
Plums:		
canned syrup pack	½ cup with syrup	100
fresh	1 (2-inch diameter)	25
Popcorn, popped	1 cup	25
Pork, roasted meat only,		
ham, cured, lean	3 ounces	210
ham, fresh, lean	3 ounces	185
loin chop, lean	3 ounces	230
Potatoes:		
baked	1 medium	90
boiled, pared,	1 medium	90
french-fried	10 pieces	155
Soups:		
chicken-noodle	1 serving	55
manhattan chowder	1 serving	65
minestrone	1 serving	85
mushroom, cream of	1 serving	185
tomato	1 serving	70
vegetable	1 serving	60
Spinach, frozen, cooked	½ cup	20
Squash, cooked:		
summer	½ cup	15
winter	½ cup	65
Strawberries, fresh	½ cup	25
Sugar:		
brown	1 cup	820
granulated	1 cup	770
	1 tablespoon	40
powdered	1 cup	460
Sunflower seeds, shelled	1 tablespoon	45
Syrup, maple	1 tablespoon	50
Tangerine	1 (2½-inch diameter)	40
Tomato juice	½ cup	25
Tomatoes:		
canned	½ cup	25
fresh	1 medium	40
Tuna, canned:		
oil-pack	6½ ounce can	530
water-pack	6½ ounce can	235
Turkey, roasted:		
light meat	4 ounces	200
dark meat	4 ounces	230
Veal, roasted	4 ounces	185
Vegetable juice	½ cup	20
Waffle	1 7-inch waffle	205
Walnuts, English	8 halves	50
Watermelon	1 wedge, 4″ × 8″	115
Wheat germ	1 tablespoon	15
Whipped Topping, frozen	1 tablespoon	15
Yogurt, plain	1 cup	150

*mg = milligrams

ENERGY EXPENDITURE BY A 150-POUND PERSON IN VARIOUS ACTIVITIES

Activity	Gross Energy Spent in Calories Per Hour
Rest and light activity	***50–200***
Lying down or sleeping	80
Sitting	100
Driving an automobile	120
Standing	140
Domestic work	180
Moderate activity	***200–350***
Bicycling (5½ mph)	210
Walking (2½ mph)	210
Gardening	220
Canoeing (2½ mph)	230
Golf	250
Lawn mowing (power mower)	250
Bowling	270
Lawn mowing (hand mower)	270
Fencing	300
Rowboating (2½ mph)	300
Swimming (¼ mph)	300
Walking (3¼ mph)	300
Badminton	350
Horseback riding (trotting)	350
Square dancing	350
Volleyball	350
Roller skating	350
Vigorous activity	***over 350***
Table tennis	360
Ditch digging (hand shovel)	400
Ice skating (10 mph)	400
Wood chopping or sawing	400
Tennis	420
Water skiing	480
Hill climbing (100 ft. per hr.)	490
Skiing (10 mph)	600
Squash and handball	600
Cycling (13 mph)	660
Scull rowing (race)	840
Running (10 mph)	900

Source: President's Council on Physical Fitness and Sports, "Exercise and Weight Control," (Washington, D.C.: U.S. Gov't Printing Office, 1979).

Directions:

1. Students will determine how many calories they use when they—
   (a) watch one hour of television
   (b) walk for 30 minutes
2. The students will then play a vigorous game for 30 minutes.
3. The caloric expenditure for a vigorous game will be compared with the other two activities.
4. The class, with the teacher's assistance, will analyze the importance of vigorous activity in controlling body fat.

Activity 8. Put Your Best Fist Forward (Muscle Fatigue)

Concept/Description: A component of physical fitness is a person's ability to use muscles many times without getting tired.

Objective: The students will experience muscle fatigue which will help them understand the importance of muscular endurance.

Materials:

Clock or watch
Pencil and paper for each student

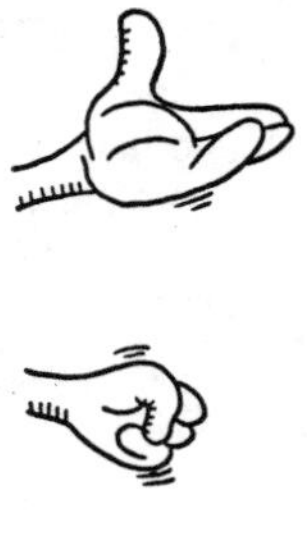

Fig. 3-3. Hand positions for fist flexion

Directions:

1. All students will place the back of one of their hands on their desk.
2. The teacher will have the students open and close their fist as many times as possible within a three-minute time period. The time period should be adjusted according to the age and maturity of the students (Figure 3-5).
3. Students will experience their muscles becoming tired and will be asked to write ways that the muscles of their bodies become tired.

4. The class will then be divided into groups and asked to give as many reasons as possible about why muscle endurance is an important part of physical fitness.
5. Each group will have the opportunity to explain its reasons to the rest of the class.

Activity 9. Flex Your Muscles (Arm Flex and Overload)

Concept/Description: A muscle will become stronger only if it is worked at higher than normal levels.

Objective: Students will understand the overload principle as it applies to physical fitness.

Materials:

Books or other heavy items that can be held in a student's hand.

Directions:

1. Students will stand and rapidly flex one of their arms for two minutes.
2. Students will then put a book or other heavy object in the hand of their other arm and repeat the two-minute exercise.
3. The teacher will discuss why the second arm became tired sooner and explain the benefits to the overloaded muscle.
4. The students will then be guided in sharing ideas about why it is important to overload a muscle.

Fig. 3-4. Arm Flexion

Activity 10. These Feet Are Made for Walking (Benefits of Walking)

Concept/Description: Walking is one of the best physical fitness activities.

Objective: To develop a walking habit.

Materials:

Walking log (See Activity 11.)
Wall Map of U.S.

Directions:

1. Use a running track or measure a specific distance where students can walk.
2. Have the students walk for 15 minutes at a brisk walking pace on a measured course.
3. Compute the distance each pupil walked during the 15-minute period.
4. Give all students a walking log and have them keep a record of the time that they walk each day and compute the distance.
5. Use a wall map of the U.S., and chart the cumulative distance walked by the members of the class each week. Start at the location of the students' school and go to designated places that are being studied in another class or that students establish as a goal.
6. A variation would be to divide the class into teams and have the teams compete to see who walks the greatest distance each week or which team can reach a designated location first.

Activity 11. A Walking We Will Go (Family Walk Chart)

Concept/Description: People of all ages will benefit from walking.

Objective: Children will share with their family the enjoyment of walking.

Materials:

Walking log
Promotional materials emphasizing the value of walking and designating a school walking week.

Directions:

1. One week before the school walking week, children will take home to their families promotional materials about walking and an explanation of the school's walking week activity.
2. During the school walking week, each member of the class will be encouraged to take a daily walk with as many members of his or her family as possible.
3. The approximate total distance that is walked by *all* members of the family will be recorded by each student.
4. At the end of the school's walking week, the class will compute the total distance that was walked. This information will be publicized in the school and in the community.
5. The students may also want to compute the total caloric expenditure during the week and convert this figure to the numbers of pounds that were taken off during the week.

Name ____________

Date	Distance Walked		Number of Family Members		Total Distance
___	______	×	______	=	______
___	______	×	______	=	______
___	______	×	______	=	______
___	______	×	______	=	______

Total Miles ______

Fig. 3-5. Walking log

Activity 12. A Portion of Contortion (Flexibility Tableau)

Concept/Description: It is important to maintain good flexibility in all joints of the body.

Objective: To demonstrate flexibility of as many joints as possible.

Materials:
(None)

Directions:
1. Divide the class into groups of five or six.
2. Each group is instructed to make up a tableau (representation of a scene) which will depict activities that require extensive flexibility.
3. Each group will present their tableau to the rest of the class, which will guess what it represents. The performers will explain why their activities required flexibility.

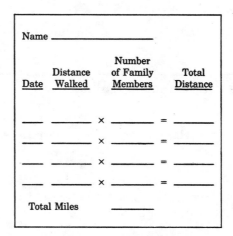

Variation:
Groups will demonstrate activities that are difficult if a person is not flexible.

Activity 13. I Can Do It! (Strength Collage)

Concept/Description: Muscular strength is important to develop as part of being physically fit.

Objective: Students will recognize that muscular strength is needed in daily activities as well as when carrying out challenging tasks.

Materials:
Newspapers and magazines
Scissors
Glue
Posterboard

Directions:
1. Have students go through newspapers and magazines and find pictures of people successfully carrying out a task or performing some activity that requires muscular strength.
2. Have each student, or a group of students, develop a collage which tells a story about the need for strength.
3. After sharing collages with the rest of the class, display them in a prominent spot in the school.

Readers are referred to pages 111–129 of the authors' book, *You'll Never Guess What We Did in Gym Today* (Parker Publishing Company, 1984) for additional physical fitness activities designed for the classroom. Activities also include those that test the skills-related parts of fitness, such as agility, balance, power, foot-eye coordination, hand-eye coordination, and speed and reaction time. In addition, there are many games in other chapters of the book and in the authors' first book, *What Are We Doing in Gym Today?* (Parker Publishing Company, 1983), that cover skill-related components of fitness. If time permits, games that emphasize different skills, such as agility or hand-eye coordination, can be played to assist the children in understanding the different skill-related components of physical fitness when they are studying their physical fitness health unit.

UNIT 4

"NO THANKS, I'M WATCHING MY WEIGHT"

Activities Highlighting Proper Nutrition

Appropriate eating habits are an important element of good health. More and more research is indicating the importance of good diet at a young age. This is important not only for good health when young but also because the habit establishes a pattern that stretches through the teen years into adulthood. Activities on nutrition in this unit move students from the abstract to the practical. They actually plan meals and assume roles that force them to look at food in terms of its ability to provide needed nutrients for them and their families.

There are many nutritional problems even in countries that are rich in food products. Some of the activities have been developed to stimulate students to investigate some of these problems and to gain an understanding of factors that cause people to eat foods that have deficiencies. Students also need to understand how often food is associated with social events in their lives. Also, different nationalities eat different kinds of foods. It is important that students know that the kind of food isn't the important factor—it's the nutritional value.

The goal of this chapter is to broaden the students' perspective of food. Food becomes more than a box of spaghetti that is picked off the grocery shelf or a carton of milk that is in the refrigerator. Food is viewed from the impact it has on a person's health and the nutritional value that it has. Furthermore, the activities assist students in selecting food for nutritional balance and different body needs.

Activity 1. 1, 2, 3, 4—This Is What We're Looking For! (Learning the Four Basic Food Groups)

Concept/Description: There are four food groups that should be included in a person's daily diet.

Objective: Students will know foods that belong to each food group.

Materials:

Empty containers of food products
Large garbage bag

Directions:

1. Have students bring to class clean, empty containers of food products from the four basic food groups. Examples would be milk cartons, fruit and vegetable cans, frozen food packages, cereal boxes, and egg cartons.

2. Place the items in a large garbage bag.
3. Set up four desks or areas in the room with a food group designation sign at each location: Dairy Group, Meat Group, Fruit and Vegetable Group, and Grain Group. As a class project, let students make up the signs.
4. Students take turns reaching into the bag, removing a food item container and then placing the container with the proper food group.

Variation:

Place the containers in a location where they are visible. Divide the class into teams of 4 or 5 students. Let the teams alternate picking up a container and have the students arrange the containers so that they represent a balanced daily diet for breakfast, lunch, and dinner.

Activity 2. Calories Come and Calories Go (Computing Your Caloric Balance or Imbalance)

Concept/Description: Caloric intake needs to be kept in proportion to caloric output.

Objective: Students will keep a record of their caloric intake and caloric output for a day and understand how they relate to each other.

Materials:

Personal Calorie Chart (See 4-1)

Directions:

1. Have each student write down everything he or she eats during a designated day.
2. Have all students keep a log of their activity for the same day.
3. Have students then compute the number of calories consumed and number of calories used. Supply calorie charts for students to use in computing their caloric intake for the day. (Emphasize that this is not an exact measurement and that more accurate information can be obtained by keeping a record over a longer period of time.)
4. Have each student determine his/her caloric balance for the day. Indicate as *plus* (+) if more calories were consumed, and *minus* (−) if more were used.
5. Add the caloric balance figures for all of the students to see if more calories were consumed or expended. Explain the ramifications. For example, for each 3500 calories consumed that were not expended, the class weight gain would be one additional pound.

Variations:

1. Compute the total number of pounds that were "lost" during the day from the combined activity of all members of the class (3500 calories to a pound).
2. Compute the total number of pounds that would have been gained during the day if there had not been any activity to counterbalance it.

Activity 3. Jello, Toast and Tea Is Really Not For Me! (Hospital Menu Planning)

Concept/Description: People differ in the types of diet they should have.

Objective: To make up menus for people who have specialized dietary needs.

Materials:

Hospital Menu Planning Worksheet for each team (See 4-2)

Directions:

1. Divide the students into teams of 4 of 5.
2. Each team will be nutritionists employed at a local hospital. The team's responsibility will be to plan meals for all types of patients. Meals must be well balanced and enjoyable.
3. A one-day diet (breakfast, lunch and dinner) is planned for four patients using the Hospital Menu Planning Worksheet, which lists the foods available at the hospital.
4. The nutrition teams are to consider each patient's problem and then design the day's diet.
5. This activity requires a basic knowledge of nutrition, and it also requires the teams to cooperate in order to analyze and solve the problems at hand. The teacher should watch how the various groups work, discuss the problem, and arrive at methods that are used in solving the problem.
6. Ask the groups to explain their reasons for choosing each food item.

Activity 4. Nutrition Mission! (Basic Nutritional Facts)

Concept/Description: There are nutritional facts that are important for students to know.

Objective: Students will know several facts about different nutritional terms.

Name ______________________________ Date __________________ (4-1)

Personal Calorie Chart

CALORIC INTAKE **CALORIC OUTPUT**

FOOD ITEM	AMOUNT	CALORIES CONSUMED	ACTIVITY	AMOUNT OF TIME	CALORIES USED

TOTAL __________ TOTAL __________

Name ______________________ Date ______________

Hospital Menu Planning

YOUR JOB: Choose breakfast, lunch, and dinner for each of these patients from the food choices available below. Meals must be appropriate to the patients' special needs, well-balanced, and enjoyable.

PATIENTS:

Patient #1

67-year-old man
Has no teeth
Has an ulcer

Patient #2

7-year-old girl
Had her tonsils out yesterday
Has a sore throat

Patient #3

45-year-old man
Very overweight
Has a serious heart ailment

Patient #4

52-year-old woman
Recovering from a broken arm
Going home the next day

HOSPITAL MENU:

Breakfast

Eggs	Waffles	Grapefruit half	Tomato juice
Oatmeal	Bacon	Orange juice	Donut
Cold cereal	Sausage	Coffee	Toast and jelly
Pancakes w/syrup	Ham	Tea	English muffin

Lunch

Soup	Hamburger	Soda	Lemonade
Salad w/dressing	Chili	Iced tea	Jello
Cottage cheese	French fries	Tea	Cake
Egg salad	Potato chips	Coffee	Ice cream
Tuna salad	Vegetable	Milk	Fruit
Hot dog			

Dinner

Chicken	Soup	Salad w/dressing	Tea
Pork chops	Broccoli	Soda	Strawberry shortcake
Hamburger	Peas & carrots	Iced tea	Cheese cake
Turkey	Stewed tomatoes	Lemonade	Jello
Spaghetti & sauce	Mashed potatoes	Milk	Ice cream
Liver	Baked potato	Coffee	Pudding
Fruit			

Materials:
3 × 5 cards

Directions:
1. Select a number of nutrition terms, and put each term on a 3 × 5 card. (The sophistication of the terms will depend on the grade level of the students and the material that has been covered in class). Examples of such terms are—corn, vitamin A, iron, protein, malnutrition, dehydration, ice cream, bulimia.
2. Have each student pull a card when it is his or her turn.
3. Use this as a review for your nutrition unit by having each student give one nutritional fact about the term he or she has drawn. For example, "Corn—Part of the fruit and vegetable group."
4. Mix the nutritional terms and let the students get another term for the next round.
5. If a student is stumped, let the next person tackle the same term.

Variations:
1. Divide the class into teams and have teams or representatives from teams compete by being the first to have an answer when the term is announced by the teacher or a student who serves as moderator. Set up the activity like a TV show, and use different techniques for teams to indicate they have the answer.
2. Have students write up nutritional terms and give point values according to what they think are the best nutritional facts. Run a contest patterned after the TV show, "Family Feud," and call it "Family Food". (See Unit 1).

Activity 5. Encore! Encore! (Using Video to Teach about Nutrition)

Concept/Description: Students need to be aware of nutritional issues and problems.

Objective: To have students present a short play or skit covering a nutritional problem or issue.

Materials:
VCR
Video tape
Video camera

Directions:
1. Divide the class into groups of 7 to 10.
2. Each group will be performing a song, dance, or play. Have them select a name for their group that relates to nutrition (examples: The Veggies, The Four Seasonings, The Pasta Pals).

3. Have each group stage a 5 to 10 minute performance depicting a nutritional problem or issue that is designated by the teacher. Each skit or act should include 4–5 facts about the group's particular subject. Examples:
   (a) A student who selects primarily junk foods.
   (b) A fad diet that is being prominently advertised.
   (c) Interpreting nutritional labels on food packages.
   (d) Eating for performance in the Olympics.
   (e) Hazards in the food supply (for older children).
4. Tape each group.
5. Show the video to other classes, on back-to-school nights, or in the school lunchroom if this is permitted.

Variations:

1. Let the students select their own topic. They might be asked to choose what they think is the number one nutritional challenge, misleading food labels, or some nutritional area that is being discussed in class. Tape each group as they perform, and evaluate the information that each acting group presents.
2. Make the video presentation a class project. Cover nutritional information from class. Make duplicate tapes. (Some parents will usually have the equipment to do this if the school does not.) Send tapes home so the students can view the tapes with their parents.

Activity 6. Have I Got a Deal for You! (Selling a New Food Product)

Concept/Description: There are many factors other than nutrition that determine whether people will eat a food product.

Objective: Students will be able to experience how a new food product is promoted.

Materials:

Paper and pens
Material determined by students

Directions:

1. Divide the class into teams.
2. Have each team develop a new kind of breakfast bar that will provide nutritional value equal to a breakfast of—
   6 oz. glass of orange juice
   2 slices of buttered whole wheat toast
   1 poached egg
   1 peach
3. Make up a name and label for the new breakfast bar.
4. Design a full-page advertisement telling the public about your product.

Variations:

1. Younger children can draw pictures of their new product.
2. Invent other food products.
3. Turn empty boxes inside out (by unfolding the flaps and seams and then retaping the box together). Cover with paper and/or draw the new label directly on the box.

Activity 7. A Corny Idea! (From the Raw Material to the Finished Food Product)

Concept/Description: Producing food involves many stages and different tasks.

Objective: Students will make a flow chart which will show the steps that precede a food product appearing on the kitchen table.

Materials:

Newsprint
Pens
Drawing materials

Directions:

1. Make a flow chart showing the steps that are taken from the time the farmer prepares the soil for a crop until the food product arrives on the table (Figure 4-1).
2. The flow chart can be a pictorial one for younger children.
3. Older children can research the steps that are followed and write a description for each.

Variations:

1. Have the class develop a production flow chart for a food of their choice. Divide the class and have different students or groups of students research the various steps that lead up to the food arriving on their table. Place this information in a flow chart.
2. Have the students write letters to farmers (or agriculture departments), manufacturers, shipping companies, and grocery stores requesting additional information that they can put on their flow chart.

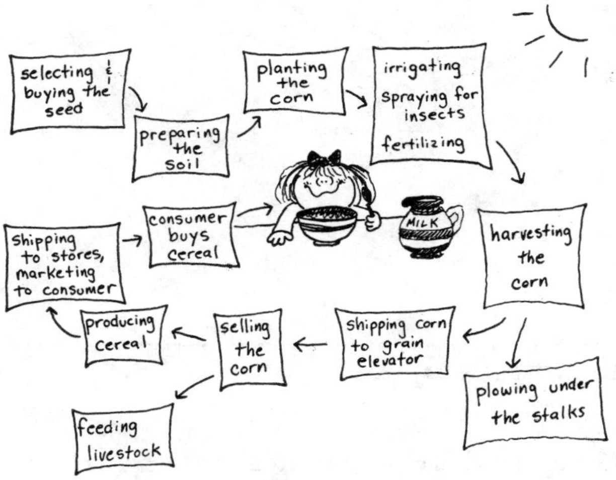

Fig. 4-1. Corn production flow chart.

Activity 8. It's a Small World (Nutritional Value of Different Foods)

Concept/Description: People in different parts of the world have different dietary habits. Different diets can have similar nutritional value.

Objective: To have students develop dinner menus for several different nationalities.

Materials:

Recipes for different foods
Nutritional values of different foods

Directions:

1. List a typical dinner menu derived from one of several different ethnic backgrounds. (This is an ideal project in which to involve parents. Ask parents to share menus that would be typical for their nationality.)
2. Compare the different menus.
3. Discuss how different foods have similar nutritional values.
4. Research reasons why certain types of foods are characteristic of specific ethnic groups or nationalities.
5. Prepare the foods and bring to class (extra credit) for all to sample.

Variation:

Have students make up a nutritional breakfast menu that does not include toast, cereal, eggs, bacon, juice, pancakes, or other traditional breakfast items. Discuss why this menu is not commonly served in the United States.

Activity 9. 'Tis the Season (Special Foods)

Concept/Description: Food is closely related to celebrations and special occasions.

Objective: To compare the kinds of foods that are eaten during holiday seasons.

Materials:
Recipes

Directions:

1. Have all students bring in a recipe which is traditionally used on a holiday in their home.
2. Compare the recipes to see the kinds of food that are commonly eaten on holidays. Are they mostly sweets? Are they nutritious? Why are special foods eaten during holidays?

Variations:

1 Select a specific holiday and have all the students bring in recipes for that holiday.
2. Have students write reports on the way that food is viewed in different cultures (for older students).

Activity 10. How Much Is Enough? (Proper Amounts of Carbohydrates, Fats, and Proteins)

Concept/Description: Many Americans need to reduce the percentage of fats and increase the carbohydrates in their diets.

Objective: To compare a class survey of carbohydrates, fats, and proteins consumed with recommended percentages.

Name ______________________ Date ______________ (4-3)

Nutrient Survey

Estimate what percent of your diet is composed of each nutrient:

CARBOHYDRATES (Examples: Breads, cereals, pasta, rice, vegetables, fruit, sugar)			
FATS (Examples: Butter, margarine, cheese, ice cream, whole milk, eggs, fried foods, nuts, salad dressing)			
PROTEINS (Examples: Beef, pork, chicken, fish, dairy products, beans)			
TOTAL	100%	100%	100%

Materials:

Nutrient Survey Worksheet. (See 4-3)

Directions:

1. Have each student survey three adults and have the student fill out the Nutrient Survey Worksheet for each of the adults surveyed.
2. Compile the answers of all the surveys to get a mean for each category: proteins, fats, carbohydrates. (This would be a good project to complete as part of a mathematics assignment.)
3. Have students research the percentage of each of the nutrient classifications that is recommended by various authors and health organizations.
4. Compare the results of your surveys with your research findings.
5. Have the class write a special edition of a newspaper highlighting the findings. (Other nutritional facts could also be incorporated into the newspaper.)

Variation:

Have adults guess the recommended adult percentage of each nutrient.

Activity 11. Vitamin C for Me (Nutrient Needs)

Concept/Description: Different foods must be eaten to supply needed nutrients.

Objective: Students will be able to match different foods with the appropriate nutrient quality.

Materials:

Food cards (See 4-2)
Nutrient Charts (See 4-4)

Directions:

1. Have your class draw or paint the picture of different foods on cards or construction paper of identical sizes (Figure 4-2). Have 12 foods that are in the carbohydrate group, 12 that are in the fat group, and 12 from the protein group. (This project could be coordinated with the art department.) Collect and place the cards on the teacher's desk.
2. Divide the class into teams and give each team a nutrient chart.
3. Mix up the cards and let the Team A draw a food card and place it in an appropriate spot on the team's Nutrient Chart. Team B follows. Should a team not be able to use a card, it must be placed at the bottom of the pile. The next team then draws.
4. The team filling all their spaces first is the winner. (Cards not needed are put at the bottom of the pile of remaining cards.)

Fig. 4-2. Sample food cards.

Variations:

1. Make cards that tell what each nutrient does. (Example: Main source of energy—to match with carbohydrates.)
2. Make up a Bingo-type board with the spaces filled in with different nutrients (Figure 4-3). The student covering the entire board or all of one nutrient will be the winner.
3. Cards could be hidden around the classroom for small children to find when they play this game.
4. Include other nutrients that are being studied in class, such as vitamins, minerals, etc.

CARBO-HYDRATES	VITAMIN A	FATS	PROTEIN
VITAMIN C	VITAMIN D	CALCIUM	FATS
PROTEIN	CARBO-HYDRATES	WATER	POTASSIUM
IRON	VITAMIN A	FATS	WATER

Fig. 4-3. Nutrition Bingo card.

Nutrient Chart

CARBOHYDRATES		
FATS		
PROTEINS		
VITAMIN A		
VITAMIN C		
VITAMIN E		
IRON		
CALCIUM		
POTASSIUM		
WATER		

Activity 12. So Full and Yet So Empty (Nutritional Value of Snack Foods)

Concept/Description: Too many snack foods are high in caloric value, but have little or no nutritive value.

Objective: Students will realize the lack of nutritional value in a snack-food diet.

Materials:

Pencils and paper
Types of Snacks Worksheet (See 4-5)

Directions:

1. Have all students list all the snack foods that they eat.
2. Have students put their snack foods in the appropriate food group.
3. Use the results to discuss the dangers of too many snack foods.
4. Have all students make up a list of healthy snack foods that they could substitute for their current snack-food diet.

Name ______________________________ Date ____________________ (4-5)

Types of Snacks

DIRECTIONS: List all the snack foods you eat in the appropriate boxes below.

Dairy Group	Meat Group
Fruit and Vegetable Group	**Grain Group**

Fats and Sweeteners (Primarily just a source of calories)

UNIT 5

"RING AROUND THE COLLAR"

Activities Stressing Appropriate Personal Grooming

Will I be accepted? How do I look? Will I be liked? Although these questions aren't always asked out loud, they express typical concerns of elementary-age children, as well as those of adolescents and adults. The activities in this chapter place a heavy emphasis on helping children understand that others have the same concerns they have and helping these children accept themselves.

Nothing causes more concern to children as they approach the upper elementary grades than acne and other types of skin blemishes. There are many myths about acne, both its causes and cures. Activities in this unit deal with these issues. They help students debunk myths and realize that other students have the same problems and similar fears about how others view them because of acne.

Personal grooming is an important factor in the way we are viewed. Teeth and hair care, cleanliness and clothing, the way we carry ourselves — all can send messages to others. Activities to help students in each of these areas are presented in a nonthreatening, but informative, manner.

Activity 1. Skin Scams (Acne Causes and Cures)

Concept/Description: Students have many misconceptions about what causes and "cures" acne.

Objective: To have students understand the causes of acne and explore legitimate treatment procedures.

Materials:

Paper
Pens or pencils

Directions:

1. Have all students list all the "causes" and "cures" for acne that they have heard or read about.
2. Tabulate the responses to determine the frequency with which each "cause" and "cure" is listed.
3. Categorize the "causes" and "cures" that the students list. For example, categories for causes will probably include foods, lack of personal cleanliness, and anti-

social behavior. Categories for cures range from different kinds of skin care to specific foods to medical treatment.

4. Discuss the validity of each "cause" and "cure." Convey to the students that there is no known cause or cure—just procedures that can alleviate some of the difficulties with acne.

Variations:

1. Have students research the accuracy of the causes and cures that were listed.
2. Invite a dermatologist to come to your class and discuss the causes and cures that were listed.

Activity 2. You Need Acne-Off (Advertising For Acne Cures)

Concept/Description: There are many so-called "cures" for acne that do not withstand close scrutiny.

Objective: To help students become knowledgeable consumers of products designed to cure acne.

Materials:

Acne cure advertisements

Directions:

1. Have students collect all the advertisements they can find about acne cures.
2. Analyze the appeal that each advertisement has for a young person. (Most advertisements seem to indicate that to be popular, you cannot have pimples.)
3. Compare costs of different acne cures.
4. Determine the success rate that is claimed for each treatment.
5. Discuss the merits of each product that is advertised. Benzoyl peroxide seems to be helpful, while products containing alcohol actually dry out the skin, causing more oil to be produced.

Variations:

1. Collect products that are for acne treatment, and read the labels and accompanying materials.
2. Ask a physician to point out misleading statements commonly found in acne advertisements.

Activity 3. Howdy Doody with Acne? (Puppet Show on Skin Care)

Concept/Description: There are acceptable skin-care procedures that will contribute to healthy skin.

Objective: Students will understand how to care for their skin properly.

Materials:

Materials to make puppets
Blanket or similar item to use for puppet show

Directions:

1. Plan a class puppet show that will emphasize appropriate skin care. For example, puppets might show appropriate washing techniques, procedures that will prevent sun burn, acne treatments, or means of protecting the skin when exposed to cold, windy weather. The students should write a dialogue for the puppets to use during the show. Included in the dialogue can be various aspects of skin care that have been discussed in class.
2. Let the students make puppets that will be needed for the show.
3. Present the show at a school assembly or for different classes.

Variation:

Have groups of 5–7 students present a puppet show to the rest of the class on different aspects of skin care. For example, one group might cover sun tanning; another, acne; and a third, skin cleanliness.

Activity 4. Accepting Different Skin Conditions

Concept/Description: Much of the anxiety about skin appearance emanates from misconceptions.

Objective: Students will have a realistic understanding of various skin problems.

Materials:

Props determined by groups

Directions:

1. Form two or three groups in the class.
2. Have each group prepare a skit to present to the rest of the class. The skit is to emphasize the following:
   (a) Skin differs according to age, heredity, climate, exercise, and diet.
   (b) Acceptance of others who have skin problems.
   (c) Overcoming personal anxiety about perceived or actual skin problems.

Activity 5. P.U., Who Smells Y.O.U.! (Controlling Body Odor)

Concept/Description: There are different causes of body odors and varied steps to follow in order to control such odors.

Objective: Students will know how to control offensive body odors.

Materials:

Body Odor Game Board (See 5-1)
Controlling Body Odor; Body-Odor Cause Cards (See 5-2)
Playing pieces such as Bingo chips, pennies, etc.

Directions:

1. Have students pair up to play this game.
2. Have a Body Odor Game Board and a set of Keeping Clean Cards available for each pair of players.
3. Mix the cards thoroughly and lay them face down.
4. Let the players alternate drawing cards.
5. Controlling Body-Odor Cards permit the player to move forward two spaces. Body-Odor Cause Cards require the player to move back one space. A Controlling Body-Odor Card must be drawn to start the game.
6. When a card has been used, put it aside. When all the cards have been used, mix them again, and continue playing.
7. The winner is the first player to have a pleasing presence for others (the final block).

Variations:

1. Give different point credits for the cards. For example, using soap when washing might be worth three spaces forward, and not washing regularly might cause the player to move back four spaces.
2. Have students make up lists of phrases to place on the Keeping Clean Cards.

Body Odor Game Board

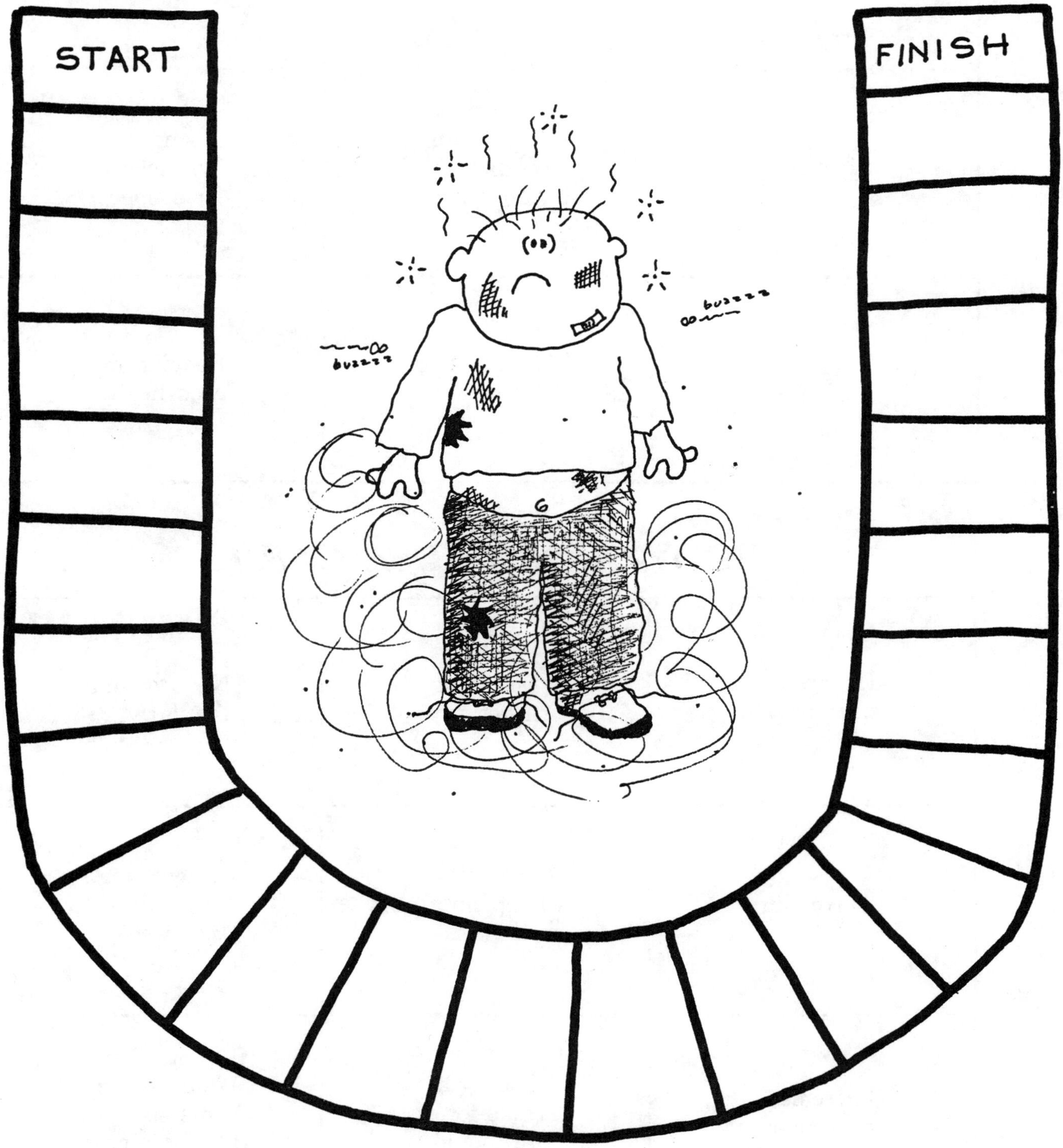

CONTROLLING BODY-ODOR CARDS

(5-2)

Using a deodorant	Taking a bath	Wearing light, loose clothes in hot weather
Showering	Applying an underarm anti-perspirant	Using a washcloth or sponge
Washing with soap	Wearing clean clothing	Keeping in good health

BODY-ODOR CAUSE CARDS

Heavy perspiration	Sports on a hot day	Not washing regularly
Dirty skin	Sweat mixing with pollutants on the skin	Showering only once per week
Extreme nervousness	Riding a bike for an hour	Wearing the same socks for three days

Activity 6. Maybe It's Your Breath (Bad Breath)

Concept/Description: There are different causes of bad breath and ways to maintain pleasant breath.

Objective: Students will understand how to prevent bad breath.

Materials:
None

Directions:

1. After a discussion of the causes of halitosis and methods of prevention, divide the class into small groups.
2. Have each group compose a jingle, poem, or limerick on the topic of bad breath.
3. The groups will present their literary efforts to the class.
4. Use the presentations as a basis for a follow-up review of halitosis. Cover causes such as the eating of foods like garlic and onions, gum disease, tooth decay, illness, fever, improper brushing of teeth, and stomach disorders. The halitosis prevention review should mention diet, regular visits to the dentist, appropriate care of teeth and gums, and medical assistance for sore throats and stomach disorders.

Activity 7. The Tooth, the Whole Tooth, and Nothing but the Tooth (Parts of a Tooth)

Concept/Description: Each part of a tooth needs appropriate care to prevent problems.

Objective: To know the different parts of a tooth and dental problems that relate to each part.

Materials:
Materials selected to make a tooth model
Paper and pencils or pens

Directions:

1. Have the students in your class make a large model of a tooth. They can choose to make different kinds of models. A model might be constructed of cardboard, wood, play dough, paper, or some other material.
2. Next, have the students label each part of the tooth.

3. Have groups of students select different parts and make a diagram of that part. Have them indicate possible dental problems, causes of these problems, and preventive care that is needed.
4. Display the diagrams and tooth models in the classroom.

Activity 8. Tooth or Consequences (Caring For Teeth Throughout Life)

Concept/Description: There is general tooth care needed at all times and special care at different stages of a person's life.

Objective: To become aware of the type of care that is needed to keep good teeth throughout life.

Materials:

Tooth-Care Time-Line Worksheet (See 5-3)
Newsprint
Paints and/or marking pens

Directions:

1. Have students use the Tooth-Care Time-Line Worksheet to construct a time line on tooth care for the baby years through adulthood. Emphasize special care that is needed at each age on the time line.
2. As a class, create a larger time line on the newsprint.
3. Display the time line, and let members of the class explain its significance to the principal or visitor to the school.

Variations:

1. Use pictures with captions to form the time line.
2. Feature health professionals who assist with dental care on the time line.

Activity 9. Metal Mania (Orthodontic Work)

Concept/Description: Orthodontics is a valuable branch of dentistry.

Objective: Students will understand how teeth can be aligned properly.

Materials:

(None)

Name ______________________ Date ______________

Tooth-Care Time-Line

DIRECTIONS: Place items from the list below (and any others you feel are appropriate) on the time line.

- Proper nutrition
- Taking care of baby teeth
- Learning to brush teeth
- Regular dental checkups
- Flossing teeth
- Emphasize diets with sufficient calcium
- Filling decayed teeth
- Using plaque-preventing mouthwash
- Protecting teeth with fluoride
- Pulling wisdom teeth, if necessary
- Orthodontic work, if indicated
- Pulling baby teeth
- Appropriate gum care
- Calcium additives, if indicated
- Cleaning teeth

1 year	2 years	5 years	10 years	15 years	20 years	30 years	40 years	50 years	60 years

Directions:

1. Arrange for an orthodontist to visit your class and show pictures or slides of different orthodontic problems.
2. Have the orthodontist explain how teeth can be properly aligned and why this is important.
3. Proper care of teeth should also be covered. It works effectively for students to write out questions that they want to ask before the orthodontist's visit.

Activity 10. Hair Today, Gone Tomorrow (Hair Grooming)

Concept/Description: Good looking hair is an important facet of good grooming.

Objective: Students will know how to properly care for their hair.

Materials:

Hair Care Survey (See 5-4)

Directions:

1. Have students investigate the do's and don'ts of hair care.
2. Have each student complete the Health Care Survey by getting the opinions of family members or friends.
3. Request the same information from a barber and a beautician.
4. Compare the family-friend survey with the barber-beautician survey.

Activity 11. Walking Tall (Body Carriage)

Concept/Description: A person's posture tells you something about that person.

Objective: To present a clear picture of how important good body carriage is.

Materials:

VCR
Video camera and tape
Paper and pencils
Props for different roles

Name ______________________________ Date ________________ (5-4)

Hair Care Survey

Family/Friends' opinions

DO's for hair care	DON'Ts for hair care
1.	1.
2.	2.
3.	3.
4.	4.
5.	5.

Barber/Beauticians' opinions

DO's for hair care	DON'Ts for hair care
1.	1.
2.	2.
3.	3.
4.	4.
5.	5.

COMPARE the two sets of responses above. What similarities and differences do you see?

____

____

____

____

____

____

Directions:

1. Have members of the class assume different roles. Examples would be a lazy person, someone who slouches in his/her seat, a politician, an athlete, a tired person, a dynamic city mayor, a trapeze artist, a magician, a conductor, etc.
2. Videotape students as they pantomime their roles.
3. Watch the video and give students time to write down their impressions of each person based on his/her body carriage.
4. Discuss how impressions are formed by messages received from body language.

Variation:

Have students watch a video tape or TV program without audio and have them write down what kind of a person they think each person is that they see on the tape. Their observations will be based on their watching a few minutes of the tape. Compare lists and discuss how important body carriage is in giving a perception about a person.

Activity 12. You Look Maaavelous! (What Clothes Tell Us about a Person)

Concept/Description: Clothes tell many things about the person who wears them.

Objective: To use pictures to show how clothes can affect perceptions about someone.

Materials:

Pictures

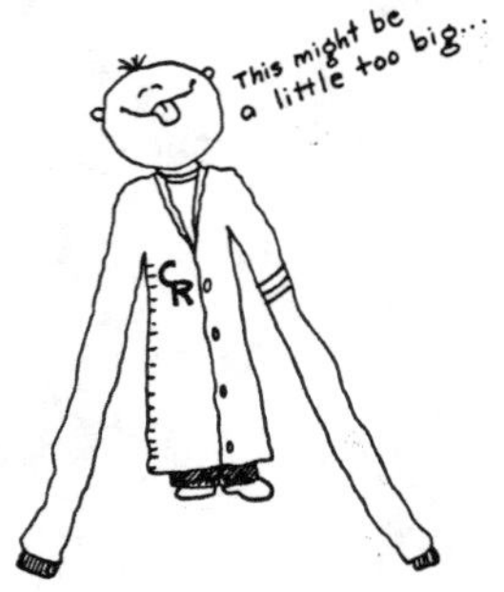

Directions:

1. Have students bring to class some pictures that show the clothes fashions of different age groups.
2. Group the pictures by age.
3. Lead a discussion on why different age groups dress differently.
4. Have students share their ideas about why people of the same age group might wear different styles of clothes.
5. Discuss how clothes affect one's perception of another person.

Variations:

1. Discuss what clothes can tell us about another person.
2. Invite a psychologist to speak to the class on how clothes can be an indicator of a person's feelings and personality.
3. Have a fashion designer discuss color choices in clothing with the class.

Activity 13. March Down the Aisle in Style (Fashion Show)

Concept/Description: Models place a high priority on good grooming.

Objective: To have students learn grooming techniques by being models.

Materials:

Clothes to model from a store

Directions:

1. Arrange with a local clothing store to have a fashion show at the school that will feature the students in your class.
2. Invite parents and other members of the community to attend.
3. After the show, have students discuss what they learned about good grooming as a result of being models.

Variations:

1. If it isn't possible to arrange for a store to sponsor the fashion show, put on your own show. Try to arrange for a professional to assist in preparing the students. (Remember to use parents as resources.) Your home economics department can also be an excellent resource.
2. Arrange for students to attend a fashion show and have them critique the show. What good grooming features did the models exhibit?

Activity 14. Department Store (Dressing a Mannequin)

Concept/Description: Clothes do make a difference.

Objective: To use a mannequin to show how vital appropriate attire is in making a good impression.

Materials:

Two store mannequins
Clothes

Directions:

1. Borrow a male and female mannequin from a store. Select mannequins that represent the approximate ages of students in your class.
2. Divide the class into groups of six to eight.
3. Have each group bring clothes to dress the mannequins in a manner that would make the best impression on adults attending an orchestra concert.
4. Have each group dress the mannequins and explain their choice of clothes.
5. Have the class discuss the importance of clothes in giving a positive message.

Variations:

1. Dress the mannequins for different types of occasions.
2. Have students dress mannequins to make a good impression and to make a poor impression.

Activity 15. A Display of Good Taste (Clothing Displays)

Concept/Description: The way clothes are presented determines the impact they have.

Objective: To use store displays as a way of evaluating good and poor messages that are received from clothes.

Materials:

Store Window Display Evaluation Worksheet (See 5-5)

Directions:

1. Give this assignment several weeks in advance of teaching your grooming unit.
2. Give each student an evaluation worksheet.
3. Have each student report on one outstanding and one poor store display of clothes. (It can be a window display or a display within a store).
4. Have the students share the results listed on their worksheet.
5. Ask students to compare the clothing displays with grooming habits of students their age. Emphasize the impact of good and poor grooming.

Activity 16. Groomed to Perfection (Good Grooming Characteristics)

Concept/Description: There are many facets to good grooming.

Objective: Students will list characteristics that they feel are important for good grooming.

Name ______________________________ Date ______________ (5-5)

Store Window Display Evaluation

DIRECTIONS: Evaluate two store window displays: one that you think is outstanding, and another you consider poor.

Store visited ______________________________

Type of display ______________________________

____

This was a ______ good ______ poor display. (Check one)

Explain why: ______________________________

____

____

____

What message did the display give to you? ______________________________

____

____

____

Store visited ______________________________

Type of display ______________________________

____

This was a ______ good ______ poor display. (Check one)

Explain why: ______________________________

____

____

____

What message did the display give to you? ______________________________

____

____

____

Materials:

Good Grooming Profile Worksheet (See 5-6)
Transparencies
Overhead projector

Directions:

1. Have all students complete a good grooming profile.
2. After students have completed their profile, list each category on a separate transparency, and have the students print their good grooming characteristic on the appropriate transparency.
3. Discuss the results of the cumulative profile which evolves on the transparencies.
4. Have groups of students make up a good grooming profile for a student of their age.

Activity 17. Look Like a Million (Desirable Grooming Goals)

Concept/Description: Students need to have personal grooming goals.

Objective: To establish good grooming goals.

Materials:

Good Grooming Profile Worksheet (from Activity 16) (See 5-6)

Directions:

1. Give all students a copy of a Good Grooming Profile Worksheet. Have them list one desirable characteristic about each category that they feel describes themselves.
2. Have students write one personal grooming goal that they have in each area.
3. Emphasize that the worksheet is for them to use and that it will assist them in establishing good grooming goals. It will not be handed in or shared with the class.

Activity 18. I Don't Want You to See Me This Way (Personal Grooming Problems)

Concept/Description: There are many grooming problems that concern people.

Objective: Students will state their grooming concerns in a non-threatening environment that allows for open discussion of possible solutions.

Name ____________________ Date ____________ (5-6)

Good Grooming Profile

Directions: Indicate at least one desirable characteristic for each grooming category below.

Hair care	
Clothing	
Skin	
Fingernails and hands	
Breath	
Body cleanliness	
Teeth	
Posture	
Feet	
General appearance	

Materials:

Sheets of paper, half size
Pens or pencils
Basket or other container

Directions:

1. Have all students write anonymously on the paper that is given to them the personal grooming problem that most concerns them.
2. Put the sheets of paper in a basket, hat, or other container, and draw out one sheet at a time.
3. Have class members give suggestions for solutions to the grooming problems. It may be necessary for the teacher to read the concerns first and rephrase them so that no student will be recognized by other members of the class.

Activity 19. Shower to Shower (A Good Grooming Booklet)

Concept/Description: A summary of good grooming techniques will be valuable to the authors and students for whom it is written.

Objective: To select grooming topics and write a booklet containing good grooming tips on each topic.

Materials:

Paper and writing utensils
Printing or photocopying facilities

Directions:

1. Have students write the Good Grooming Booklet for a lower grade to prepare the students in that grade for the following school year.
2. Have students determine what topics should be included.
3. Elect an editorial board that will make writing assignments and put the booklet together.
4. Give a copy to each student in your class; also to members of one class in a lower grade. It usually works best to write the guide for students who are one grade lower.

UNIT 6

NEVER SAY "QUACK" TO A DOCTOR

Activities for Consumer Health

An important goal for schools is to make students informed consumers. The long-range goal is to have adults who are intelligent consumers. This goal can be best attained by covering the principles of consumerism throughout students' school years. Children of all ages are consumers, and television advertising, as well as other forms of advertising, makes extensive use of this fact. Children are susceptible to misleading and false advertising. They are also impressionable. It's easy to persuade them that they want a wide range of items.

This chapter provides activities which will assist students in understanding that producers of goods are constantly using techniques to try to get them to buy their products. The second purpose of the activities is to help students recognize misleading information in advertising, as well as advertising that is not true. Quackery is a problem for all ages, and children feel the impact of quackery as extensively as do adults. They will be better adult consumers if they are wise consumers in childhood and adolescent years.

There is concern about the millions of dollars that are wasted on products and programs each year. This affects almost every household. Of even more concern is the negative effect that some products have on people's health. Activities in this chapter can be used to help make children consumers who will recognize danger signals as they are peppered with advertising slogans and other appeal techniques.

Americans are bombarded with over 300 advertisements each day. It is important that students realize the profound effect advertising has on each and everyone of us.

Activity 1. "And Now a Word from Our Sponsor . . ." (Slogans and Symbols)

Concept/Description: We are affected by ads whether or not we consciously realize it.

Objective: Students will realize the impact that advertising has on their knowledge about products.

Materials:

Slogans or logos (See sample slogans p. 130.)
Paper
Pens or pencils

Directions:

1. Read each slogan aloud (or show a company's logo) and ask students to try to identify the product. Most will be able to identify some, if not all.
2. Check the answers. If students can identify even one product, then advertising has made an impression on them.
3. Discuss how their knowledge of these products could influence their decisions when shopping (e.g., if they're in a hurry, or if they don't know which of three brands of orange juice to buy, or when they want to buy "the best" to impress their friends.)

Sample Slogans:

1. Mmmmm, Mmmmm, good (Campbell's Soups)
2. When it rains, it pours (Morton Salt)
3. Cookies made by elves (Keebler)
4. Mr. Whipple (Charmin)
5. Thank you for your support (Bartles and James)
6. Have it your way . . . (Burger King)
7. I'm *not* going to pay a lot for this muffler! (Meineke)
8. Silly rabbit, ______________ are for kids! (Trix)
9. The first and last name in popcorn (Orville Redenbacher)
10. It takes a tough man to make a tender chicken (Perdue)

Activity 2. That's Appealing! (Appeal Techniques)

Concept/Description: Advertisers appeal to our emotions and senses in a variety of ways.

Objective: Students will recognize different advertising techniques that are used to encourage them to make purchases.

Materials:

Video recordings (or audio recordings of TV commercials)—approximately 10–20
Appeal Techniques Reference Sheet (See 6-1)

Directions:

1. After a discussion on advertising techniques, have the class view (or listen to) the various commercials.
2. While the tape is playing, have groups of students categorize the ads according to the appeal technique being used to sell each product. More than one technique may be used in each ad. Some popular categories are described in the Appeal Technique Reference Sheets (See 6-1). Other categories can be developed by the class.
3. Discuss how and why advertisers try to target certain groups of people.

Appeal Techniques Reference Sheet

1. Nostalgia—plainfolks, "down home," back-to-nature, the way Grandma used to make it.

   Examples: Ivory soap, Old-Fashioned Cookies, Grape Nuts, Country Time Lemonade

2. Bandwagon—Everyone is buying this product because it's the best. Don't be left out!

   Examples: car commercials, pain relievers

3. Transfer/Fantasy—White knights, green giants, super athletes, handsome men, beautiful women, rich people, etc., are featured. Buyers tend to transfer these qualities to the product and themselves if they use the product.

   Examples: Grey Poupon mustard, colognes, alcohol, Wheaties, clothing

4. Humor—People tend to remember an ad that makes them laugh and may buy a product because of the positive association with it.

   Examples: some beer commercials, Wendy's

5. Sense appeal—Sounds or pictures that appeal to the senses.

   Examples: hamburgers shown being grilled, food commercials, getaway vacation commercials

6. Statistics—Bombardment with "facts" or statistics that may have little or no meaning, but sound impressive. Statements such as "3 out of 4 doctors recommend . . ." fail to tell how many doctors were surveyed, who conducted the survey, etc.

   Examples: pain relievers, weight loss products, allergy medications, medications in general

7. Testimonial—When important or well-known people testify that they use the product, and therefore so should you.

   Examples: Bill Cosby for Jell-O pudding, Michael Jackson for Pepsi, etc.

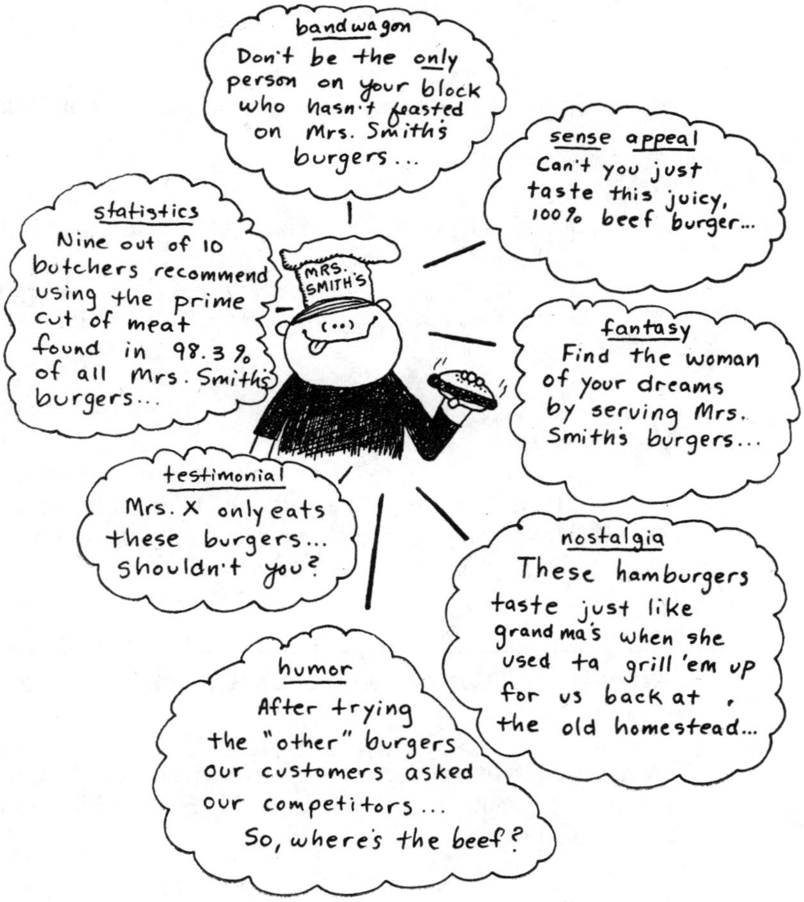

Activity 3. Marketing Magic (Make Your Own Advertisement)

Concept/Description: By understanding how advertisers construct ads that appeal to our emotions and senses, students may be able to separate "facts" from "claims."

Objective: Students will devise a commercial using one of the appeal techniques they have learned, and they will recognize other appeal techniques used by classmates.

Materials: Will depend on type of ad student chooses.

Directions:

1. Divide students into groups of 4–5, and ask them to devise their own commercial to be performed for the class.
2. On the day of performance, have the class try to determine the type of advertising approach the group was using. (Refer to the Appeal Techniques Reference Sheet listed in Activity 2.)

Variations:

1. Assign the group a specific type of advertising technique (nostalgia, humor, etc.).
2. Have individuals cut ads out of magazines and list the techniques used.
3. Have students make their own ads using construction paper, newsprint, etc., and display them in the classroom.

Activity 4. On the Lookout (Quack Claims)

Concept/Description: Quack devices and claims provide false hope to victims and may delay proper medical treatment. Being able to identify quackery can save money, time, and health.

Objective: Students will be able to demonstrate visually that a health product or program is quackery.

Materials:

Will depend on student's choice of ad in magazines, newspapers, tabloids.

Directions:

1. Go over the Signs of Quackery List with your students. (See below.)
2. Have each student find a questionable ad in one of the tabloids, magazines, or newspapers—for example, an ad for quick weight loss, hair restoration, restoring youth, good fortune, etc.
3. Have groups or individuals design a test model or prototype of a product that will perform according to the ad's claims. Use boxes, string, Christmas lights, etc. Allow for individual creativity.
4. Attempt to "sell" the product to the class. Each sales pitch should include one or more signs of quackery.
5. Have members of the class tell how they knew the product was quackery.

Signs of Quackery List:

1. Products offered as "secret" remedies or "not available elsewhere."
2. A sponsor who claims he is fighting the medical profession that does not accept his "wonderful" discovery.
3. Products sold door-to-door by so-called "health advisors."
4. Products called "miracle" drugs, devices, or diets sold in sensational magazines by faith-healer groups or by crusading lay people.
5. Promoters who tell you about the wonderful miracles their products or services have performed for others.
6. Products or services good for a wide variety of real or imagined illnesses and disorders.

NOTE: Additional information is available from your physician, the county medical society, the FDA (Food and Drug Administration), the Better Business Bureau and, if a quack product is promoted by mail, the U.S. Postal Services.

Variation:

Allow students to invent their own product. (In past years, students have "invented" the invisible doll complete with invisible clothing, as well as the miracle-cure-all shower cap designed to take care of all ailments, especially the "heartbreak of psoriasis.") The important point is for the students to understand that beyond the humor, quackery is a very serious problem. It results in a waste of money and time and can even have a serious effect on the health of many people.

THE ANTI-BALDNESS MIRACLE
CAP AVAILABLE ONLY BY MAIL...
LOOK WHAT IT DOES FOR MR. X!

Activity 5. Weight a While (Weight Loss)

Concept/Description: The *only* safe, effective way to lose weight is to eat less, eat a balanced diet, and exercise.

Objective: Students will become familiar with different diets and be able to evaluate the merits of each.

Materials:

Copies of diet plans, such as—

KLB-6 Diet	The Bran Diet
Herbal-Life	The Stillman Diet
9-Day Wonder	Weight Watchers
10 Day Fast	Lean Line
The Rotation Diet	Nutri-System

Directions:

1. Have the students study different diet plans.
2. Students will evaluate the diet plans that were selected for study and discuss questions such as the following:
   (a) Which diets are nutritionally balanced?
   (b) Which diets are nutritionally deficient?
   (c) Which diets include behavior modification?
   (d) Which diet plans include a balanced diet, reduction in quantity of food consumed, and exercise?

(e) Do the diets have anything in common?
(f) How many pounds can you lose each week on each diet?
(g) What is the length of time you are expected to stay on each diet?

Variations:

1. Have the students survey their parents to find out about diets they have tried and report back to the class.
2. The students can write to weight loss centers and other weight loss organizations for literature and investigate the information they receive.

Activity 6. To Market, To Market (Supermarket)

Concept/Description: By reading the nutrition labels on products, we can become better comparison shoppers.

Objective: Students will learn to read labels and become familiar with the contents of various food products.

Materials:

Empty cartons, boxes, jars, and cans with nutrition labels
Shopping lists

Directions:

1. If possible and before starting this activity, request a home economics teacher, a nutritionist, or farm extension home economist to speak to your class on the nutritional value of various foods.
2. Set up a supermarket somewhere in your room with empty containers that either you or your students provide.
3. Put prices on all containers.
4. Give all students a shopping list and have them choose the items with the best nutritional qualities.
5. Compare items that were selected by the students, and point out buying practices that will increase the nutritional value of the groceries of the typical shopper.

Variations:

1. Discuss the following with the students:
   (a) What measurement is used to designate the amount of salt and/or sugar in a product?
   (b) What products contain the most salt and sugar? (The results will probably be surprising to the students.)
   (c) Which products contain the most calories per serving?
   (d) Which products use BHA and BHT? For what purpose are they used? (preservatives)

(e) How much does each product cost per serving?
(f) What does RDA stand for? What does it mean?
(g) Which products contain the greatest amounts of saturated fats?

2. Have the students do their shopping on the basis of minimum expenditure, while still meeting nutritional standards.

Activity 7. Survey the Situation (Conducting a Product Survey)

Concept/Description: The ability to analyze a product will help us to become more careful, knowledgeable consumers.

Objective: Students will be able to compare the ingredients of different brand names of the same product.

Materials:

Pain Reliever Survey Worksheets (See 6-2)

Directions:

1. Have students survey various supermarkets or drug stores and compare pain relief products such as aspirin, Ibuprofen and Acetaminophen.
2. Emphasize basic rules for buying products:
   (a) Compare prices based on the same quantity of each product.
   (b) Compare ingredients.
   (c) Review package labels for harmful ingredients.
   (d) Look for possible side effects that are noted on package.
   (e) Compare recommended dosage.
   (f) Note shelf life.
   (g) Review claims of the manufacturers that appear on package or labels.
   (h) Examine the tamper-proof qualities.
3. After the survey is completed, have the class determine which product is the best buy, which one is the safest, and which will last the longest. Also compare other products such as shampoo, mouthwash, acne medications, etc. by developing survey sheets for them.

Variations:

1. Have students suggest different categories to compare.
2. Attempt to determine the purpose of one or more ingredients included in each product.
3. Have students discuss the stores where they found they could get the best prices for the same products.
4. Have students compare ingredients of some highly advertised brands with lesser-known brands. (Students will be surprised to find that the ingredients are the same, but the cost differs significantly.)
5. Have students figure out why highly advertised brands frequently have much higher price tags.

Name ______________________ Date ______________ (6-2)

Pain Reliever Survey

Store(s) surveyed: ______________________________

PRODUCT	AMT. OF ASPIRIN	AMT. OF CAFFEINE	OTHER PAIN RELIEVERS	NO. OF TABS	PRICE

Activity 8. I Get Your Vibes (Alternative Healing Methods)

Concept/Description: Many non-traditional medical treatment methods exist, but are not always accepted by traditional medical science.

Objective: Students will recognize that there are proponents of healing methods that have varying degrees of acceptance by the medical profession.

Materials:

Literature or guest speakers on psychic healing, zone therapy, acupuncture, healing diets, exercise plans, and other healing techniques.

Directions:

1. Review the basic concepts of several healing methods and discuss their acceptance in modern medicine. Be sure to note that the medical profession does change its position with time. Point out areas in which positions have become modified with time, research, and experience. An example would be the initial acceptance of unlimited jogging mileage per week as compared to the more recent rejection of this jogging approach. Other examples would be acceptance of the use of aspirins to prevent heart attack in men over forty and the rejection of the intake of megadoses of Vitamin C.
2. Have students obtain information from the American Medical Association and other medical groups on their positions on the various healing methods.
3. Have students write to organizations that promote non-traditional medical treatment and obtain their literature.
4. Compare the positions of the medical societies and non-traditional medical treatment organizations.

Variations:

Invite guest speakers to come to class to present their views.

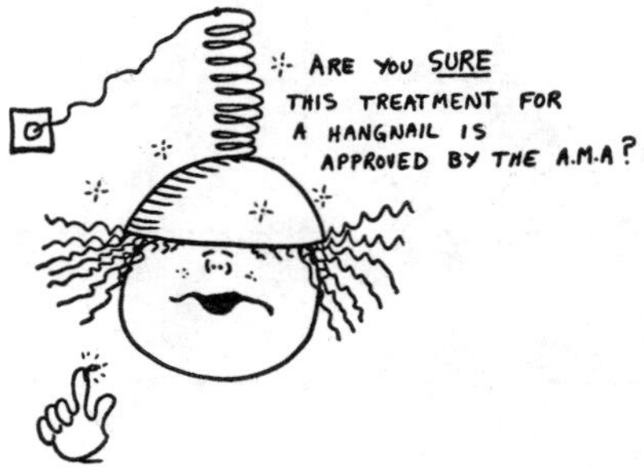

UNIT 7

FROM THE WOMB TO THE TOMB
Activities on Human Growth and Development

The activities in this unit cover the total life span of a human—from birth to death. Students have many questions, and, unfortunately, much misinformation about the birth process, adolescence, dating, aging, and death. Sexuality is a central issue for adolescents, of course, and activities in this unit will afford them the opportunity to discuss sexual topics in a positive way and to gain the knowledge they need to make informed decisions. Other activities help students to understand the implications of aging and work to create a healthy attitude towards those who are older. Finally, students have an opportunity to discuss death and the special circumstance of the death of a loved one.

Before using the activities in this chapter, make sure that they are appropriate for the grade-level curriculum that has been approved by the local Board of Education or other equivalent organization.

Activity 1. What a Trip! (Birth of a Baby)

Concept/Description: The birth process can be understood by use of a simulation model.

Objective: To present the concept of birth in a clear, yet comfortable, manner.

Materials:

Small baby doll
String
Piece of material cut into a circle
Uterus model made of two pieces of material, constructed as shown in Figure 7-1.

Directions:

1. Construct the model as shown in Figures 7-1 and 7-2. Use this "non-threatening" model to explain labor and childbirth. (Using a fully clothed doll with a full head of hair usually elicits a laugh and allows for a very comfortable atmosphere.)
2. Begin by placing the *placenta, cord*, and *attached baby* inside the uterus. As you explain a normal delivery, you can bring the baby's head out of the vaginal canal. Once the baby is out, show that the umbilical cord is still attached to the placenta. Cut the cord, and then explain how the placenta (afterbirth) is delivered, etc.
3. Explain breech birth, caesarian section, and twins, if you desire. The amount of detail you go into is up to you and should be dependent on the age of your students, as well as your curriculum guidelines.

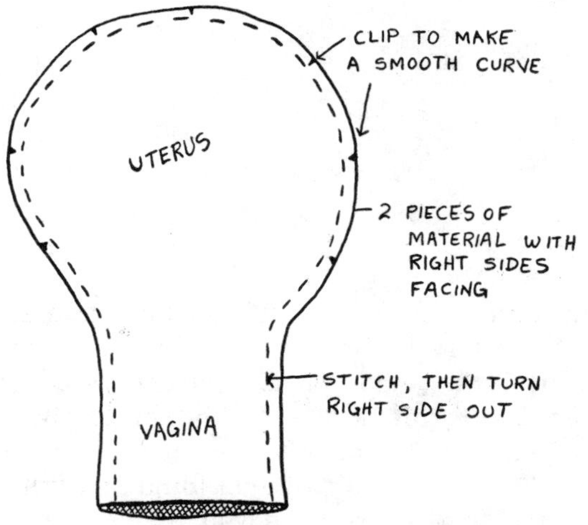

Fig. 7-1. Construction of a uterus model.

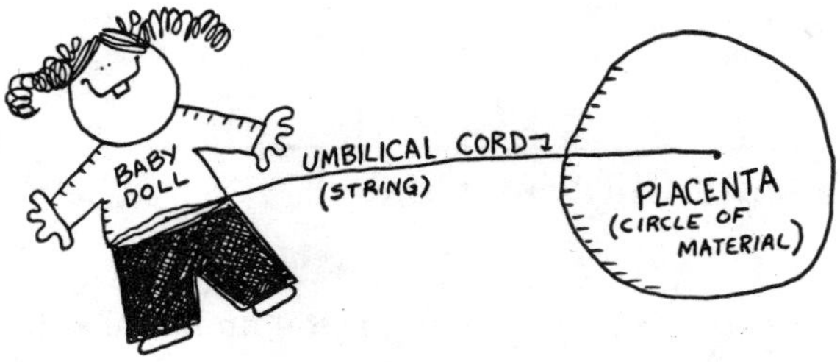

Fig. 7-2. Be sure the doll fits inside the uterus you've constructed.

Activity 2. How Egg-Citing! (Ovulation to Menstruation)

Concept/Description: Ovulation and menstruation are taught while students learn about the parts of the female reproductive system.

Objective: To have students trace the path of a mature egg cell from the ovary to the outside of the female body.

Materials:

Female Reproductive System Worksheet (See 7-1)
Overhead transparency of Worksheet
Overhead projector
Pens or pencils
Crayons or markers
Overhead transparency markers (optional)

Directions:

1. While referring to the overhead transparency, have students label and color in their worksheets as you explain the female reproductive system as follows:
   (a) The *ovaries* produce egg cells. Label and color in both ovaries. (Point out their location on the transparency or color in with the transparency markers as you speak.)
   (b) During the process of *ovulation*, a mature egg cell leaves an ovary and enters one of the *Fallopian tubes*. There are two tubes. Label them and color them in.
   (c) For a few days, the egg cell travels down a Fallopian tube. In preparation for the egg's arrival, should it be fertilized, the lining of the *uterus* begins to thicken. Label the uterus, and color the uterus and the lining.
   (d) In this example, the egg is not fertilized by the male sperm cell, so it leaves the body together with the lining of the uterus. This is called *menstruation*.
   (e) The passageway to the outside of the body is the *vagina*. Menstrual blood leaves by way of this organ. Label and color in the vagina.

Answer Key:

1. Fallopian tube
2. Ovary
3. Uterus
4. Cervix
5. Vagina

Variation:

Depending on the age of the student, you may wish to go into more or less detail. Other organs you may wish to explain would be the *labia, cervix, clitoris*, and *hymen*.

Activity 3. Journey to the Outside (Production and Release of Semen)

Concept/Description: Locating the parts of the male reproductive system on a worksheet can be used effectively in teaching about the male reproductive system.

Objective: To have students trace the path of a mature sperm cell from the testes to the outside of the male body.

Materials:

Male Reproductive System Worksheet (See 7-2)
Overhead transparency of Worksheet
Overhead projector
Pens or pencils
Crayons or markers
Overhead transparency markers (optional)

Name ______________________ Date ______________ (7-1)

Female Reproductive System Worksheet

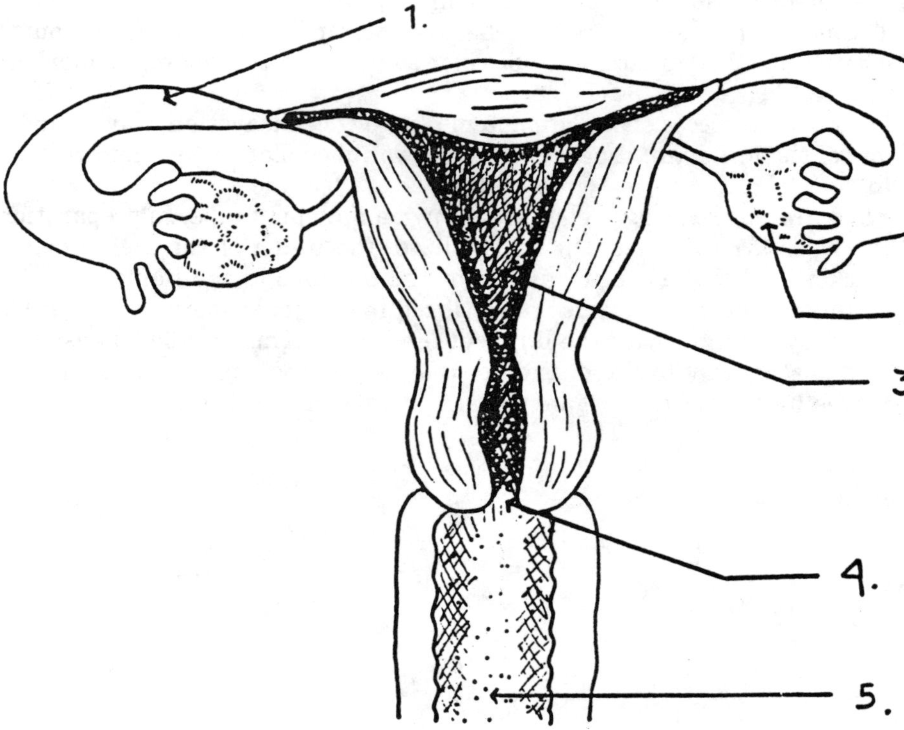

Directions: Match terms from the box at right with the numbers indicated above. Write the terms below.

1. ______________________
2. ______________________
3. ______________________
4. ______________________
5. ______________________

cervix
Fallopian tube
ovary
uterus
vagina

Directions:

1. While referring to the overhead transparency, have students label and color in their worksheets as you explain the male reproductive system as follows:
   (a) The *testes* produce sperm cells. Label and color in the testes. (Point out the location on the transparency or color in with the transparency markers as you speak.) NOTE: Explain that this is a side view and that there are two testicles.
   (b) On each *testicle*, there is an organ that stores sperm while they mature. This is called the *epididymis*. Label and color this organ.
   (c) As the sperm prepares to leave the body, it travels up a small tube called the *vas deferens*. Label and color.
   (d) The sperm then receives fluids from two glands. First, it receives a sugary fluid from the *seminal vesicle* for nutrition. Color in and label this gland.
   (e) Next the sperm and seminal fluid join an acidic fluid from the *prostate gland*. Color in and label the prostate. The *bulbo-urethral glands* also secrete a clear mucous lubricant that makes up much of the fluid portion of what is now called *semen*.
   (f) The semen leaves the body by way of a tube called the *urethra*. The urethra is a tube that runs through the *penis*. Color and label both the urethra and the penis.

Answer Key:

1. Seminal vesicle
2. Vas deferens
3. Prostate
4. Penis
5. Urethra
6. Foreskin
7. Bulbo-urethral glands
8. Testicle
9. Scrotum

Variation:

Depending on the age of the student, you may wish to go into more or less detail. You may also wish to explain ejaculation, erection, and masturbation.

Activity 4. A Tough Decision (Debate on Teenage Pregnancy)

Concept/Description: There are several options that can be followed when teenage pregnancy occurs, and each option requires careful evaluation of the consequences.

Objective: To look at the negative and positive aspects of four possible choices should teen pregnancy occur.

Name ______________________________ Date ____________________ (7-2)

Male Reproductive System

Directions: Label numbers 1–9 below with the correct terms from the box below.

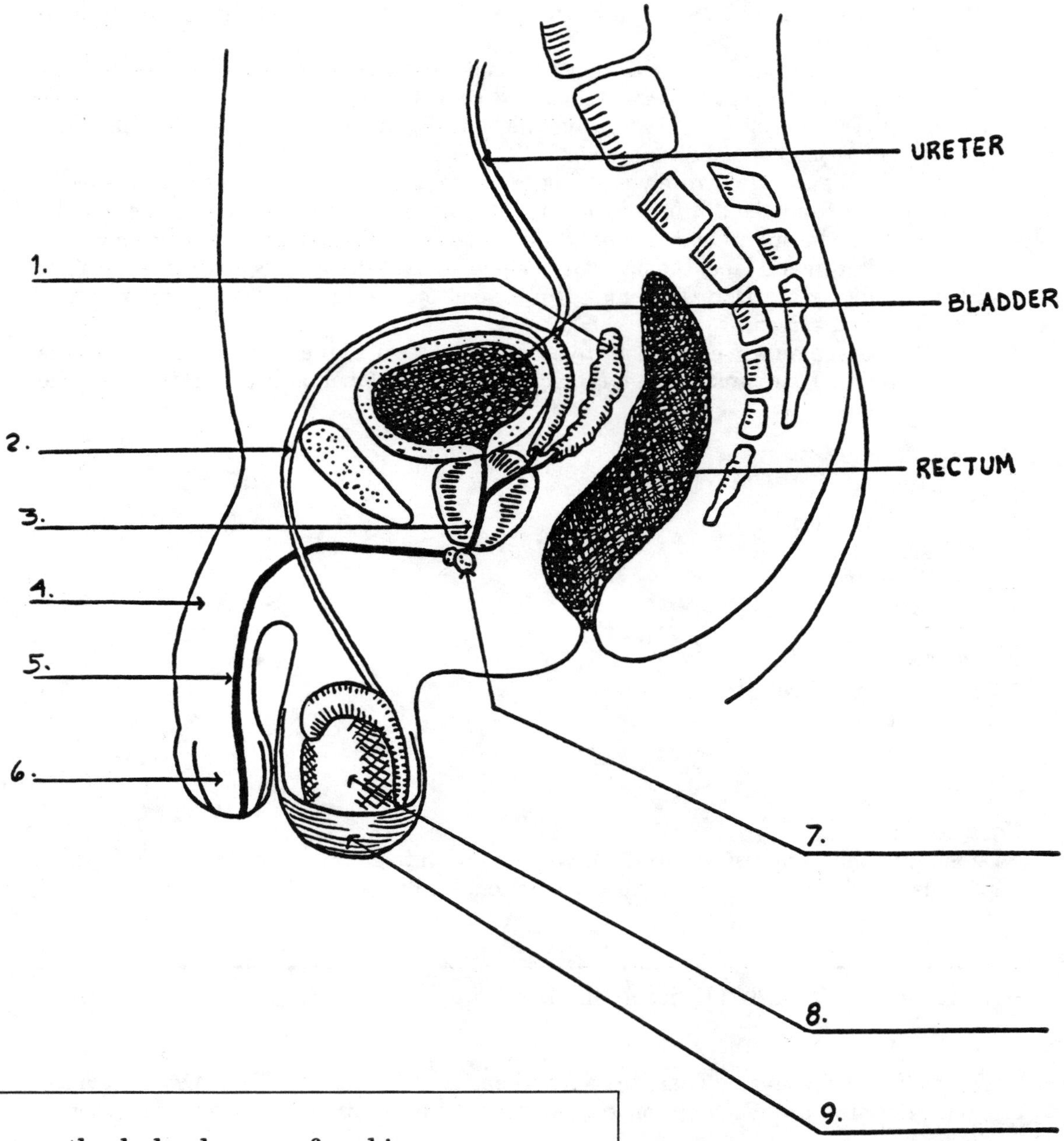

bulbo-urethral glands		foreskin
penis	prostate	seminal vesicle
scrotum	testicle	urethra
vas deferens		

Materials:

Resource books
Pamphlets from various organizations

Directions:

1. Assign groups of students *one* of the following options to research concerning teenage pregnancy:
   (a) Teenage mother keeping her baby without getting married
   (b) Giving the baby up for adoption
   (c) Having an abortion
   (d) Teenager getting married and raising the baby
2. Encourage the group to obtain information that might present both sides of the issue. (For example, information from anti-abortion leagues as well as pro-choice groups.)
3. Have each group prepare an opening argument supporting the assigned option. (They may disagree with teen marriages, for example, but they must look for ways to support this viewpoint as part of the debate.)
4. Instead of a debate, you may wish to choose a panel discussion format, or a large group discussion.
5. As a follow-up, ask all class members to write an essay on the choice they found to be the most viable option and have them support their opinion.

Variation:

Run the class as a TV talk show, complete with guests, a host, and an audience, and videotape it.

Activity 5. Board Meeting (A Values Continuum)

Concept/Description: There are many differences of opinion on value statements.

Objective: To have the students accept the values of others and gain insight into why values differ.

Materials:

Chalkboard
Chalk

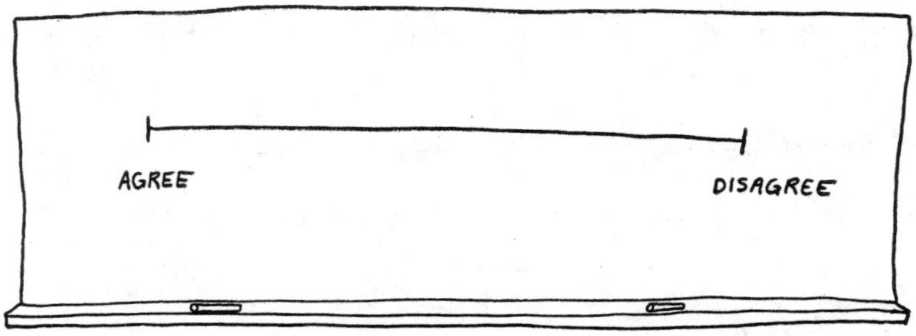

Directions:

1. Draw a continuum line on the chalkboard as shown in Figures 7-3: Use the largest chalkboard available. (Or use a long piece of butcher paper, with a line drawn in marker, and tape it across the wall.)
2. Divide the class into groups of 10–12.
3. Read one of the value statements from the list that follows or devise your own.
4. Have one of the groups stand, and ask all persons in the group to place themselves under the continuum line according to whether they agree or disagree with the statement made.
5. Ask various individuals why they feel the way they do. Discuss with the class.
6. Continue until each group has had a chance to respond to a statement.
7. Encourage the groups to listen to each other's opinions before forming set opinions.

Examples of Value Statements:

1. People who are *really* in love won't fight, argue, or disagree.
2. It is impossible for teenagers to experience real true love.
3. It is not harmful for a couple to have intercourse before marriage if they are really in love.
4. What my friends think of me is currently more important than what my parents think.
5. Fathers should not kiss their sons after about age 10.
6. Women should not work, but should stay at home with the children if at all possible.
7. Abortion should be illegal.
8. Friends should understand if you choose to spend most or all of your time with your boyfriend or girlfriend.
9. Parents should help their teenage children choose a method of birth control.
10. Girls should pay for a date if they ask a guy out.

Activity 6. My Dreamboat (The "Perfect" Date)

Concept/Description: Students will benefit by learning how others view the person they want to date.

Objective: To discuss what girls and boys look for in another person.

Materials:

Paper
Pens or pencils

Directions:

1. Have students write a few paragraphs about what they would consider "the perfect date."

2. Have them explain where they would go, what they would do, with whom they would go (they may be shy about this, so make it optional), and their expectations. Note: On occasion, you may get a few sarcastic or sexual comments about their "expectations." Use these to develop a class discussion on sexuality.
3. With the students' permission, read a few of the exceptional dates to the class.
4. Discuss.

Variations:

1. Discuss why some dates may be less than "perfect."
2. Discuss the role movies and TV can play on our perception of romance and dating.

Activity 7. A Path to Choose (Where a Sexual Decision May Lead)

Concept/Description: Responsible decisions concerning sexual intercourse involve consideration of many factors and consequences.

Objective: To show students all the other factors that must be taken into consideration once they have chosen to have intercourse.

Materials:

Where a Sexual Decision May Lead Worksheets (See 7-3)
Where a Sexual Decision May Lead Worksheet Answer Key (See 7-4)
Pens or pencils

Directions:

1. Pass out the worksheets.
2. Refer to the answer key, and begin at the top of the worksheet where the first decision is to have intercourse or practice abstinence. As you explain, have the students fill in each possible decision and its consequences until the worksheet is completed.
3. Discuss the worksheet, and point out the number of decisions that have to be considered if a person decides to have intercourse.

Variation:

Discuss the possibility of not only pregnancy but also of contracting sexually transmitted diseases, including AIDS, if the choice is to have intercourse.

Name ________________________ Date ________________ (7-3)

Where a Sexual Decision May Lead

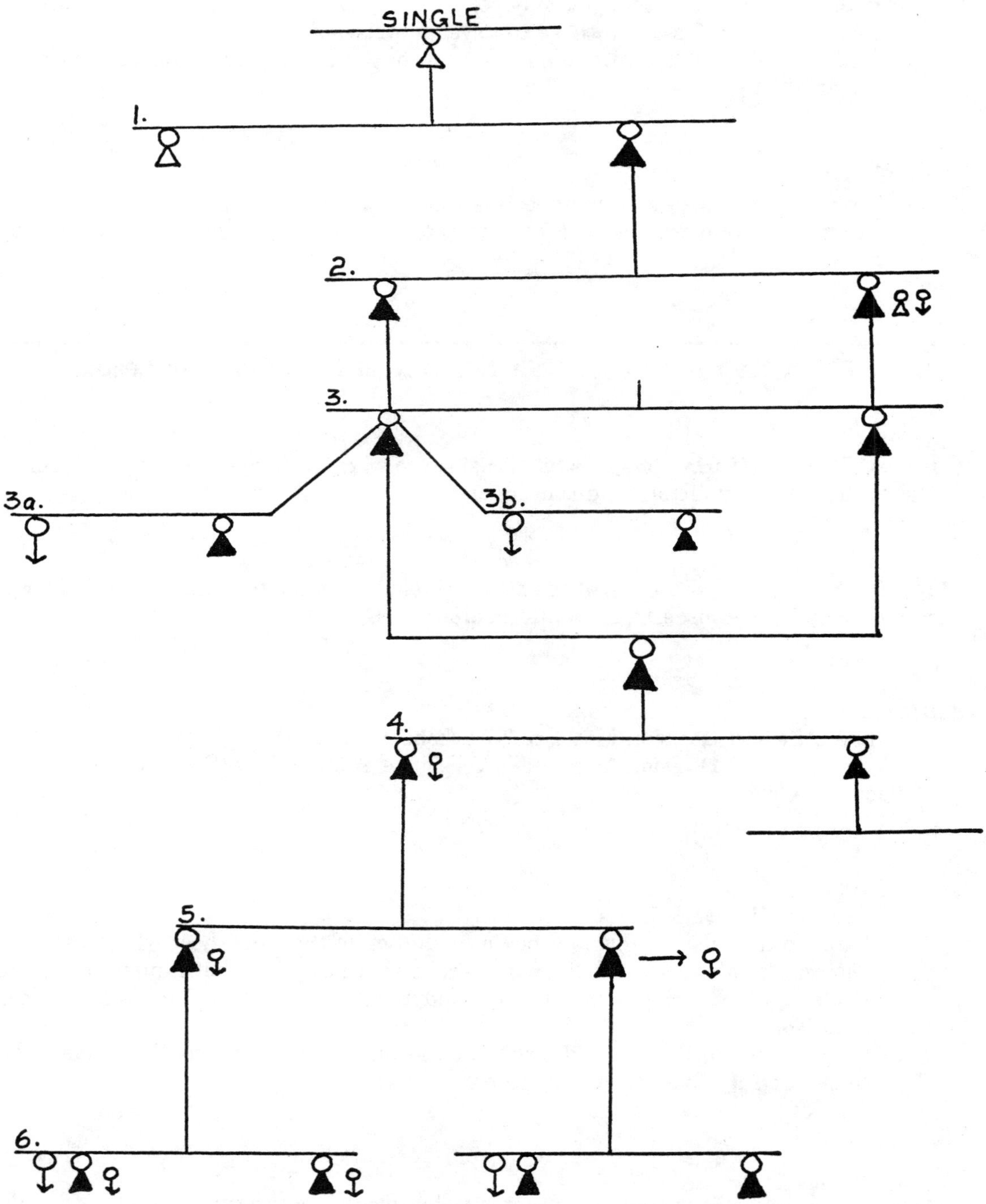

Where a Sexual Decision May Lead Answer Key

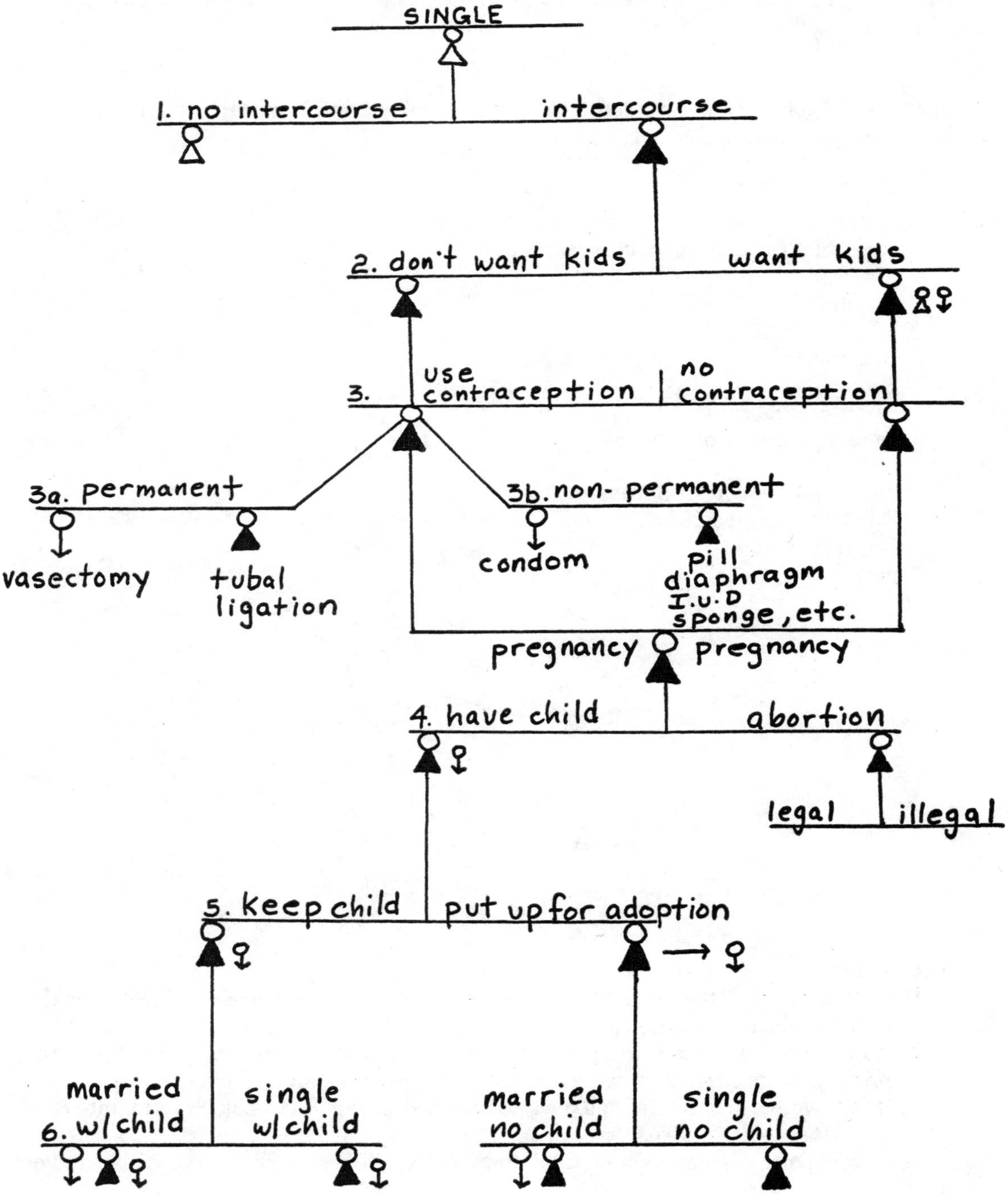

Activity 8. What Is That? (Birth Control and Hygiene Products)

Concept/Description: Students are frequently poorly informed about birth control and hygiene products.

Objective: To have older students compare the effectiveness of various birth control and hygiene products and discuss their use.

Materials:

- Various birth control products, such as—
  - Condom
  - Diaphragm
  - I.U.D.
  - Contraceptive foam, jelly
  - Sponge
  - Birth control pills
- Various hygiene products, such as—
  - Douches
  - Feminine deodorant sprays
  - Deodorant suppositories
  - Deodorant wipes
- Paper
- Pens or pencils

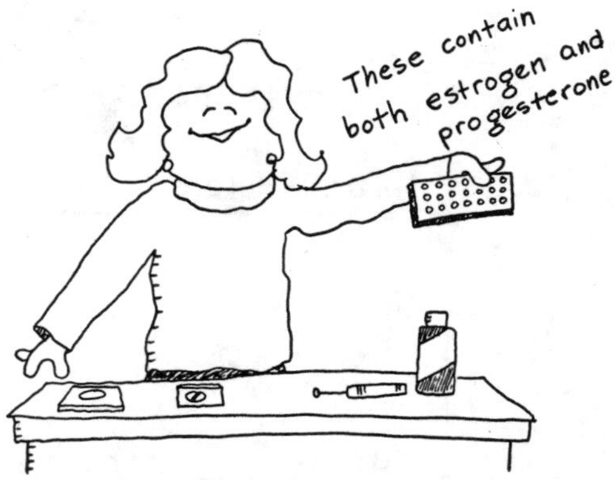

These contain both estrogen and progesterone..

Directions:

1. Obtain some of the products listed above. (NOTE: Many are available over the counter, from a gynecologist, or a family planning center.)
2. As you hold up one of the products, ask students to guess what they think the product is or what it is used for. Have them write down their guesses.
3. When work is completed, go back to the first product and ask class members to *volunteer* their guesses.
4. Explain and discuss each product and its effectiveness, risks, and positive and/or negative points.

Variation:

Explain how advertisers "push" certain products with questionable value. (For example, products such as feminine deodorants or douches are not necessary and may even cause problems.)

Activity 9. I Hate When That Happens! (Boys'/Girls' Opinions)

Concept/Description: Young people frequently have misconceptions about what qualities are desired by members of the opposite sex.

Objective: To come to an understanding about what boys and girls look for in the opposite sex.

Materials:

Paper
Pens or pencils

Directions:

1. Divide the class into boys and girls and assign one secretary and one spokesperson for each group.
2. Ask the girls to complete the following sentences: "I like boys who ______________." "I dislike boys who ______________."
3. At the same time, ask the boys to complete the following sentences: "I like girls who" ______________. "I dislike girls who ______________."
4. Have the "secretaries" jot down all the responses, and have the spokespersons read them aloud (you may wish to screen them first).
5. Discuss. (Sometimes answers that are "sexual" or "immature" can be used to spur discussions on appearing "macho" or "experienced.")

Activity 10. Hey, Sexy! (Sex In Advertising)

Concept/Description: Sex is a powerful selling strategy used to tout many products.

Objective: To show ads to students that attempt to portray a certain image using sexual overtones. To discuss and analyze each ad.

Materials:

Magazines
Scissors

Directions:

1. Have students cut out ads that use sexual images or associations to sell their products. (Perfume ads, wine and champagne ads, blue jean ads, and ads with scantily dressed persons are a few examples.)
2. Discuss the ads and analyze the image the manufacturers are trying to attach to the products.
3. Ask students if they feel they are getting adequate product information from the ad.
4. Ask whether they feel that sex does help to sell products, and why or why not.

Variation:

Videotape commercials of the type described above, and analyze them.

Activity 11. Act Their Age (Effects of Aging)

Concept/Description: Young people find it difficult to relate to many of the problems of aging.

Objective: To help students become aware of the problems some people face as they grow old.

Materials:

Ear plugs (hearing impairment. For sanitary reasons, one pair of plugs per person)
Glasses smeared with petroleum jelly (cataracts)
Thick gloves or mittens (arthritis)
Gum balls or jaw breakers (dental problems)
Unflavored seltzer water (loss of taste)
Unsalted pretzels or crackers (loss of taste)
Cups
Leggos or small toys
Tape recorded instructions
Tape recorder
Pens, papers
Children's book
Needles and thread

Directions:

1. Divide the class into small groups. Have the groups rotate to the stations as explained below. After each station, have students jot down their feelings and comments to discuss at a later time.

   Station #1: Hearing Impairment—Have the students place the ear plugs in their ears to simulate loss of hearing. Play a taped set of instructions at a very low volume. Have each person attempt to follow the instructions. (For example, the tape could say, "Write your name in capital letters. Now, circle the third letter of your last name. Draw two squares. . . .")

Station #2: Cataracts—Have students wear an old pair of glasses smeared with petroleum jelly to simulate cataracts. Ask them to thread a needle.

Station #3: Arthritis—Have students put on thick gloves or mittens to simulate arthritis. Ask them to build something with Leggos or small toys.

Station #4: Dental Problems—Ask students to place a gum ball or jaw breaker behind their front teeth and hold it there using their tongue. Ask all students to read aloud a paragraph from a children's book; then pass the book to the next person to read aloud, and so on.

Station #5: Loss of Taste—Give each student unflavored seltzer water (colored, if you wish) and unsalted pretzels or crackers. Ask them to sit down and enjoy their "snack."

2. Ask students to refer to their notes from each station and to relate some of their feelings and frustrations. Have them share their experiences with the class.
3. Discuss the frustrations elderly persons face and ways in which others can help them.

Activity 12. Let's Discuss It! (Death Discussion Groups)

Concept/Description: Feelings about death are frequently neglected.

Objective: To have students openly discuss death and issues related to death.

Materials:

3 × 5 Death discussion cards (See p. 156)
Pens, pencils
Paper

Directions:

1. Divide the class into equal small groups. Give each group a discussion card.
2. Ask groups to discuss the problem given and jot down their comments.
3. Have the members of each group share their problems and thoughts with each other.

Questions for Discussion Cards:

1. If given a potion that would let you live for 100 more years, would you take it? Why or why not?
2. If given one year to live, what would you do in that year?
3. How would you like to be remembered when you die?
4. What is your greatest fear about dying?
5. Do you think anyone has the right to take a "hopeless case" person off a life-support machine? Who has the right? When?
6. Would you want to know if you were dying of a serious illness? Why or why not?
7. Should young children be allowed to talk about death or attend funerals? Why or why not?
8. Would you like to donate your body to science after you die? Why or why not?
9. Should a dying person who is in a lot of pain be allowed to die if he or she wants to?
10. Do you think abortion should be considered if a fetus is shown to have a serious handicap or problem?

Activity 13. Hear Me, Hear Me! (Guest Speakers)

Concept/Description: There are some professions that must confront life and death situations on a regular basis.

Objective: To gain a better understanding of death by meeting with people who deal with death frequently.

Materials:

Guest speakers, such as—
- Funeral director
- Rescue/ambulance squad member
- Fire fighter
- Doctor
- Nursing home director

Directions:

1. Invite various people who deal with death to speak to your classes.
2. Have students jot down their questions ahead of time.
3. Later, discuss how various professions must deal with death on a daily basis. Ask students for their reactions and comments. Ask how many of them would consider a profession that must deal with life and death circumstances.

UNIT 8

TURN OFF, TUNE OUT, DROP IN!

Activities Designed to Discourage Substance Abuse

One of the most difficult issues that confronts young people is the pressure to use tobacco, alcohol, or some other drug. This pressure begins at a younger and younger age. This makes it imperative that health units dealing with substance abuse be included in health curricula beginning with the lower grades and continuing throughout a student's school years.

The activities in this unit include some that are designed to provide information so that students become more aware of the complexity and extent of drug use. More important are the activities that increase understanding of societal pressures to use drugs.

Students must realize the impact that drugs have not only on individuals but also on communities. It is for this reason that several of the activities make use of community resources.

Prescription and non-prescription drugs must also be used with care. To develop a total picture of drugs, activities designed to inform about these kinds of drugs are also included in this unit. Teachers are encouraged to use and modify the activities that are presented so students will have an accurate picture of all kinds of drugs, good and bad, that are part of our culture.

How does a student withstand the pressure to use illegal drugs? The answer to this question is of critical importance. Several activities are designed to assist students in recognizing different kinds of pressures and to give them skills to withstand such pressures. Of equal importance are activities which are designed to show that a student who does not want to use drugs is not unique. There are many other students who feel the same way! This can lead to opportunities for the teacher to provide activities that will contribute to understanding the need to be accepted and activities that demonstrate healthy outlets for group acceptance. You will find activities that do this in Unit 2. They can be used effectively in conjunction with this unit or as follow-up activities.

Activity 1. Accidents Don't Have to Happen (Scrapbook)

Concept/Description: Many accidents are caused by alcohol and other drug usage.

Objective: To make students aware of the number of drug- and alcohol-related problems nationwide.

Materials:

Daily newspapers
Construction paper
Glue

Directions:

1. At the start of the unit, have students keep a scrapbook of drug- or alcohol-related incidents or accidents by having them cut out items from the newspaper and paste them onto construction paper.
2. Have the students choose a drug- or alcohol-related accident and tell how the story's outcome could have been different if alcohol or drugs were not involved.
3. Discuss.

Activity 2. Speak to Me! (Guest Speakers)

Concept/Description: There are many community people who can serve as resources for a unit on substance abuse.

Objective: Students will receive pertinent information about substance abuse from guest speakers.

Materials: (None)

Directions:

1. A few weeks before the start of a unit on substance abuse, contact local agencies that will send out guest speakers, and schedule a speaker per week. Guests might include a speaker from Alcoholics Anonymous, a police officer to explain and, perhaps, demonstrate the use of the breathalyzer, a speaker from a drug rehab center, and a representative from the American Cancer Society.
2. Or, schedule all the speakers on the same day, and organize a "Substance Abuse Awareness Day" school-wide.
3. Have students prepare questions ahead of time, and write a brief evaluation or reaction after each speaker has left. Discuss.

Activity 3. Put a Lid on It! (Safety Caps)

Concept/Description: All safety caps do not offer the same degree of safety in preventing accidental openings.

Objective: To show students safety caps and explain the reason for their use.

Materials:

Clean, empty bottles, with various types of safety caps clearly numbered.
Paper
Pens or pencils

Directions:

1. Have students try to open each cap.
2. Have the students number their papers according to the number of bottles. Write a V for very safe, an S for safe, and a U for unsafe next to each bottle number after rating the effectiveness of each cap in deterring a five-year-old child. Discuss.
3. Besides young children having difficulty opening caps, who else may have a problem? (The elderly or those with arthritis.) What can be done to help the elderly or arthritic? (Pharmacists will usually replace the cap that is difficult to open with an easy-to-open one upon request.)

Activity 4. Check It Out! (Surveying Non-Prescription Drugs)

Concept/Description: It is important to read and abide by the information given on over-the-counter (OTC) or non-prescription drugs to avoid possible injury or illness.

Objective: To make students aware of the information found on OTC drug labels and containers.

Materials:

Clean, empty bottles or boxes from typical non-prescription (OTC) medications, such as pain relievers, cold remedies, nasal sprays, etc.
Non-Prescription drug survey questions (See p. 162)
Pens or pencils

Directions:

1. Place the non-prescription containers at various locations around the room.
2. Write survey questions on the board, or distribute a survey sheet.
3. Ask students to answer the questions based on the information they gained by carefully reading the labels.
   NOTE: The questions will vary according to the type of containers you have.

Sample Survey Questions:

1. Which products are dangerous to use if you are currently using tetracycline?
2. Who should *not* use Benadryl elixir?
3. What is the recommended dosage of Tylenol for children 6–12 years old?
4. How much Maalox can be taken by an adult in a 24-hour period?
5. What should you avoid doing if you are taking Dimetapp?

Activity 5. Check It Out, II! (Surveying Prescription Drugs)

Concept/Description: It is important to read and abide by the information given on prescription labels to avoid possible injury or illness.

Objective: To make students aware of the information found on prescription bottles.

Materials:

Clean, empty prescription bottles with clear, readable labels
Pens or pencils

Directions:

1. Place the prescription bottles at various locations around the room.
2. Ask students to list information found on *most* containers and special information found on *some* containers. You may want to provide paper or a survey sheet.
3. Discuss the results.
   NOTE: Activities 3, 4, and 5 can be used as learning stations. The students may then rotate from activity to activity.

Answers:

Information found on most prescription containers includes—

The person's name	The name of the pharmacy
The doctor's name	The phone number of the pharmacy
The name of the drug	Directions for use
The amount of the drug	Expiration date

Special information may include special instructions, such as—

Shake well before using.
Keep refrigerated.
Do not take on an empty stomach.
Do not take with orange juice.

Activity 6. Play It Again, Sam! (Alcohol- or Drug-Related Songs)

Concept/Description: Music is a way of expressing many emotions. Some songs include messages that are pro- or anti-drugs and alcohol.

Objective: To have students discuss the possible meanings of some songs that may be drug- or alcohol-related.

Materials:

Drug- or alcohol-related songs on tape
Tape recorder
Words to the songs dittoed

Directions:

1. Tape-record various songs dealing with (or supposedly dealing with) drugs or alcohol. (Ask students for suggestions or have them bring in the actual songs. Be sure to listen to them first.)
2. Write down the words, and pass out a copy of the words to each student.
3. Play the songs (4–5) for the class, and discuss the possible meaning and why artists might choose to sing about these topics.
4. Some suggestions are included below:
   "Another Try," by America
   "White Rabbit," by Jefferson Airplane
   "The Needle and the Damage Done," by Neil Young

Activity 7. Smoke, Choke, Eventually Croak! (Anti-Smoking Campaign)

Concept/Description: Printed materials can be used effectively in giving information about the dangers of smoking.

Objective: Students will mount an anti-smoking informational campaign throughout the school.

Materials:

Materials from your local chapter of the American Cancer Society
Hard candies
Poster board
Markers, crayons
Paints, brushes

Directions:

1. Contact your local American Cancer Society, and obtain free or inexpensive posters and pamphlets.
2. Hold a school-wide anti-smoking poster or mobile contest, and award prizes (your student council may be willing to assist).
3. Have your class design and set up a "Quit Smoking Campaign." Pass out pamphlets and hang the American Cancer Society and student-designed posters

throughout the school. In the teachers' lounges, place a few pamphlets and hard candies with the suggestion that the teachers suck on the candy rather than smoke a cigarette.

Variation:
Have the class write a newsletter to pass out in school. It could contain poems, stories, factual information, drawings, or any other component of a regular newspaper.

Activity 8. A Day in the Life (Describing An Abuser)

Concept/Description: Drug and alcohol abuse occurs in all age groups, professions, ethnic backgrounds, income levels, and in both sexes.

Objective: To have students describe their perception of a day in the life of an alcoholic or drug addict and to help them to see that alcohol and drugs affect all walks of life.

Materials:
Paper
Pens and Pencils

Directions:
1. Have students write a few paragraphs about a typical day in the life of a drug or alcohol addict. Describe the person and how they looked, dressed, acted, etc.
2. Ask students to volunteer to read their descriptions.
3. From the papers, determine if students believe the average abuser to be a skid-row alcoholic or drug addict. Did anyone describe the user as a woman? Did anyone mention a professional, such as a business person, doctor, teacher, police officer, etc?
4. Discuss how alcohol and drug addiction affects all ages, professions, ethnic backgrounds, income levels, and both sexes.

Variation:
For extra credit, have students ask three adults to describe a drug addict or alcoholic and jot down their responses. Discuss how adults perceive the typical abuser. What could influence their perceptions? (Knowing a relative who has a drug or alcohol problem, previous courses on alcohol or drugs, etc.)

Activity 9. "This Has Been a Public Service Announcement . . ." (Anti-Substance Abuse Ads)

Concept/Description: Designing ads can be an effective way to stimulate students to investigate the dangers of drug use.

Objective: Students will incorporate accurate information in ads planned to discourage the use of tobacco, alcohol, and other drugs.

Materials:

Video camera
VCR
Various props
Blank tape

Directions:

1. Have the class or groups within the class design a 30–60 second TV public service ad that is anti-alcohol, tobacco, or drugs.
2. Be sure to set specific guidelines—for example, no more than five per group; all people in the group must speak; a script must first be approved; or you must include five facts within your ad.
3. Tape the ads and show them to other classes, the principal, etc.

Activity 10. Go for the Gusto? (Analyzing Tobacco and Alcohol Ads)

Concept/Description: Advertising for tobacco and alcohol products varies according to the population that the manufacturer is trying to reach.

Objective: To show students the image tobacco and alcohol manufacturers attempt to portray to increase sales of their products.

Materials:

Alcohol and tobacco ads from magazines
Analyzing Tobacco and Alcohol Advertisement Worksheets (See 8-1)

Directions:

1. Give each student two ads promoting alcohol or tobacco.
2. Have the students study the ads, and then have them fill in the worksheet.
3. Discuss the ads and their observations with the class.

4. Ask what type of image each product is trying to portray (for example, wine ads are perhaps portraying a sophisticated, romantic image; beer ads are more masculine; cigarette ads vary from a cool, sophisticated image to the rough and tumble cowboy image, etc.)
5. Do the ads give an honest portrayal of their products? Why or why not? Discuss.

Variation:

Videotape alcohol ads and analyze. Use magazine ads for cigarettes, pipe tobacco, chewing tobacco, etc.

Activity 11. What You See Isn't What You Get (How Drugs are Cut)

Concept/Description: Other ingredients are added to drugs to stretch them further and to increase the amount of money the drug dealer makes. Many ingredients are unsafe, and one cannot be sure what they are or know the amount that is added.

Objective: To show students that the person who buys drugs can never be certain what he or she is purchasing.

Materials:

Containers of various white powders such as baby powder, powdered sugar, flour, cleanser, white cake mix, etc.
Waxed paper or dish
Spoon

Directions:

1. Have students gather around a desk or table and place all the powders listed above on the table.
2. Ask them to watch carefully as you mix a little of each powder together into the dish or wax paper. Continue taking a little powder from each container, and then mix your pile together thoroughly.
3. Ask the students to tell you exactly how much baby powder or some other component is in the mixture.
4. Relate this to the way drugs such as heroin and cocaine are cut with other ingredients. Explain that, unless you are a chemist, it is impossible to know exactly what is in the mixture. Discuss how this could be dangerous. (The body can tolerate approximately one to four percent of a pure drug in a mixture. A person would not know and could die if a higher percentage were added. Also, a poisonous substance could be used to stretch the drug.)

Name ______________________ Date ______________ (8-1)

Analyzing Tobacco and Alcohol Advertisements

DIRECTIONS: Analyze two ads, fill in this form, and staple your ads to it.

AD #1

1. Product ______________ Description of ad: ______________
2. This ad appeals to what basic need/desire? ______________
3. Is it a realistic portrayal of life? Why or why not? ______________
4. Could another product be substituted? If so, what? If not, why not?
5. Will the suggested results be achieved? Why or why not? ______________
6. List three alternatives to meet the need suggested in the ad: ______________

AD #2

1. Product ______________ Description of ad: ______________
2. This ad appeals to what basic need/desire? ______________
3. Is it a realistic portrayal of life? Why or why not? ______________
4. Could another product be substituted? If so, what? If not, why not?
5. Will the suggested results be achieved? Why or why not? ______________
6. List three alternatives to meet the need suggested in the ad: ______________

Activity 12. Here's Proof! (Determining Percentage of Alcohol)

Concept/Description: The proof of an alcoholic beverage is two times the percent of pure alcohol found in the beverage. The higher the proof, the stronger the beverage.

Objective: To determine the different amounts of alcohol in various beverages, and to discuss what proof is.

Materials:

Labels from liquor bottles (wine, whiskey, champagne, etc.)
Empty containers of liquor, beer cans, etc. Bring these in yourself.

Directions:

1. Have students look for the proof (or percentage) on each bottle or can. If the proof is listed, ask them to determine the percentage of alcohol. NOTE: Proof is two times the percentage of alcohol. For example, if a beverage is 50 Proof, then it contains 25 percent alcohol.
2. Have students place the bottles or labels in order, from those containing the lowest percentage of alcohol to the highest percentage.
3. Explain that one can of beer, one glass of wine, and one shot of whiskey contain approximately the same amount of alcohol. The other ingredients include fruit juices, water, etc.
4. Ask students why they think manufacturers are required to list the proof or percentage of alcohol. Ask if they think this *should* be required? Why or why not? Discuss.

Activity 13. You Can Lead a Horse to Water, But . . . (Peer Pressure)

Concept/Description: Many individuals feel obligated to conform to their peers in order to be accepted.

Objective: To show students first-hand an example of peer pressure and its possible negative effects.

Materials:

One chocolate kiss (or other candy) for every 5–6 students
Pen or pencil and paper (for two observers)

Directions:

1. Ask for two students to volunteer to help you. (They will be observers, but don't announce that to the class.) Their job will be to watch and listen to what occurs and write down comments or conversation.
2. Divide the rest of the class into groups of 5–6, and place a chocolate kiss in the middle of each group. Choose one person per group, and ask them to leave the room with you.
3. Quietly tell the chosen students that if they can go back into the group and *not* eat the chocolate kiss, no matter what their group says, they will receive extra class credit or some other teacher-determined payoff. Let these students remain in the hall, and ask them *not* to tell the group their instructions.
4. Tell the rest of the class groups that if they can persuade the chosen group member to eat the chocolate kiss, their group will each receive extra class credit or some other teacher-determined payoff. Tell them to use any strategy they wish (guilt, anger, begging, bribing, etc.), but not to touch the person at all.
5. Allow the activity to last for about 10–15 minutes so that the observers can jot down the tactics each group uses to persuade their person to eat.
6. Stop the activity and explain that this was an example of peer pressure. Ask the chosen persons how they felt and why. Ask the observers to explain what they saw and heard. Ask various group members if they felt frustrated, angry, etc. Discuss.
7. Ask the students to relate their experience to other possible peer pressure situations (drugs, alcohol, smoking, doing what the group wants, etc.) Discuss.
8. Brainstorm ways that you could get out of peer pressure situations in which you feel uncomfortable.

Activity 14. It's My Decision (Problem Solving)

Concept/Description: Looking at all aspects of a problem and thoroughly analyzing it could help students to make more sensible, clearer decisions.

Objective: To show students some basic steps in analyzing, solving, and evaluating decisions.

Materials:

Decision-Making Worksheet (See 8-2 & 8-3)
Sample Problems (See 8-4)
Pens or pencils

Directions:

1. Give each student a Decision-Making Worksheet.
2. Go over the worksheet with the class, and then give them a fairly simple problem to analyze. (Use one from the sample problems included, or design your own.)
3. Have the class fill in their guides, and then discuss their methods of solving the problem.
4. Discuss how some problems are solved and why the solutions may not be the best choice. For example, refer to number 1 of the sample problems. The actual situation between the two neighbors ended when one man shot the other. Although the problem was "solved," the gunman spent the rest of his life in jail.

Activity 15. I'm on Your Side (A Story about Drug Use)

Concept/Description: People have different reactions to drug use. It is particularly important to know the truth before making judgments.

Objective: To rank order the story characters individually from the least objectionable to most objectionable.

Materials:

Five sheets of paper
Tape
Marker
"The Marijuana Story" (See 8-5)

Directions:

1. Read "The Marijuana Story" to your class.
2. After reading the story, ask class members to rank the characters in order from the one whose actions you most approve of to the one whose actions you approve of least. (Be sure to include Jim, Patti, Patti's dad, Jim's dad, and Jim's mom.)
3. Write one of the character's names on each of the five sheets of paper and tape it to the walls of the classroom. Space the sheets as far apart as possible.
4. Ask the students to stand by the paper with the name of the person whom they feel is most at fault in the story.
5. After each person has decided, have the groups discuss why they feel the way they do.
6. Appoint a spokesperson to explain the group's feelings.
7. Discuss.

(Continued on p. 174)

Name ______________________ Date ______________ (8-2)

Decision-Making Worksheet

STEP 1. In a few sentences, define the problem to be solved ______________________

____

____

STEP 2. Educate yourself. Gather information related to the problem. Identify at least three possible solutions or alternatives.

1. ______________________
2. ______________________
3. ______________________

STEP 3. Consider the positive and negative aspects of each alternative.

Positive	Negative
1. ______	1. ______
2. ______	2. ______
3. ______	3. ______

Positive	Negative
1. ______	1. ______
2. ______	2. ______
3. ______	3. ______

Positive	Negative
1. ______	1. ______
2. ______	2. ______
3. ______	3. ______

STEP 4. List persons affected by these alternatives and any personal values that may be in conflict with these alternatives.

1. ______________________
2. ______________________
3. ______________________

(Continued on 8-3)

(Continued from 8-2)

STEP 5. Compare all the alternatives and identify your choice.

MY CHOICE IS: ______________________________

STEP 6. Design a plan to carry out this decision. List steps that need to be taken. Identify ways of handling obstacles.

____

____

____

____

STEP 7. Evaluate the decision:

1. What happened? ______________________________
2. Would you handle this situation differently next time? ______________________________

   ____

Sample Problems:

1. Mr. Brown and Mr. Smith live next door to each other. Each week, Mr. Brown mows his lawn. When he does, the grass shoots from his mower on to Mr. Smith's porch. Mr. Smith is getting tired of sweeping his porch after Mr. Brown mows. What could he say or do?
2. Sue just bought her favorite tape and has not even opened the package. Donna asks to borrow the tape for her party that afternoon. Donna has lost or broken Sue's tapes in the past, but they are good friends. What could Sue do or say?
3. Dan asks Beth to meet him at the movies. When Beth gets there, Dan buys a ticket for himself only. Beth has $3.00, and the movie costs $4.50. What could Beth do or say?
4. Bill, who is 16, asks Jamie his brother, who is 21, to buy some alcohol for him and his friends. Bill promises he won't drive, but lately Bill has been getting into a lot of trouble. What could Jamie do or say?
5. Mr. and Mrs. Wilson have a cocktail party. Their fifteen-year-old daughter Jennifer asks for a glass of wine. What do you think her parents should do or say?
6. At a party, every person there is either doing coke or smoking pot. When Jean walks in with her friend Ashley, who is new in the neighborhood, another friend offers them some drugs. Jean accepts. Ashley is very uncomfortable and has no desire to use any drugs, but wants desperately to "fit in." What could Ashley do or say?

Variation:

1. Have all groups attempt to convince the other groups of their position and allow group members to switch, if they desire.
2. Do an overall ranking of all the characters that is based on individual student rankings.
3. The teacher can also do other statistical analyses of the way each character was ranked.

THE MARIJUANA STORY

Jim, a high school student, moves with his parents to a new community in October of his senior year. He is rather shy and doesn't make friends easily. Most of his fellow students regard him as a "brain" because he is taking accelerated courses in science and math. His parents want him to go to college and have decided that he is not to go out on school nights; he must stay home and study.

Patti is in Jim's American History class. She thinks he's cute and has been trying to coax him into asking her out for a date. Jim, however, has never considered a date because Patti is a cheerleader and a member of the popular set at school, and anyhow, Jim has to stay home and study.

One Tuesday afternoon, Patti gives in to impatience and asks Jim over for the evening to listen to records. Jim eagerly accepts. At dinner that night, he tells his parents that he is going over to a friend's home to work on a science project and will be home around ten o'clock. At seven, he makes his escape.

He goes to Patti's house, and soon they are in the recreation room, talking and listening to the stereo. About eight o'clock Patti reaches into her pocket and pulls out a plastic bag. She asks Jim if he'd like to smoke some grass. Jim takes the bag and looks inside it. He is curious about marijuana. He has never seen it before.

Suddenly, Patti's father walks in. He halts and stares at the couple and then grabs the bag from Jim. He looks at Jim and then at his daughter. "Is this marijuana?" he inquires. Patti looks down, and Jim sits there, speechless. "Patti," says her father, "You go to your room, while I take this young hood to the police station. What's your name, boy?"

Jim is scared. He blurts out the name of one of the kids in his class rumored to sell drugs.

Patti's father leads Jim to the car, muttering imprecations about slum punks and bad apples that ruin the whole barrel. Once in the car, he calms down and asks Jim where he lives. Jim tells him his address, hoping he won't be taken to the police station.

Finally, they arrive at Jim's house, and in the heat of the confrontation with Jim's parents, no introductions take place. Patti's father departs, saying, "The only reason I brought Jim home is that I don't want to put a kid in jail because he's had the misfortune of a bad upbringing."

Jim's mother demands, "How long has this been going on? After all I've done for you, now you slap me in the face. We gave you everything!" His father motions him to go to his room and says, "Get some sleep. We'll talk about this in the morning when we've all calmed down."

In the morning, Jim finds that his father has gone to work early and that his mother has some news for him. "Your father and I had a long talk last night, and I finally persuaded him to go along with my decision. From now on, you'll do all your studying at home. Weekends, you'll work in your father's store, and all of your earnings will be put away for your college education."

UNIT 9

ALL SYSTEMS ARE GO! Activities to Teach about the Body's Systems

Understanding how the various systems of the body operate can be both fascinating and valuable for the student. Children are interested in their bodies and how they work. Activities in this chapter will give students a clear understanding of how the systems of the body function. This will help them understand themselves better and dispel many of the fears that children have when they think they are abnormal because of the messages they are receiving from their body.

An important educational goal is to contribute to developing healthful life styles for students. Knowing the components of their body systems and having a basic understanding of how the systems function form the foundation upon which healthy life styles can be built.

The first part of this unit contains activities that apply to several different systems. They can also be modified to teach about other systems. The second part includes specific activities for each body system. They will help students understand how each system functions by actively engaging them with a simulation of the system in operation or making them a part of the simulation. For example, in one of the activities for the circulatory system, some of the students become blood cells that flow through different parts of the circulatory system.

Activity 1. That's Shocking (Electric Game Board)

Concept/Description: All body parts are designated by words that can be either technical or common usage terms.

Objective: Students will be able to match the word that corresponds to the different body parts.

Materials:

Insulated wire
Bolts and nuts (or screws if you prefer not to drill holes)
Plywood
Acrylic paint
Brushes
Flashlight reflector head piece
6 volt battery
6 volt bulb
3 × 5 cards (or any size you wish)

Directions:

To construct an Electric Body Board (Figure 9-1):

1. Cut out a piece of plywood to the size you desire the electric game board to be.
2. Draw the design you want (in this case, a human torso).
3. Paint the design using acrylic paint.
4. On 3 × 5 cards, write the names of the body parts that you have included on your torso.
5. Set the bolts and nuts in place. Put one bolt on each body part, and distribute an equal number of bolts on the outside of the torso (Figure 9-1).

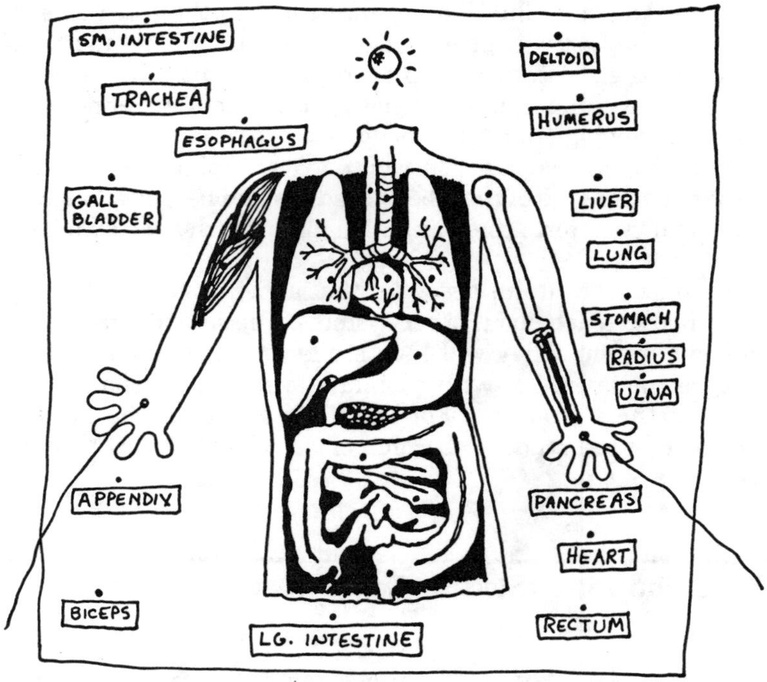

Fig. 9-1. Electric body board.

6. Attach the cards in a random fashion below the bolts that have been placed outside the torso drawing.
7. Place an electric wire to connect the bolt from a body part to the bolt just above the card designating the same body part. Secure with the nuts. (Remember to strip the wire to attach to the bolts.)
8. Drill a hole at the top of the board, and insert the flashlight reflector head and bulb.
9. Attach the battery to the back of the board.
10. Place two wires on the 6 volt battery: one on the positive post, and one on the negative post. (Remember to strip the wires to attach them to the posts.)
11. Run the wire on the negative post to the flashlight reflector for grounding.
12. Run a long wire from the positive post through one of the torso's hands, and use it for playing the game.
13. Attach a third wire to the end of the 6 volt bulb, and extend it through the other hand on the torso.

To Play:

1. Students attempt to match a card with the appropriate body part.
2. Touch a wire from one of the torso's hands to the bolt on one of the body parts.
3. Touch the wire from the torso's other hand to the bolt above the name that corresponds. If correct, the circuit will be completed and the bulb will light up.

Activity 2. I See You! (Model Making)

Concept/Description: Models can be used to assist students in understanding the composition of the human body.

Objective: Students will be able to construct models of the human body and body parts.

Materials:

Store-bought models (visible man, woman, heart, etc.)
Glue
Paint
Brushes

Directions:

1. Allow groups of students to construct store-bought models as part of a class plan, or allow students to work on them when there is free time, or as a reward for good work.
2. Display the models in the school's showcase, if possible.

Activity 3. Who Am I? (Guess the Organ and System)

Concept/Description: Students will use clues about organs and systems to recognize characteristics of the different organs and systems.

Objective: Students will learn about body organs and systems through a system of clues.

Materials:

Plywood
Hooks (screw in type)
3 × 5 Cards
Hole punch
Paints
Brushes

Directions:

To construct a game board (Figure 9-2):

1. Decide on the size of your game board, and cut the plywood to that size.
2. Paint the wood and decorate it if you so desire.
3. Write the categories on the top of the board (in this case, the systems).
4. Place approximately 5 hooks under each category.
5. Punch holes in the top of the 3 × 5 cards. On each card, write a clue describing an organ or system (Figure 9-3). End each clue with the question, "Who Am I?"

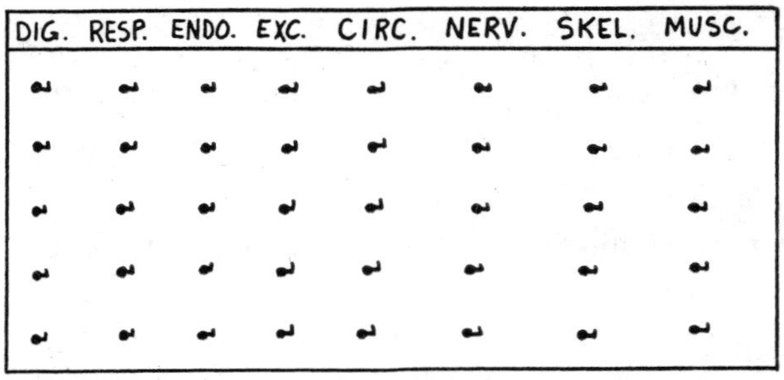

Fig. 9-2. Game board with hooks.

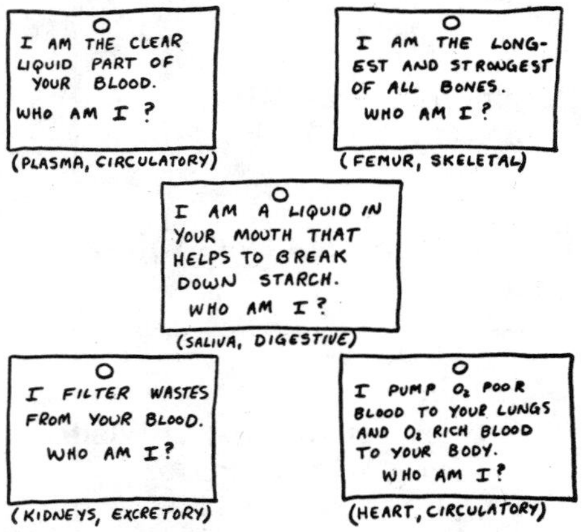

Fig. 9-3. Sample "Who Am I?" cards.

To play:

1. Lay the cards face down on the teacher's desk.
2. Divide the class into two groups.
3. Have one member of one group come up to the desk and choose a card. That person reads aloud the clue. The team has 10 seconds to give the correct answer. If the answer is an organ, the team may also opt to give the correct system to which it belongs. It is a double or nothing situation. In other words, if team members correctly guess "pancreas," they get one point. If they opt to guess the system and are correct, they get two points; if incorrect, they get no points.
4. Alternate from team to team until all cards have been used up.
5. Place any card that has been answered incorrectly back on the desk, face down.
6. Place correct answers on the hooks under the proper category (system).
7. The team with the most points is declared the winner.

Activity 4. Where are You Hiding? (Seek and Find)

Concept/Description: Word recognition helps students learn about body systems.

Objective: Students will recognize words that relate to systems of the body.

Materials:

Seek and Find Worksheets (See 9-1)
Pens or pencils

Directions:

1. Have students search for the systems-related words either diagonally, vertically, horizontally, forwards, or backwards.
2. To make it a competitive game, play a time-limit version, with either groups or on an individual basis, to see who can find the most words.

Variation:

Allow students to devise their own Seek and Find and answer key and have the students share these materials with each other.

Activity 5. WHO SAID THAT? (Talking Tapes)

Concept/Description: By writing a script for a body part that they have constructed, students will understand more about their bodies.

Objective: Students will learn about body parts by designing models and developing a script that describes the body part.

Materials:

(Will vary)
Tape
Tape Recorder

Directions:

1. Have students design a body part, such as a tooth, a heart, a pancreas, etc., and construct it out of materials of their choice (clay, papier mache, wood, construction paper, etc.).
2. Have students write out a script as if that body part were talking about itself. Record the script on a tape. Playback all the tapes to the class.
3. This activity has been used successfully with older students constructing the parts and passing them on to younger students for use in their health classes. The models have also been given to schools that are located in underprivileged areas.

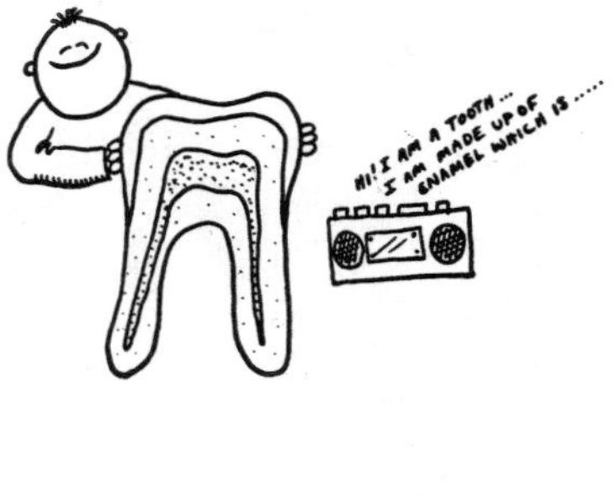

Name ______________________________ Date ________________ (9-1)

Seek and Find

FIND THESE WORDS:

SKULL
BRONCHIAL TUBE
OVARY
SPLEEN
REPRODUCTIVE
SKELETAL
TRICEPS
MUSCULAR
DIGESTIVE
CIRCULATORY
RESPIRATORY
NERVOUS
ENDOCRINE
EXCRETORY
LIVER
LUNG
TRACHEA
PANCREAS
ESOPHAGUS
BRAIN
SPINAL CORD
MEDULLA
DELTOID

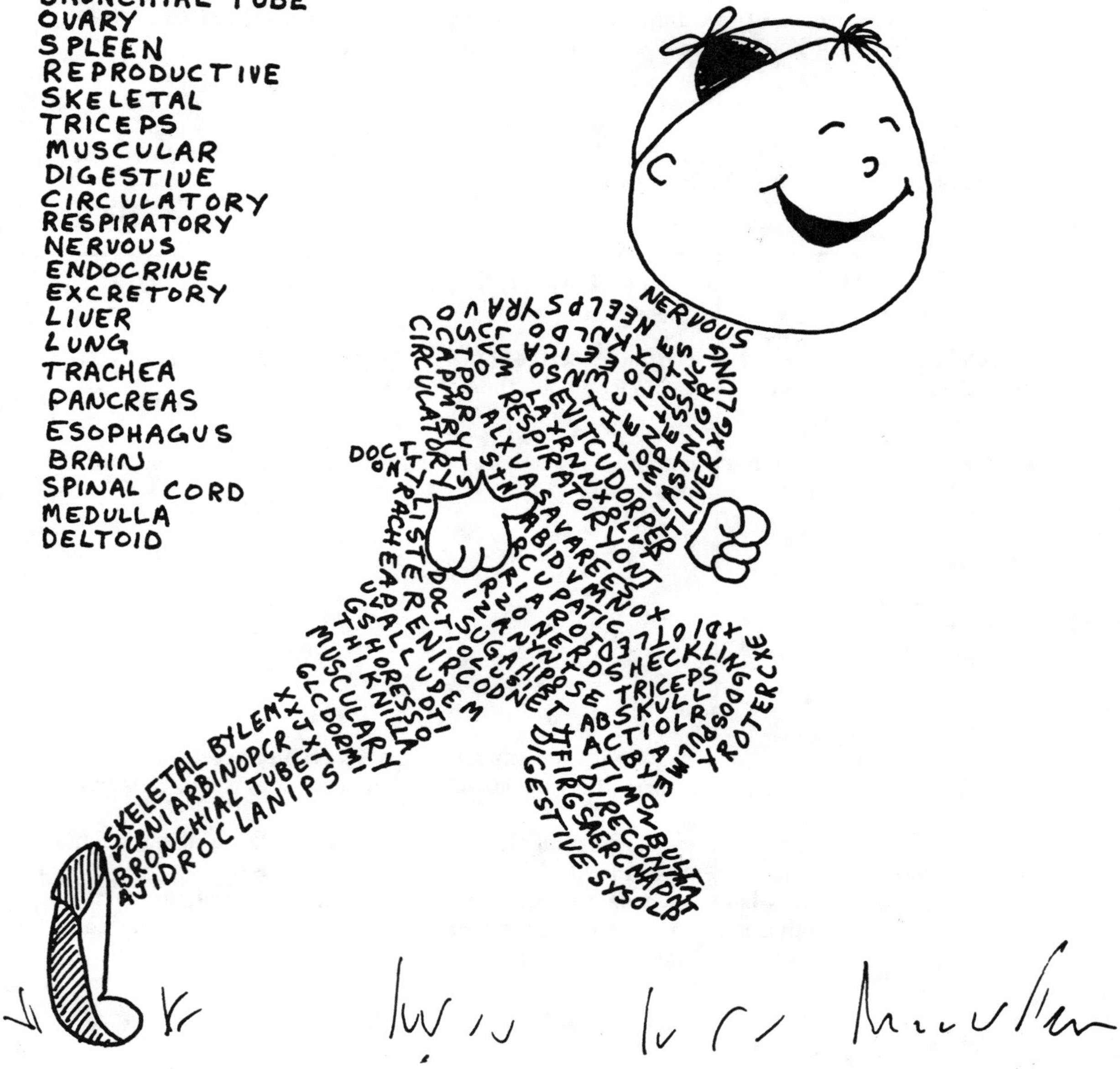

Activity 6. Bingo! (Body Bingo)

Concept/Description: A Bingo format is a fun way to learn terms relating to systems of the body.

Objective: Students will become familiar with words that describe parts of the body.

Materials:

Dittoed Blank Bingo Cards (See 9-4)
Body Bingo Checking Chart (See 9-2)
Sample Bingo Card (See 9-3)
Bingo markers (pennies, pieces of paper, chips, etc.)
Shoe box or small box
NOTE: Laminate the cards and charts for a more permanent setup.
ALTERNATE: Photocopy cards, mark them with a pen or pencil while playing, and discard them when through. (Be sure to keep at least one copy of each card, or you will have to redo the cards each time you want to play.)

Directions:

1. Refer to the Sample Bingo Card provided, and draw up your own Bingo cards using the blank.
2. Ideally, each card should be different. Refer to the checking chart and slightly vary each column. (It is not necessary to draw a picture for each square.)
   NOTE: You may wish to make your own checking chart and alter the game to meet your needs.
3. Bingo is played by calling out numbers chosen at random. The easiest way to do this is to photocopy two copies of your checking chart. (Laminate it if you desire.) Cut one chart into squares, and place them in the shoe box. Use the box when drawing numbers. Use the other chart for reference. After calling a number, place the cutout square over its corresponding square on the chart. In this way, you will know which numbers have been called should there be a discrepancy.
4. Play by regular Bingo rules; that is, pick a square and call out the number and word (e.g., "O-74: Ligaments"). Wait a few seconds for students to search. Continue to call out numbers and words until someone shouts, "Bingo!"
5. Decide ahead of time what constitutes "Bingo." Some popular versions are—
   (a) Vertical, horizontal, or diagonal rows
   (b) Four corners
   (c) X
   (d) H or T
   (e) Outside edges
   (f) Whole card
   (g) Any other version you or your class invents
6. When a student shouts "Bingo," check your chart, and award that person, or team (if you wish), a point.
7. Continue playing a time-limit or point-limit game.

Body Bingo Checking Chart

B	B1 INTESTINES DIG	B2 HEART CIRC	B3 ARTERY CIRC	B4 NEURON NERV	B5 LUNG RESP	B6 RADIUS SKEL	B7 BICEPS MUSC
B8 STOMACH DIG	B9 PANCREAS ENDO	B10 UTERUS REPRO	B11 PLASMA CIRC	B12 BRAIN NERV	B13 TRICEPS MUSC	B14 ESOPHAGUS DIG	B15 TRACHEA RESP
I	I16 LEUKOCYTES CIRC	I17 VAS DEFERENS REPRO	I18 SALIVA DIG	I19 AORTA CIRC	I20 QUADRICEPS MUSC	I21 SPINAL CORD NERV	I22 VENTRICLES CIRC
I23 HAMSTRINGS MUSC	I24 ULNA SKEL	I25 SKULL SKEL	I26 VEIN CIRC	I27 ISLET OF LANGERHANS ENDO	I28 BLADDER EXC	I29 GASTRIC JUICE DIG	I30 TRAPEZIUS MUSC
N	N31 OVARIES ENDO	N32 CEREBRUM NERV	N33 PATELLA SKEL	N34 NOSE RESP	N35 BLOOD CIRC	N36 RECTUM DIG	N37 CAPILLARIES CIRC
N38 DELTOID MUSC	N39 ULCER DIG	N40 HEART ATTACK CIRC	N41 STROKE CIRC	N42 MEDULLA NERV	N43 FALLOPIAN TUBES REPRO	N44 VENA CAVA CIRC	N45 HUMERUS SKEL
G	G46 ARTERIO-SCLEROSIS CIRC	G47 MULTIPLE SCLEROSIS NERV	G48 SCAPULA SKEL	G49 PECTORALS MUSC	G50 ALVEOLI RESP	G51 TENDONS MUSC	G52 RIBS SKEL
G53 SPINAL COLUMN SKEL	G54 MOUTH DIG	G55 SEMINAL VESICLE REPRO	G56 CLAVICLE SKEL	G57 CEREBRAL PALSY NERV	G58 TIBIA SKEL	G59 BRONCHI RESP	G60 PROSTATE REPRO
O	O61 AUDITORY NERVE NERV	O62 GASTROC-NEMIUS MUSC	O63 TONGUE DIG	O64 PERICAR-DIUM CIRC	O65 FEMUR SKEL	O66 PITUITARY GLAND ENDO	O67 META-CARPALS SKEL
O68 A.I.D.S. IMMUNO	O69 MUSCULAR DYSTROPHY MUSC	O70 LEUKEMIA CIRC	O71 EMPHYSEMA RESP	O72 OPTICAL NERVE NERV	O73 PELVIS SKEL	O74 LIGAMENTS SKEL	O75 LARYNX RESP

Sample Bingo Card

BODY BINGO

SYSTEMS OF THE BODY

B	I	N	G	O
PLASMA CIRCULATORY 11	SALIVA DIGESTIVE 18	ULCER DIGESTIVE 39	MULTIPLE SCLEROSIS — NERVOUS 47	AUDITORY NERVE NERVOUS 61
HEART CIRCULATORY 2	VENTRICLES CIRCULATORY 22	FALLOPIAN TUBES FEMALE REPRODUCTIVE 43	RIBS SKELETAL 52	TONGUE DIGESTIVE 63
ESOPHAGUS DIGESTIVE 14	VEIN CIRCULATORY 26	FREE SPACE	MOUTH DIGESTIVE 54	LARYNX RESPIRATORY 75
BICEPS MUSCULAR 7	VAS DEFERENS MALE REPRODUCTIVE 17	VENA CAVA CIRCULATORY 44	TIBIA SKELETAL 58	PELVIS SKELETAL 73
BRAIN NERVOUS 12	SKULL SKELETAL 25	NOSE RESPIRATORY 34	PROSTATE MALE REPRODUCTIVE 60	MUSCULAR DYSTROPHY — MUSCULAR 69

Blank Bingo Card

B	**I**	**N**	**G**	**O**
		FREE SPACE		

Activity 7. A Really Big Shoe (Filmstrip Shoebox Theater)

Concept/Description: A filmstrip can be made—even by young children—to cover information that is learned in class.

Objective: Students will depict various health topics on a filmstrip they make.

Materials:

Shoeboxes
White butcher paper cut into long strips
Markers, pens, pencils

Directions:

1. Cut a rectangular hole (to serve as the movie screen) in the bottom of each shoe box. Be sure to leave an edge all the way around the screen. (See Figure 9-4).
2. Next, cut an opening in each side of the box that will be large enough to slide the paper strips through.
3. Cut the butcher paper into long strips slightly narrower than the side openings.
4. Have the students design "filmstrips" telling stories or giving facts on a variety of health topics, such as fire safety and first aid, by writing and drawing on the strips. The number of frames will be determined by the length of the filmstrip desired.
5. Slide the papers into the boxes as shown, and have the students demonstrate their filmstrip to the class.

Fig. 9-4. Filmstrip Shoe Box Theater.

Activity 8. Eye See! (Systems Review)

Concept/Description: Definitions that can refer to something other than an anatomy term are a challenge for students and fun for them to try to decipher.

Objective: Students will have fun using a clue to come up with an anatomical term.

Name ______________________ Date ______________ (9-5)

Anatomy Review Fun Sheet

DIRECTIONS: Use the clue given to identify the body part.

1. A tropical tree ______________
2. Worn by kings ______________
3. Used by artists ______________
4. Musical instruments ______________
5. Bright garden flowers ______________
6. A student ______________
7. Product of a spruce tree ______________
8. Something carpenters use ______________
9. Parts of a clock ______________
10. A large wooden box ______________
11. Edge of a saw ______________
12. Covering of an apple ______________
13. Cover for pails ______________
14. Part of a stove pipe ______________
15. Part of a river ______________
16. A very small island ______________
17. Weather cocks ______________
18. Timid little animal ______________
19. A lot of negatives ______________
20. Part of a potato ______________
21. A young cow ______________
22. A place of worship ______________
23. Both ends of a tomato ______________

Materials: Anatomy Review Fun Sheet (See 9-5)
Pens or pencils

Directions:

1. Have students identify different body parts by using the clue given (e.g., tropical tree = palm).
2. Have students work individually, in pairs, or in groups.

Answers:

1. Palm
2. Crown
3. Pallette (Palate)
4. Drums (Ear)
5. Two lips
6. Pupil
7. Cones
8. Hammer
9. Face, hands
10. Chest
11. Tooth
12. Skin
13. Lids
14. Elbow
15. Mouth
16. Islet
17. Vein
18. Hare (Hair)
19. Nose (No's)
20. Eye
21. Calf
22. Temple
23. Toes

THE DIGESTIVE SYSTEM

Activity 9. Dexter Digestion (Cut and Paste)

Concept/Description: The digestive system is composed of several parts.

Objective: Students will learn the different parts of the digestive system.

Materials:
Dexter Digestion Worksheet dittos (See 9-6)
Dexter's Digestive System dittos (See 9-7)
Construction paper
Scissors
Crayons or markers
Glue or paste

Directions:

1. Have students color in the organs on the digestive system ditto.
2. Have students cut out the organs and glue them in the proper place on "Dexter" worksheets.
3. Have them clearly label all the parts and mount the picture on construction paper.

Name ______________________ Date ______________ (9-6)

Dexter Digestion

Dexter's Digestive System

DIRECTIONS: Color the digestive organs below, and then cut them out and paste them into the correct places on Dexter.

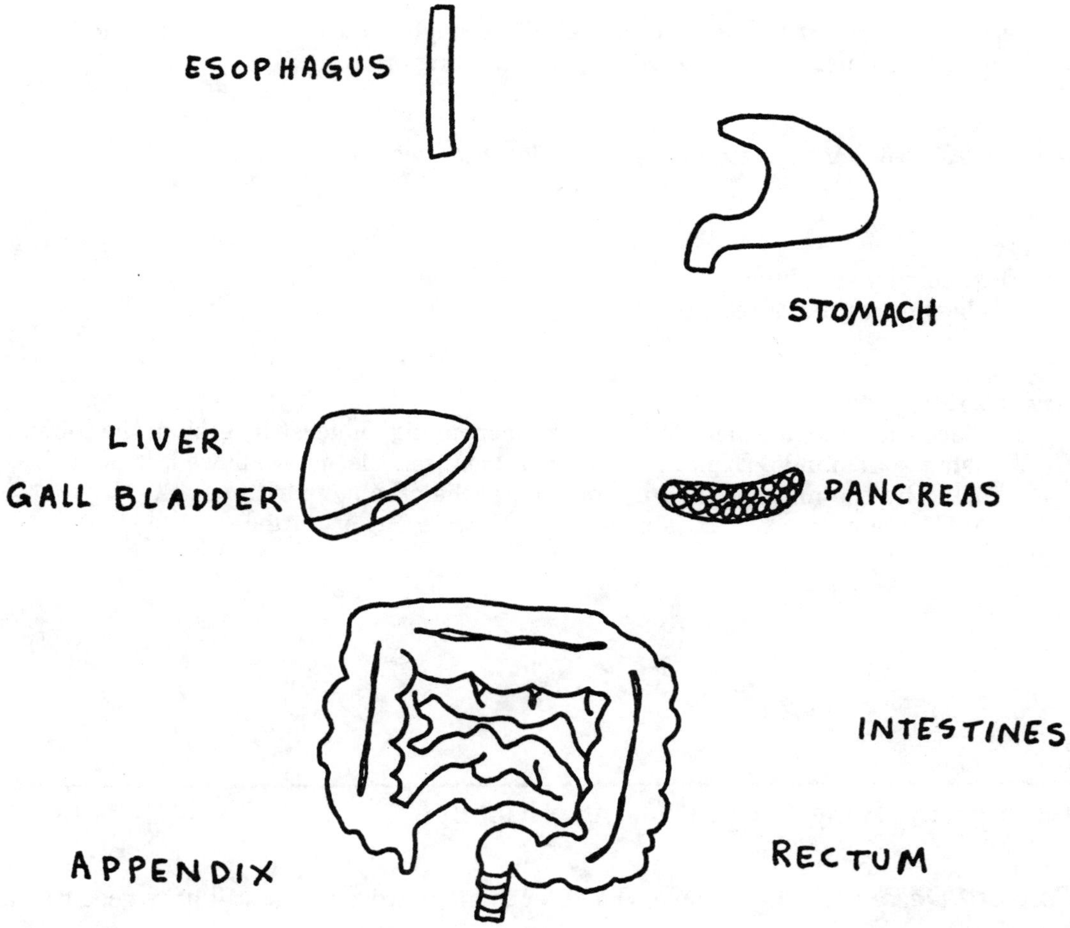

Variation:

Allow students to color "Dexter" or add any details they wish (surfboards, skates, etc.). Be sure to emphasize that proper positioning and labeling is the purpose of the activity.

Activity 10. I Feel "Squeezy" (Peristaltic Action of the Esophagus)

Concept/Description: Food is "squeezed" through the esophagus by the action of the surrounding muscles. This is called *peristaltic action.*

Objective: To demonstrate how peristaltic action works.

Materials:

Flexible rubber tubing
Marbles or a tube of toothpaste

Directions:

1. Place a marble in a piece of flexible rubber tubing. Squeeze it through the tubing, using your hands. Explain that, when food (marble) is swallowed, it is pushed along by the muscles (hands) until it reaches the stomach.
2. An alternate method is to squeeze toothpaste out of a tube.

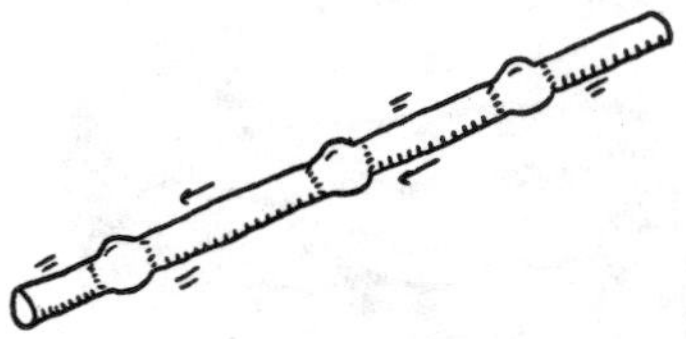

Activity 11. Hang It Up! (Making a Mobile)

Concept/Description: People who differ in many ways might still have good eating habits.

Objective: Mobiles will be used to display people with good eating habits.

Materials:

Magazines
Construction paper or poster board
Scissors
Paste or glue
String or thread
Wooden dowels

Directions:

1. Have students cut out pictures of people who have good eating habits and paste them on to construction paper (for example, a picture of a person eating fresh fruit or vegetables).
2. Attach a thread to each picture.
3. Cut a support (dowel) and suspend a picture from each end, making sure they don't touch. (Threads can be of different lengths.)
4. Tie another thread to the dowel, and support the mobile by the thread. Slide the thread back and forth until you find the point of balance. Place a spot of glue on the thread so that it remains secure. This will be your bottom picture.
5. If you want to add sections to your mobile, they should be *above* your completed section(s) since mobiles are best built from the bottom up.

Variation:

Do the same with pictures of people exhibiting poor eating habits.

Activity 12. Who Am I? (Constructing and Describing the Digestive Organs)

Concept/Description: Organs of the digestive system can be constructed of many different materials to give an understanding of that organ.

Objective: Students will be able to make models of organs of the digestive system and write a description of the organ.

Materials:

Will depend on student's or group's choice of available items.

Directions:

1. Have groups or individuals construct a particular organ of the digestive system. For example, a group could use flexible tubing for the intestines or construct the liver out of clay, etc. Include the gallbladder, liver, small and large intestines, etc.
2. Have the group write (on poster board or on 5 × 7 card) a description of the organ that ends with the sentence "Who Am I?"
3. Later, have individuals or groups view the models and try to guess which organ is being depicted or described.

Variations:

1. Work with other subject areas such as industrial arts, art, home economics, music, etc., to make projects or puzzles of wood, dough, papier mache, or even to write a song describing the organ or system.
2. Have students make a game show or video (called "Who Am I?") and use their projects and show them to other classes.

3. Have each group construct an entire digestive system, and display the projects throughout the room or school. Students could construct three-dimensional models, using balloons for the stomach and gallbladder and tubing for the intestines. Other alternatives are for them to make an entire system of clay, papier mache, etc., or construct a model using wood, paper, or some other material. Encourage their creativity.

THE CIRCULATORY SYSTEM

Activity 13. Cyrus Circulatory (Cut and Paste)

Concept/Description: Blood traveling away from the heart carries oxygen to parts of the body, and blood traveling to the heart is returning to replenish its oxygen supply.

Objective: Students will know which parts of the heart are receiving blood to renew the oxygen supply and which parts are sending oxygenated blood to parts of the body.

Materials:

Cyrus Circulatory Worksheet (See 9-8)
Cyrus's Circulatory System (heart parts) dittos (See 9-9)
Construction paper
Scissors
Crayons or markers
Glue or paste
Red and blue yarn or string

Directions:

1. Have students color in the heart as follows:
   Right atrium—blue
   Right ventricle—blue
   Left atrium—red
   Left ventricle—red
2. Cut out the parts, and glue them to Cyrus in the proper position.
3. Label all parts clearly.
4. Use string to signify blood vessels coming to and from the heart. Use red string to signify oxygen-rich blood traveling from the heart to the body by way of the arteries; use blue string to denote oxygen-poor blood traveling by way of the veins from the body to the heart and lungs. Note that this blood is *not* blue in reality.
5. Mount the worksheet onto construction paper.

Name ____________________ Date ____________ (9-8)

Cyrus Circulatory

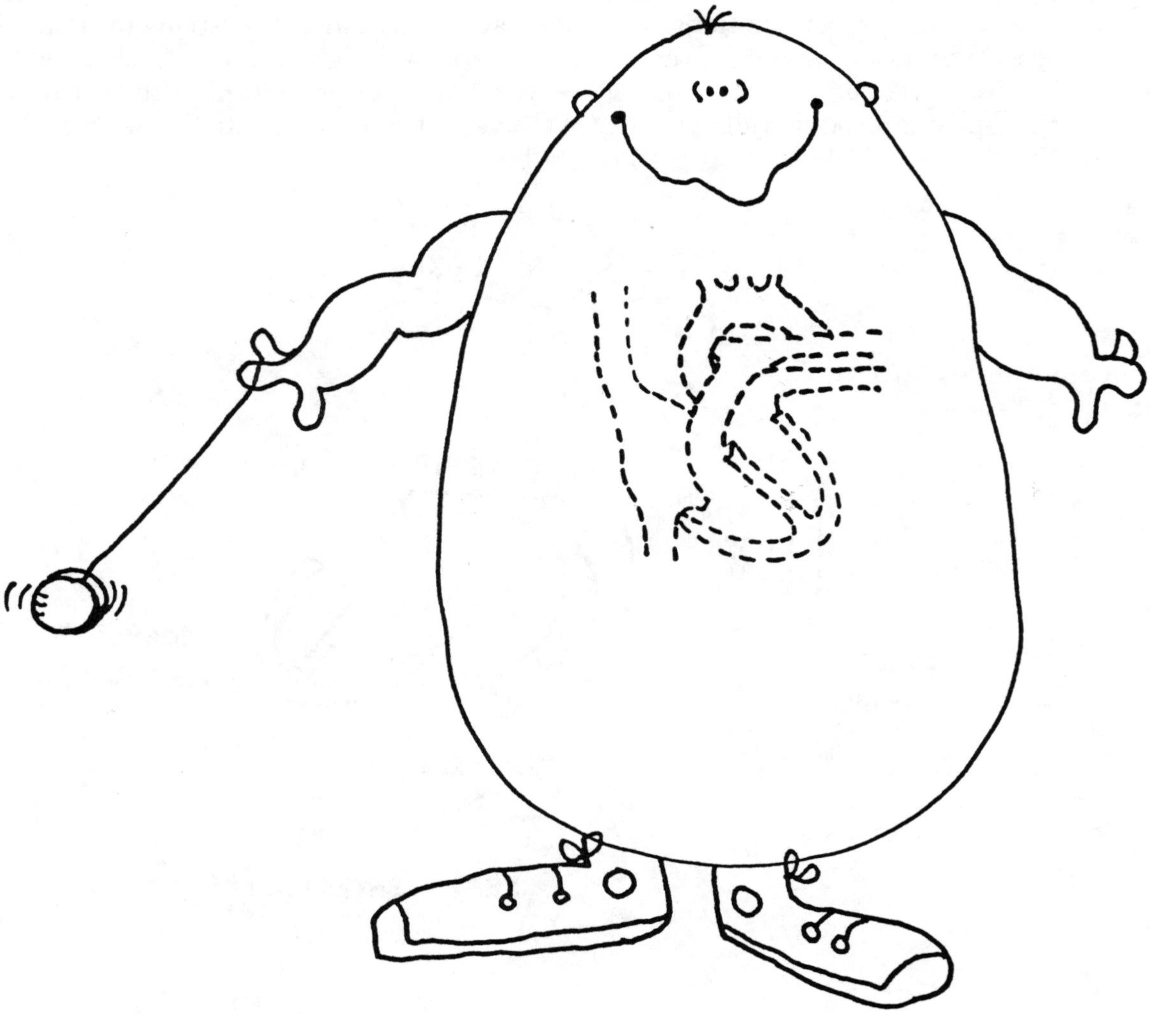

Cyrus's Circulatory System

DIRECTIONS: Color in the parts of the heart below as indicated. Cut out the parts, and glue them to Cyrus in the proper positions. Then label all parts clearly. Use string to signify blood vessels coming to and from the heart—red string to signify oxygen-rich blood traveling from the heart to the body by way of the arteries; and blue thread to signify oxygen-poor blood traveling by way of the veins from the body to the heart and lungs. NOTE: Oxygen-poor blood isn't *really* blue!

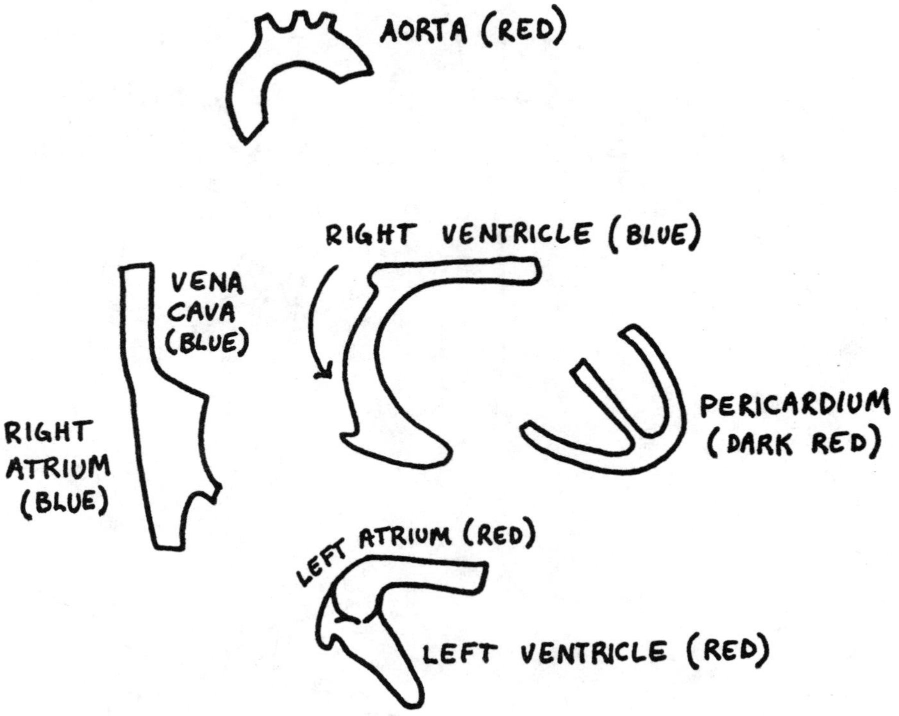

Activity 14. Heartbeat (A Game That Teaches Circulation)

Concept/Description: Blood circulation serves to send oxygenated blood throughout the body.

Objective: Students will understand how the blood circulates by simulating the flow of the blood.

Materials:

10 chairs
10–15 discs approximately the size of a 45 r.p.m. record. Color the top of the disc blue and the flip side red.
Drum (optional)
4 signs: Right Ventricle, Right Atrium, Left Ventricle, Left Atrium.

Directions:

1. Set up the chairs and signs as shown in Figure 9-5.
2. Have 10 volunteers sit in the chairs.
3. Give 10–12 other volunteers the discs (blue side *up*), and inform them that they are blood cells depleted of oxygen. They must replenish their oxygen (O_2) and get rid of the carbon dioxide (CO_2) by visiting the heart and then the lungs.
4. As the teacher beats the drum (heartbeat), students "flow" from the body to the *right atrium* (a few at a time), on to the *right ventricle*, and on to the lungs to pick up oxygen. When they reach the "lungs," the two "lungs" (students) turn their discs so that the red side is *up*, signifying the exchange of carbon dioxide and oxygen that takes place in the alveoli of the lungs. The oxygen-rich blood then must go back to the heart to be pumped out to the body. The students now enter the *left atrium*, then the *left ventricle*, and then go back out to the body. The disc is eventually flipped back to the blue side since oxygen is used up, and the process starts again.
5. To show the action of the valves, have the students in the corner chairs hold hands (valves closed) and drop hands (valves open).

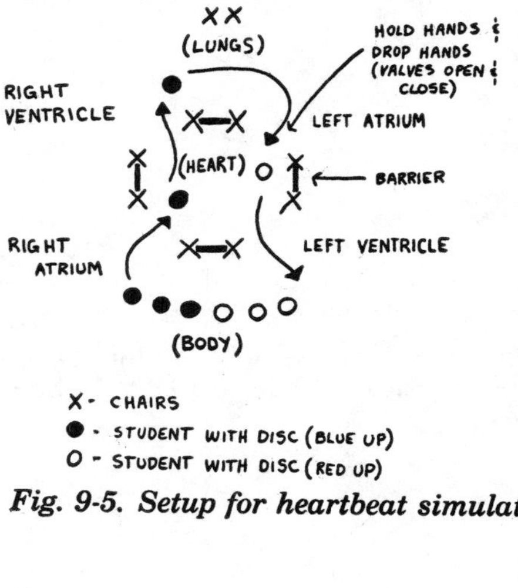

Fig. 9-5. Setup for heartbeat simulation.

Activity 15. Fill Me In (Heart Diagram)

Concept/Description: The heart is two separate pumps. The right-side pump takes in oxygen-poor blood and sends it to the lungs for oxygen while the left-side pump takes the oxygen rich blood from the lungs and sends it to the body.

Objective: To show how blood flows through the heart, lungs, and rest of the body.

Materials:

Heart Diagram Worksheet dittos (See 9-10)
Red and blue crayons or markers

Directions:

1. As you explain the circulation of the blood, have students color in the heart diagram using blue for oxygen-poor blood and red for oxygen-rich blood.
2. Start by coloring the inferior and superior vena cava blue. Next, color in the right atrium and right ventricle blue. Continue by coloring the pulmonary arteries (to the lungs) blue.
3. As the carbon dioxide and oxygen are exchanged in the lungs, the blood returns to the heart by way of the pulmonary veins (from the lungs). Color them red. Next, color the left atrium and ventricle red. Finish by coloring the aorta red. Now oxygen-rich blood is sent back out to the body's cells.

Activity 16. Collage Prep (Making a Collage)

Concept/Description: Life styles affect the health of a person's heart.

Objective: Students will recognize life styles that contribute to healthy and unhealthy hearts.

Materials:

Magazines
Construction Paper
Scissors
Paste or glue

Directions:

1. Have groups or individuals cut out pictures of people who look as if they have healthy hearts (people exercising, eating right, etc.).
2. Have others cut out pictures of those likely to have unhealthy hearts (people smoking, overweight, etc.).

(Continued on p. 202)

Name ______________________________ Date ______________ (9-10)

Heart Diagram

DIRECTIONS: Label the parts of the heart and color them. Use blue for oxygen-poor blood and red for oxygen-rich blood.

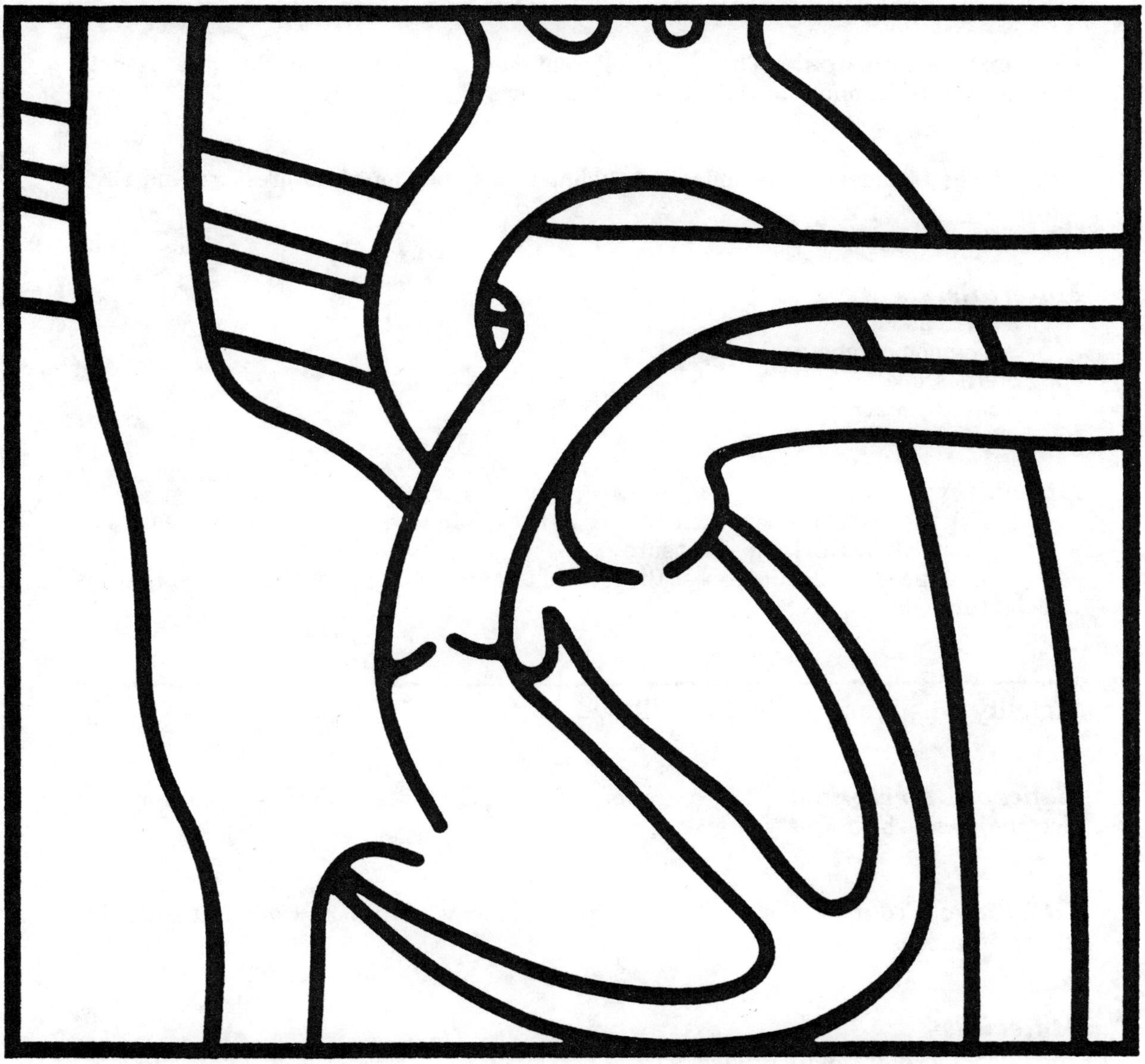

3. Make individual collages or huge classroom collages.
4. Follow up by discussing which healthy habits lead to healthy hearts.

Activity 17. What's Up, Doc? (Medical Instruments)

Concept/Description: There are different pieces of equipment that are used to measure the functioning of the circulatory system.

Objective: Students will understand what terms such as blood pressure and EKG mean.

Materials:

EKG readouts
Syphgmomanometer (blood pressure)
Stethoscope
Guest Speaker Follow-Up Worksheets (See 9-1)

Directions:

1. Ask the school nurse or local physician to explain what blood pressure means and what EKG, EEG, etc., measure.
2. Use the worksheet to assess the level of understanding after the guest speaker is through.

Activity 18. You're My Type (Blood Types)

Concept/Description: There are four basic blood types, and it is important that doctors know which type you are.

Objective: To show that some blood types can mix while others would cause blood to clump if mixed.

Materials:

Blood Typing Chart (Figure 9-6)

Directions:

1. Explain that there are four blood types (O, A, B, AB), and ask students if they know their types.
2. Explain what a blood transfusion is and why it might be necessary.

Name ______________________ Date ______________ (9-11)

Guest Speaker Follow-Up Worksheet

DIRECTIONS: List five facts you have learned from your guest speaker.

1. ____

____

2. ____

____

3. ____

____

4. ____

____

5. ____

____

WRITE A PARAGRAPH about thoughts or feelings you have as a result of what you learned from your guest speaker. Use statements such as "I thought," "I feel," "I believe," and so on.

____

____

____

____

____

____

____

____

____

____

____

3. Have students refer to the blood typing chart (Figure 9-6). Explain to them that certain blood types are compatible while others agglutinate (clump) when mixed and can cause death.
4. Ask the students if they can determine which type of blood is the universal donor. (O) Which is the universal recipient? (AB) What happens if a person with type AB blood donates blood to a person with type B, etc.?

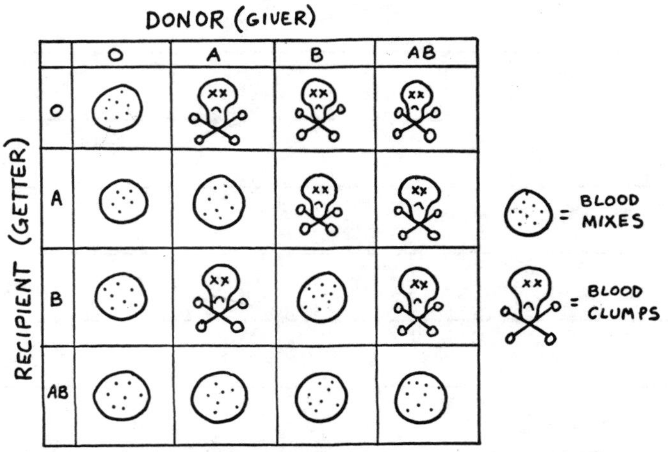

Fig. 9-6. Blood-type chart.

Activity 19. I Don't Believe It! (Early Beliefs)

Concept/Description: Our beliefs about the circulatory system change as scientific information becomes available.

Objective: Students will understand how people's views of the circulatory (and other) systems change over time.

Materials:

Encyclopedia
Books on early medical beliefs, such as Life Science Library's *The Body*, by Time-Life Books (1980).

Directions:

1. Prior to the lesson, ask the school librarian to suggest books that might delve into the early beliefs about the human body.
2. Have groups of students research the beliefs, especially those dealing with the circulatory system.
3. Topics could include blood letting, the four humors (blood, phlegm, black bile, and yellow bile), leeches, trephination, pulse taking, cauterization, etc., or research

scientists, such as Malpighi (1657), Harvey (17th Century), or German Forssman (1929).

4. Have them report back to the class on their findings.

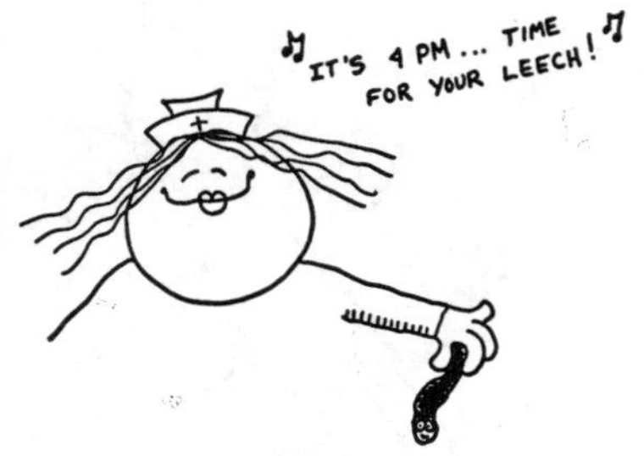

Activity 20. You've Got a Lotta Heart (Heart Dissection)

Concept/Description: Heart models and diagrams can accurately represent a real heart.

Objective: Students will realize that models and diagrams are the equivalents of actual hearts.

Materials:

Various dissection tools (for teacher use)
Steer heart
Human heart model or diagram (from local hospital, high school, etc.)

Directions:

1. Obtain a steer or calf heart form a local meat-packing house, slaughter house, or a butcher.
2. If possible, obtain a human heart model, diagram, or poster.
3. Compare the similarities and differences between the two hearts. Show the chambers, valves and, if possible, the tissue under a microscope.

THE NERVOUS SYSTEM

Activity 21. Norman Nervous (Cut and Paste)

Concept/Description: The nervous system is composed of different parts.

(Continued on p. 208)

Name ________________________________ Date ________________ (9-12)

Norman Nervous

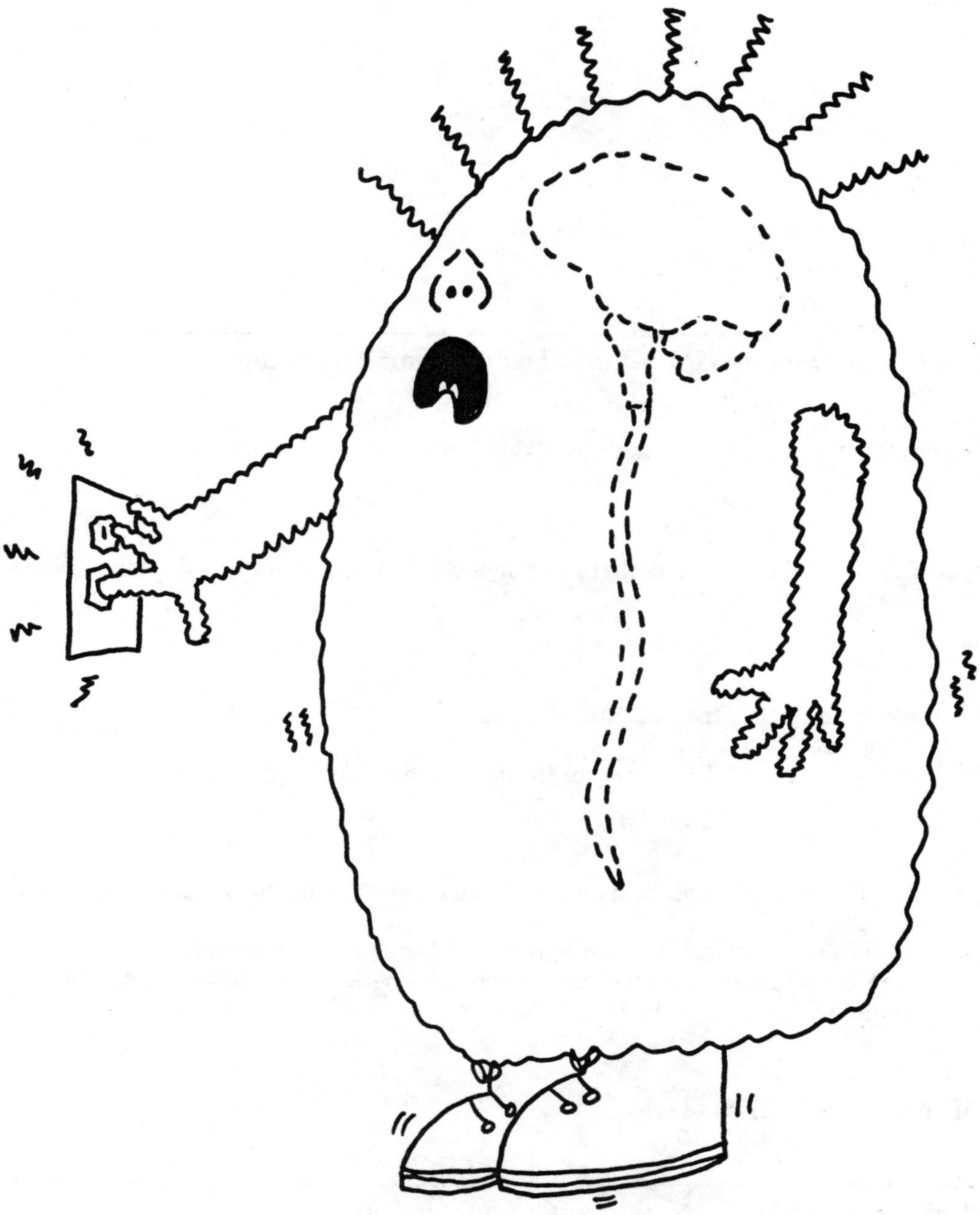

Norman's Nervous System

DIRECTIONS: Color, cut, and paste these parts where they belong on Norman.

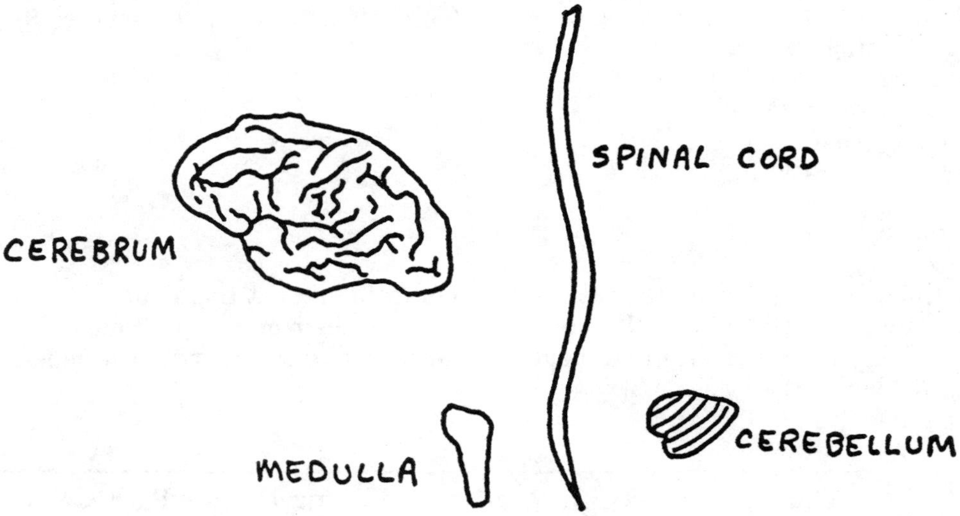

Norman's Nervous System

DIRECTIONS: Color, cut, and paste these parts where they belong on Norman.

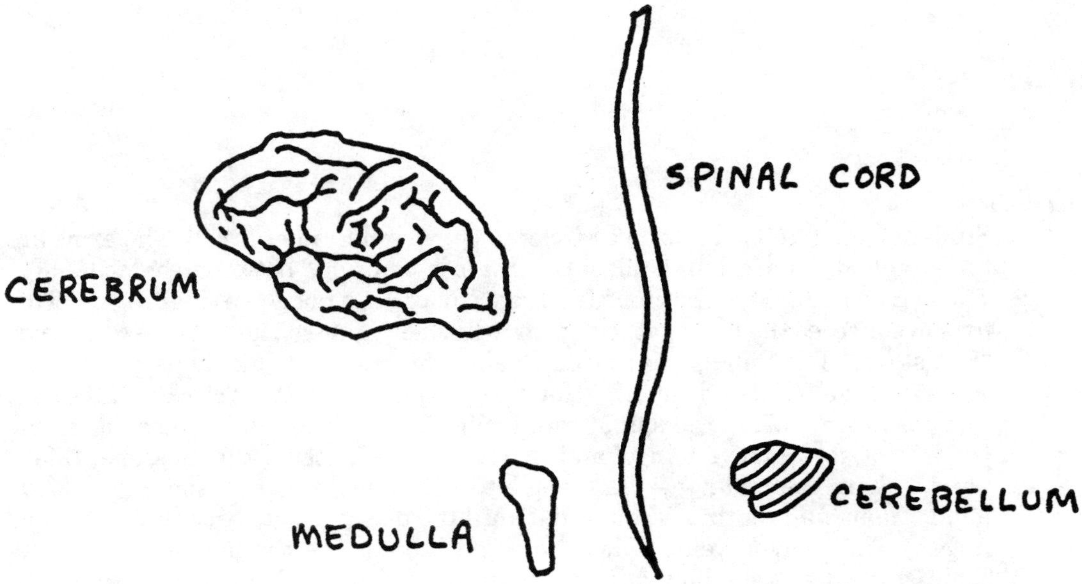

Objective: Students will be able to make a paste-up of the nervous system.

Materials:

Norman Nervous Worksheets (See 9-12)
Norman's Nervous System (parts) dittos (one-half sheet per student) (See 9-13)
Construction paper
Scissors
Crayons or markers
Glue or paste

Directions:

Have students—

1. Color in the parts on the nervous system ditto and cut them out.
2. Glue the parts onto a "Norman" worksheet in their proper position.
3. Label all parts clearly and mount the worksheet onto construction paper.
4. Display in the classroom.

Activity 22. You Take the High Road . . . (Sensory/Motor Pathways)

Concept/Description: Impulses are sent through the nervous system to and from the spinal cord and brain by way of the sensory and motor nerves at high speeds.

Objective: Students will physically experience, in slow motion, the way in which the nervous system functions.

Materials:

(None required)

Directions:

1. Students join hands and form a circle. Each person is a nerve cell. The arms are the ganglion. Joined hands form the *synapse* or bridge between the cells.
2. The person at 12:00 in the circle is a finger touching a hot stove (Figure 9-7). This person squeezes the hand of the person to his/her right (sensory nerves) and says, "Hot stove." The impulse is passed around the circle as quickly as possible by squeezing the hand and saying, "Hot stove." The person at 6 o'clock is the spinal cord (or brain). When the spinal cord (or brain) receives the impulse, he or she yells, "Hot stove, move hand," and then continues passing the message, "Move hand," along the motor nerves (people to the right). Each person says, "Move hand," aloud and continues squeezing until the message gets back to the "burned finger." That person yells, "Ouch," to signal the end of the message.
3. Time students to see how quickly this can be done. Inform them that in the nervous system, impulses and messages travel at extremely high speeds of up to

approximately 120 meters per second—that is, the length of a football field in one second.

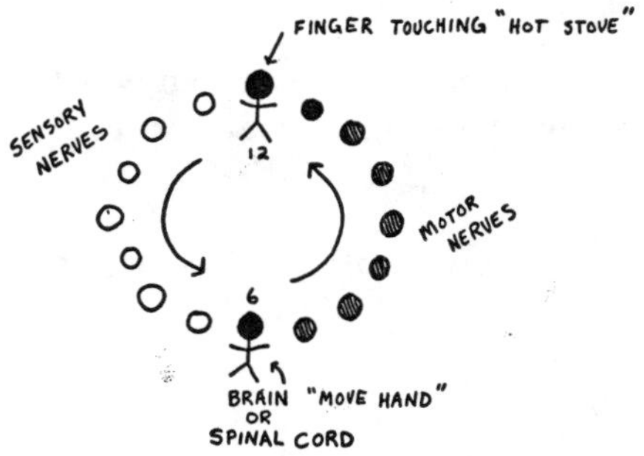

Fig. 9-7. Sensory/motor pathways circle.

Activity 23. Flex and Reflex (Testing Your Knee-Jerk Reflex)

Concept/Description: Reflexes are involuntary reactions in which the information gets processed by the spinal cord and bypasses the brain. Voluntary actions are processed by the brain.

Objective: To explain and demonstrate the knee-jerk reflex (involuntary) and compare it to a voluntary action.

Materials:

A sturdy table or desk for every two people

Directions:

1. Divide the class into pairs. Have one person sit on the desk or table and dangle his or her legs over the edge.
2. The other partner, using his/her open hand, taps just below the sitting partner's knee. (You may have to try a few times to get the proper spot.)
3. Explain how this impulse is processed by the spinal cord and does not need to go to the brain. (It is involuntary.)
4. Give other examples of reflex actions, such as pulling away from a hot object, blinking, gagging, etc.
5. Ask students to perform a simple task, such as raising their hands, writing their names, etc. Explain that this is a voluntary action. The ear sends the information to the brain, and the brain signals the muscles and nerves to complete the task.

Activity 24. I Still See You! (After Images)

Concept/Description: An after image is produced when the cones in the retina tire of a color—from a person staring at it—and produce a complementary color.

Objective: To have students discover what occurs when the cones tire of a certain color.

Materials:

8 × 10 construction paper
Scissors
Glue
Wall clock with a second hand

Directions:

1. Decide which color combinations you will use, and cut a design (star, triangle, square, circle, etc.) in one color (Figure 9-8).
2. Glue the design on a page of 8 × 10 construction paper. Place a black dot in the center of the design.
   NOTE: The following color combinations produce the best results: black/white, red/green, yellow/blue.

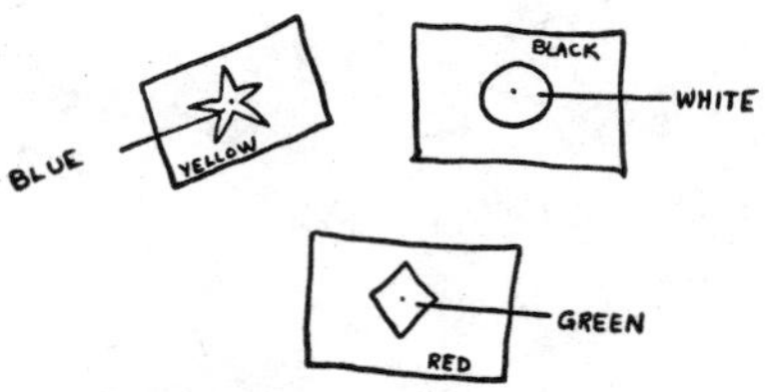

Fig. 9-8. After-image sheets.

3. Make one after-image design per student, if possible.
4. Have students stare (without blinking) at the black dot for approximately 40–60 seconds. When time is up, ask them to stare at a wall (white) or white sheet of paper.
5. Ask what they see. (It will take a few seconds before the after-image appears.)
   NOTE: Students should see the opposite of what they first stared at. For example, if looking at a red circle on a green sheet, they should then see a green circle on a red sheet since green and red are complementary colors.

Variations:

1. Have students cut and paste their own designs in the colors they choose.
2. To add to the lesson, bring in optical illusions, photos of common objects magnified (available in many game magazines), and have a sense-of-sight "lab."

Activity 25. Name That Sound (Sound Effects)

Concept/Description: Humans store information that they can use at a later time.

Objective: Students will understand that sensory messages are interpreted by the brain.

Materials:

Tape recorder
Tape of sounds or sound-effects record
Record player
Paper
Pencils or pens

Directions:

1. Record or have students record 10–15 sounds, such as traffic going by, basketballs being dribbled in the gym, dishes being washed, etc.
   NOTE: If you allow students to do their own sounds, be prepared for the inevitable "toilet being flushed," which so many of them find enjoyable!
2. Play the sounds, and have students write down their guesses. Later, give the answers.
3. Explain how sounds are brought in by the ear and processed in the brain. Their guesses are possible because their brains have stored information that helps them recall the sounds or similar ones.

Activity 26. I Hear Ya Loud 'n Clear (Constructing an Ear—Sense of Hearing)

Concept/Description: In the ear there are many parts which function together to make hearing possible.

Objective: Students will know the parts of the ear and understand how hearing is produced.

Materials:

Ear Construction Function Cards (See 9-14)
Various household objects that could depict ear parts. For example—

1. Funnel = outer ear
2. Paper towel tube = ear canal
3. Drum = ear drum

4. Hammer = hammer
5. Block of wood = anvil
6. Rubber horseshoe = stirrup
7. Snail shell = cochlea—(perhaps this isn't your basic household object—a drawing could suffice)
8. Three circular objects (large rings, hula hoops, etc.) = semi-circular canals
9. String = auditory nerve

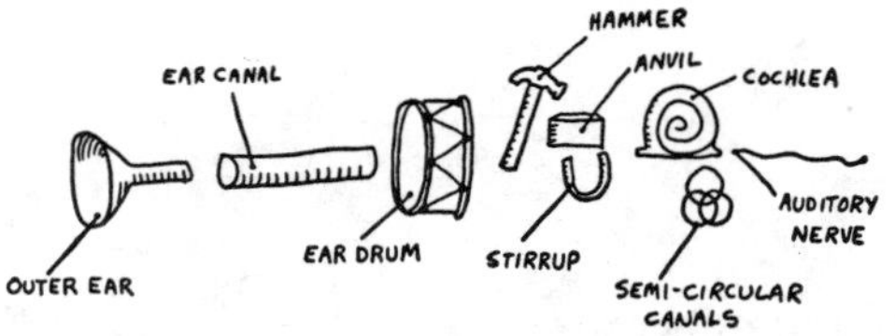

Directions:

1. Use the above items to construct an "ear," or devise your own parts.
2. Give different students the pieces of equipment described, and have them stand next to each other in front of the room in the order the items (1–9) are listed above.
3. Give other class members the function cards numbered 1–9.
4. Ask the person holding Card #1 to read the card while Person #1 steps forward.
5. Continue reading cards until they have all been read.
6. When finished, discuss how sound travels through the ear to the brain for processing.

Activity 27. Dot's Incredible Braille (Aids for the Blind)

Concept/Description: Blind people are able to read through the Braille system.

Objective: Students will experience aids that assist the blind to function without the sense of sight.

Materials:

Braille alphabet (available from local Association for the Blind)

Directions:

1. Explain various causes of blindness (birth defect, injury from accident, disease, etc.) and explain how some people rely on Braille to read.
2. Have the students feel the Braille lettering and discuss how important the sense of touch is to someone who must read Braille.

Variation:

1. Various magazines such as *Reader's Digest* are available in Braille. Have students try to decipher a paragraph or so.

Ear Construction Function Cards

1. OUTER EAR I collect sound waves and funnel them into the ear canal. I am the outer ear.	2. EAR CANAL I am a canal that goes to the ear drum. I am coated with wax for protection. I am the ear canal.	3. EAR DRUM Sound waves strike me, causing me to vibrate. I set up movements in the three bones of the ear. I am the ear drum.
4. HAMMER I am a bone shaped like a hammer. I am the beginning of the middle ear. I am the hammer.	5. ANVIL I am an anvil-shaped bone between two other tiny bones. I relay the vibrations from the hammer to the stirrup. I am the anvil.	6. STIRRUP I am the smallest bone in your body and the last to receive the vibrations. I send them on into the inner ear. I am the stirrup.
7. COCHLEA I am the beginning of your inner ear. I am filled with fluid and receive the sound waves. I am a snail-shaped structure. I am the cochlea.	8. SEMI-CIRCULAR CANALS I am three circular canals that help you to maintain balance and equilibrium. I am the semi-circular canals.	9. AUDITORY NERVE I connect the inner ear to the brain and send the impulses to the brain. I am the auditory nerve.

2. Discuss or have a guest speaker from the local Association for the Blind show various other items used to help the blind, such as beeper softballs, etc.
3. Take the students to a walking trail that has been designed for the blind.

Related Activity: Invite a speaker from the Association for the Deaf to talk about hearing impairment, deafness, sign language, noise pollution, etc.

Activity 28. A Tasty Map (Mapping the Basic Tastes)

Concept/Description: Different regions of the tongue have receptors for the four basic tastes of salty, sweet, sour, and bitter.

Objective: This experiment will prove to the students that receptors for the different tastes are located on different parts of the tongue.

Materials:

4 Cotton swabs *per person*
4 Small cups (bathroom size) per group
Lemon juice (sour)
Strong, cold coffee (bitter)
Sugar water (sweet)
Salt water (salty)
1 Tongue Map Worksheet per person (See 9-15)
Pens or pencils
Answer Key (See p. 216)

Directions:

1. Divide the class into small groups (4–5), and give each person 4 swabs and a map.
2. Give each group four cups. Put a small amount of lemon juice in one, coffee in another, sugar water in another, and salt water in the last.
3. Have all students dab the swab in the sweet solution and touch it to the various areas of their tongues as shown on the map. First, have them touch the tip of their tongues. Then, without closing their mouths (this would spread the solution over all areas of the tongue), have them indicate if they can taste "sweet." If so, have them indicate it on the tongue map by placing an "S" (sweet) in the proper space.
4. Then, have them touch the sides and the back of their tongues with the same swab. (Do not allow the students to put the same swab back into the solution once it has been in their mouths.) Have them indicate if the sweet taste is present in those areas.
5. Discard the swabs.
6. Next, have them pick up new swabs and continue testing for salty (X), sour (R), and bitter (B).
7. Discuss how closing their mouths will spread a taste over their tongues. Compare the results within the class.

Name ______________________________ Date ________________ (9-15)

Tongue Map

DIRECTIONS: Dip a *clean* swab into one of the small cups, and touch it to the different areas of the tongue indicated on the map below. AVOID closing your mouth because that spreads the solution over all the areas. Discard the swab, and repeat the process with a clean swab and a new cup. Label the tongue map with the following letters:

B = BITTER
R = SOUR
X = SALTY
S = SWEET

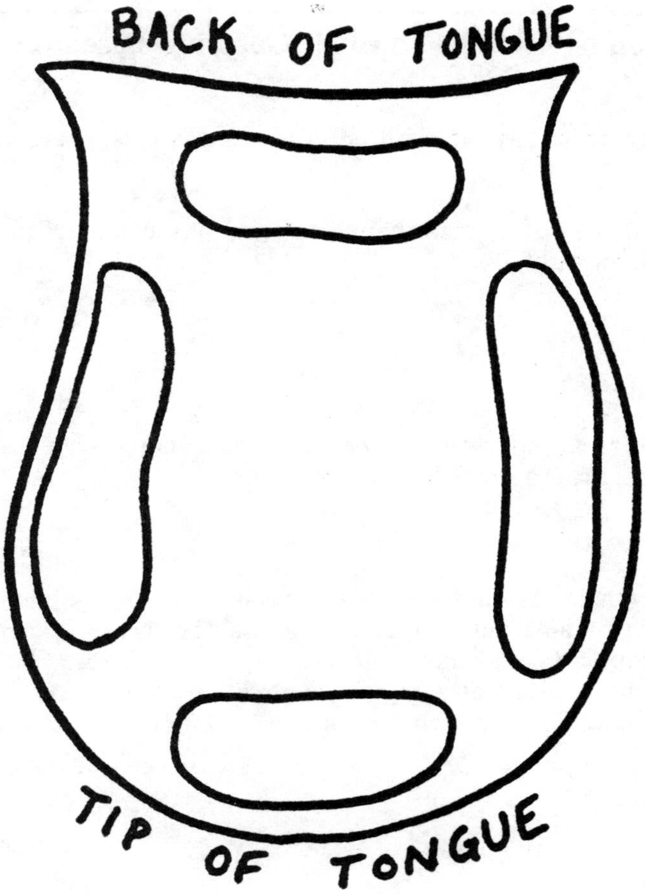

Answer Key:

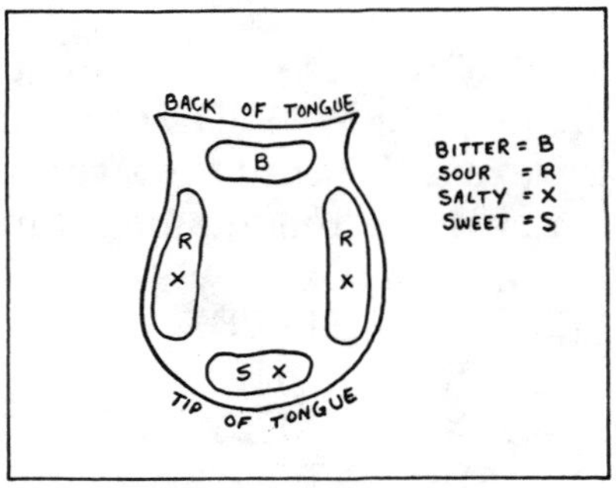

Activity 29. You're Awfully Touchy! (Guessing Based on Touch)

Concept/Description: We depend on other senses to support our sense of touch.

Objective: Students will realize that their sense of touch is frequently supported by other senses, such as sight.

Materials:

6 Tin cans w/covers
Blindfolds
Various familiar objects with different textures (sandpaper, metal keys, satin material, Leggos, grapes, marbles, gummy worms, etc.)

Directions:

1. Place the objects in the tin cans and cover them until students are blindfolded.
2. Blindfold a student and have him/her guess what is in each tin can using *only* the sense of touch. Record these guesses.
3. Discuss why it is easier to use a combination of senses.
4. Have students decide which senses they rely on the most. Why is this the case?

Activity 30. The Nose Knows (Olfactory Adaptation)

Concept/Description: The receptors in the nose will tire of the same odor and will no longer be able to detect that odor. They can, however, pick up a new scent.

Objective: Students will experience the occurrence of olfactory adaptation.

Materials:

Peppermint extract (available in supermarkets)
Strawberry extract (available in craft stores)
Wall clock with a second hand
Paper and pen or pencil
Cups (1 per group)

Directions:

1. Place a *very few* drops of peppermint extract in small cups (one per group). Also place a few drops of strawberry extract in another cup (one per group).
2. Have one student hold one nostril shut while smelling the peppermint from the cup. Time how long it takes before that person can no longer smell the peppermint.
3. Jot down the time (how long it took for olfactory adaptation to occur).
4. Have the student raise the cup with the strawberry scent to his or her nose. Can the student detect the scent?
5. Compare time differences among the group and the class.
6. Repeat the process with the other nostril. Is there a difference?

Activity 31. A Potato a Day Keeps the Doctor Away? (Smell and Taste)

Concept/Description: Taste is dependent on the sense of smell.

Objective: Students will find that they need to use their sense of smell, as well as sense of taste.

Materials:

Small, cut-up pieces of potato (in water)
Small, cut-up pieces of apple (placed in water with lemon juice)
Blindfolds

Directions:

1. Have students select partners.
2. Have one partner blindfolded and have him/her pinch his/her nose shut tightly.
3. Have the other partner feed the first either a piece of potato or apple and ask the blindfolded partner to tell which it is.
4. They will be unable to tell since taste is dependent on smell. They may try to guess using sense of touch (tongue sensation).
5. Have partners switch jobs.
6. Discuss the difficulties each partner had.

Variations:

Try the same task using different textured foods, such as peanut butter, spongecake, etc., and discuss how they were forced to try to use their sense of touch (feel of food against their tongues).

THE SKELETAL SYSTEM

Activity 32. Skeeter Skeletal (Cut and Paste)

Concept/Description: The skeletal system contains many different bones.

Objective: Students will learn to recognize different bones.

Materials:

Skeeter Skeletal Worksheet dittos (See 9-16)
Skeeter's Skeletal System dittos (See 9-17)
Construction paper
Scissors
Crayons or markers
Glue or paste

Directions:

Have students—

1. Color in the bones (any color).
2. Paste the bones, in the proper position, onto the worksheet.
3. Label all bones neatly.
4. Mount on construction paper.
5. Display.

Name ______________________________ Date ________________ (9-16)

Skeeter Skeletal

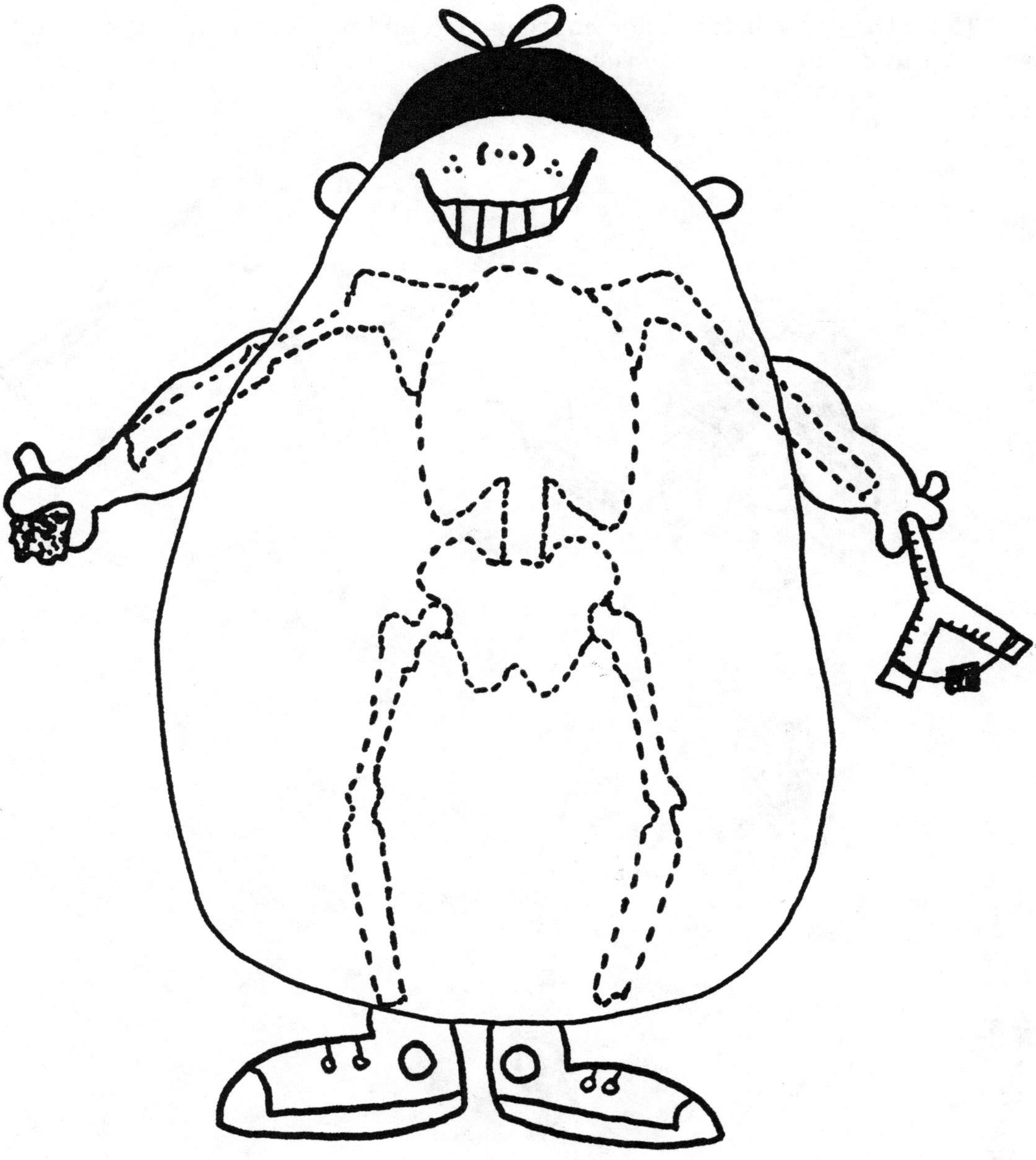

Skeeter's Skeletal System

DIRECTIONS: Color the bones below. Then cut them out, and paste them into the correct locations on the Skeeter Skeletal Worksheet.

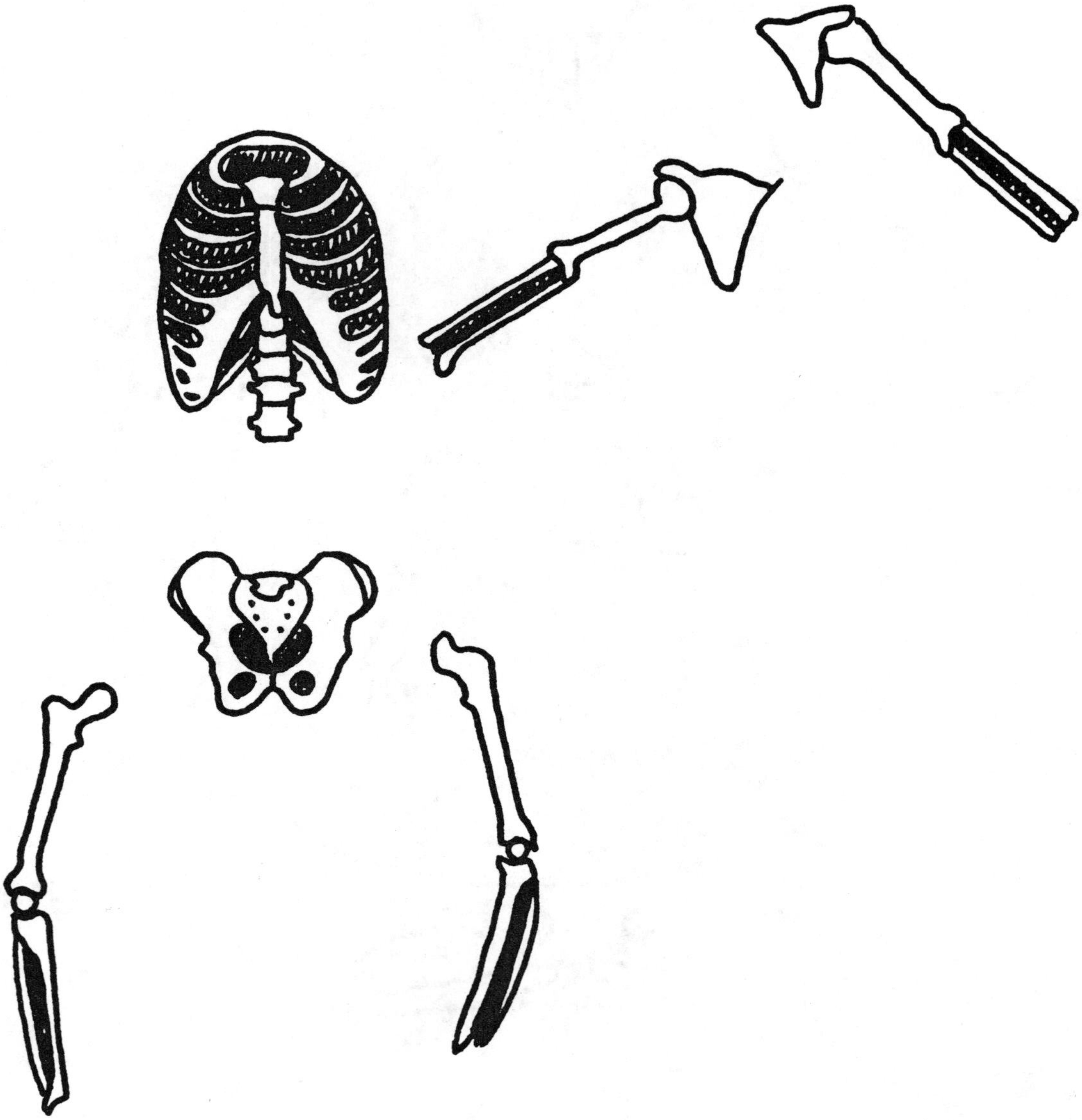

Activity 33. X-Ray Eyes (Viewing X-Rays)

Concept/Description: Bones differ for a variety of reasons.

Objective: Students will recognize differences in bones through the use of X-rays.

Materials:

X-rays of children, adults, elderly persons, or of broken bones (obtained from doctors, hospitals, or students themselves)
Overhead projector

Directions:

1. Place the X-ray on the overhead projector, and observe the bones, looking for differences, breaks, etc.
   NOTE: Do not leave the X-rays on too long, for they will begin to fade.

Variation:

See if you can obtain ultra-sound photos, "cat" scans, EKG readouts, and EEG readouts, and show them to the class. Although most of these cannot be shown on an overhead projector, perhaps you have access to an opaque projector, or you could pass the readouts around the class.

Activity 34. Cut It Out! (Constructing a Skeleton)

Concept/Description: Labeling the different bones will help students learn the parts of the skeletal system.

Objective: Students will become familiar with the names of various bones.

Materials:

Bones I, II, and III Dittos (See 9-18, 9-19, 9-20)
Scissors
Paper Fasteners
Glue

Directions:

Have students—

1. Cut out the bones.
2. Label each bone.

3. Attach bones to each other in the proper position with glue or with fasteners if you desire movement.
4. Display throughout the classroom. (Halloween is an excellent time.)

Variations:

1. Use different kinds of materials, such as card board or wood.
2. Have groups of students make a skeleton.

Activity 35. Make No Bones About It (Designing T-Shirts)

Concept/Description: A T-Shirt skeleton will serve effectively as a teaching device about the skeletal system.

Objective: Students will each have a T-shirt depicting the skeletal system.

Materials:

T-shirts
Mechanical drawing of desired design (camera-ready art work done with black ink on white paper to the exact size)
Overhead transparency of the upper skeleton
Overhead projector
White butcher paper
Tape

Directions:

Although this activity is a difficult one, it has proven to be one of the most rewarding for both students and teachers. Unless your industrial arts or art department can assist you, it may be necessary to design the shirts, collect money from the students, and send the design out to be printed.

1. Have a back or front view (depending on whether you want to print the front or back of a shirt) of the skeletal system put onto an overhead transparency.
2. Tape large sheets of butcher paper (white, preferably) to the blackboard, wall, or any other *smooth* surface.
3. Line up the projector so that the picture of the skeletal system focuses on the butcher paper. Using pencil, have students trace the bones onto the butcher paper as neatly as possible. When the overhead is turned off, you will have an enlarged drawing of the skeletal system.
   IMPORTANT NOTE: To save money and time, you must be sure the image is the size you want on a T-shirt. Hold up a shirt or have the image projected on a student's back while he or she is standing against the butcher paper, and adjust the distance from projector to the paper until the image fits onto the shirt.

(Continued on p. 226)

Bones I

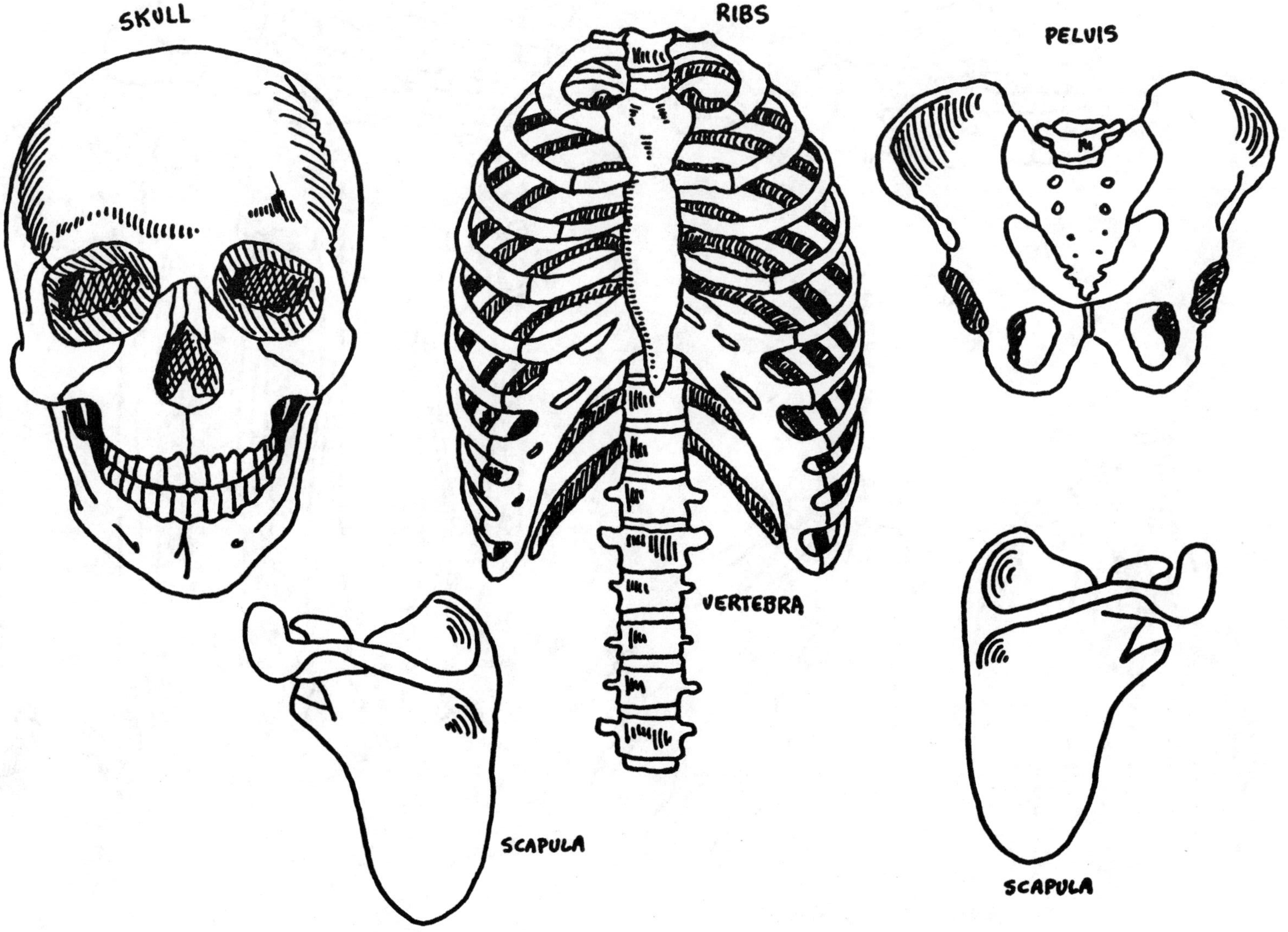

Bones II

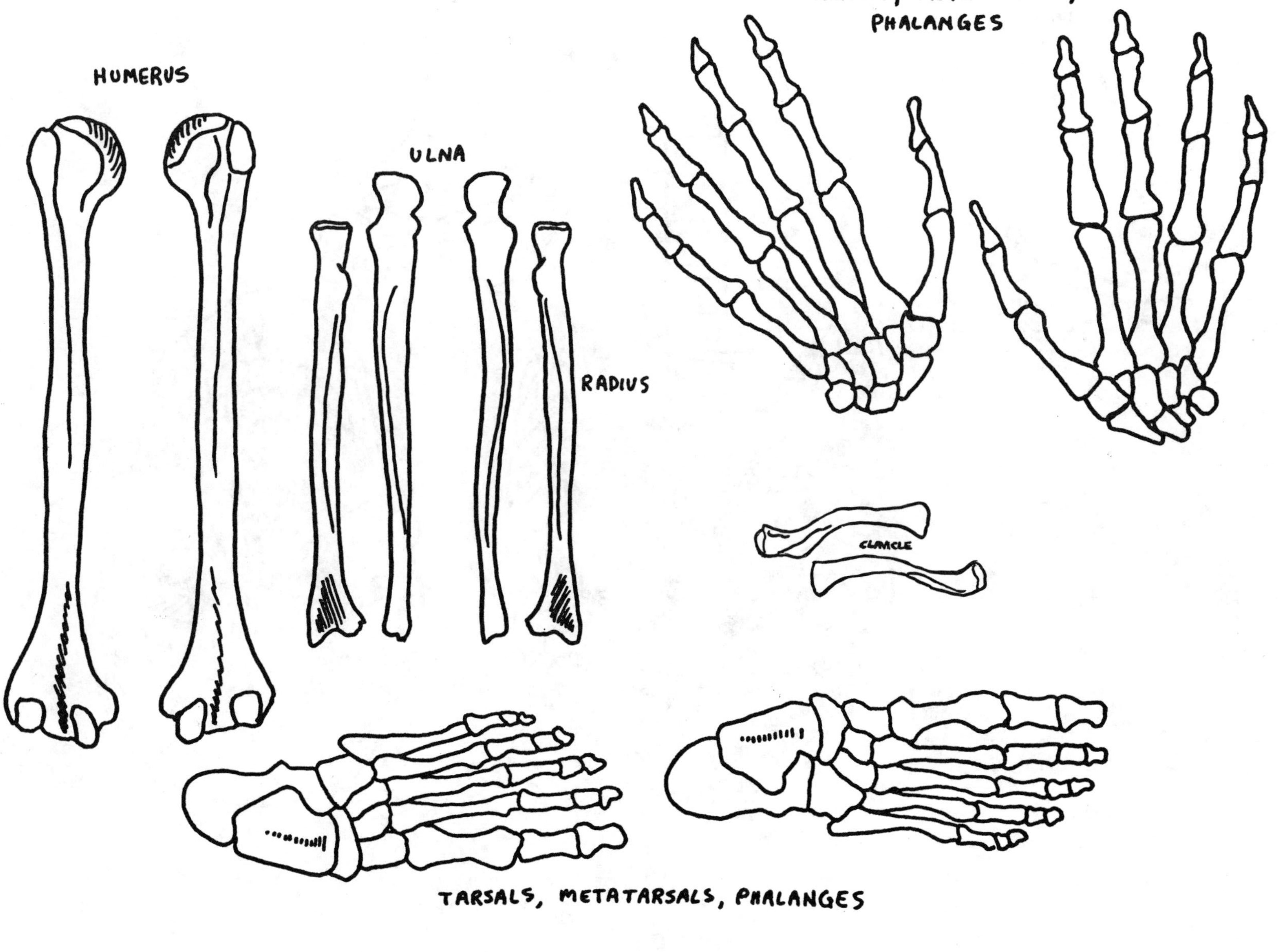

HUMERUS
ULNA
RADIUS
CARPALS, METACARPALS, PHALANGES
CLAVICLE
TARSALS, METATARSALS, PHALANGES

Bones III

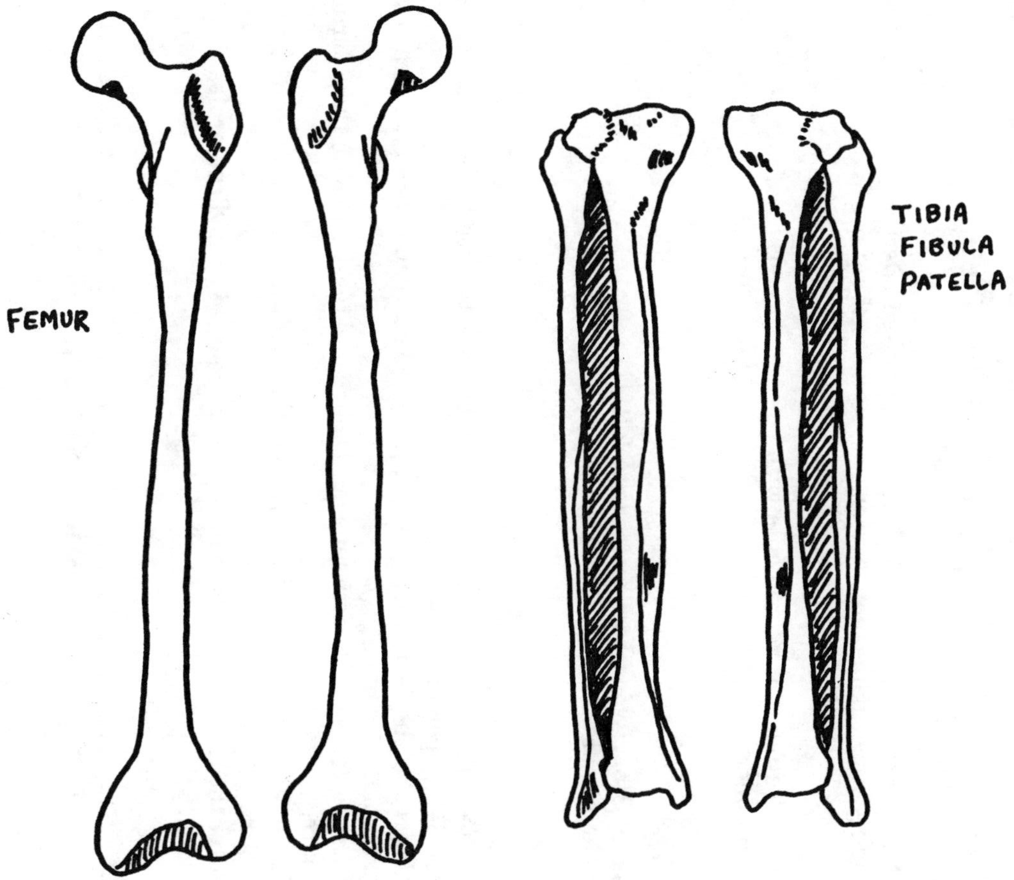

DIRECTIONS:
1. Cut out the bones.
2. Label each bone.
3. Attach bones to each other in the proper position (with glue or with fasteners if you desire movement).

4. Carefully go over the drawing with black India ink (not marker or pen) and erase the pencil marks. It is then ready for a T-shirt printer to reproduce on the T-shirts. (For a better quality job, the printer's artist can refine the rough pencil sketch, but this will be more expensive.)
5. If possible, your industrial arts or art department may assist by silk screening the drawing for you—perhaps each child can bring in his/her own T-shirt. NOTE: This activity can be used successfully for the muscular, digestive, circulatory, and respiratory systems as well. For obvious reasons (and if you value your job), we do not suggest this activity when studying the reproductive system.

Variation:
Label the parts you have drawn if you wish the labeling to show up on the T-shirt.

Activity 36. TELL ME A STORY (A Skeletal Story)

Concept/Description: A story format can be used effectively to assist students in exchanging technical names for laymen's terms describing bones.

Objective: To familiarize students with some of the technical names for bones in a humorous manner.

Materials:
Skeletal Story Worksheet dittos (See 9-21)
Pens or pencils

Directions:
1. Write a story that will involve various bones of the body, such as a story about an accident, sporting event, etc.
2. Underline the words that can be changed to their more technical names (for example, *hips* to *pelvis*).
3. Include names of students in your classes and teachers (with their permission of course).
4. Have students translate by writing the medical names above the underlined words.
5. After the underlined words have been translated to medical terms, read the story aloud.

Activity 37. That's Knot Possible (Knotting a Bone)

Concept/Description: The hardness of bones is due to the minerals (especially calcium) of which bones are composed. Removing the calcium will result in softening of the bones. *(Continued on p. 228)*

Name ________________________________ Date ________________ (9-21)

Skeletal Story Worksheet

One day, I decided to take up skateboarding. "How difficult could it be?" I thought. "It's only a board with four wheels." So I went to the store to buy myself a skateboard.

I scratched my ______________ (head) in amazement. Then putting my ______________ (hands) on my ______________ (hips), I said, "Hey, can someone pick out a skateboard for me?"

The salesperson picked out a beauty. I paid for it and started to leave. Before I was out the door, I banged my ______________ (knee) on a display, tripped, and dropped the board on someone's ______________ (foot). That someone was my "old friend," Mr. Dunn.

"Hey, watch it," he said. Then, realizing who it was, he decided to come skateboarding with me.

We went to the steepest hill we could find, and I said, "Let's do ______ ______________ (hand) stands!" So, down the hill I went. But . . . there was a tree. Not wishing to hit the tree, I rolled onto my ______________ (back) and landed on my ______________ (tail bone). Boy, did that hurt!

Next, it was Mr. Dunn's turn . . .

Objective: Students will understand that bones can become soft and brittle because of disease or age.

Materials:

Clean chicken bones
Container (glass jar) filled with vinegar
Lid for container

Directions:

Clean off the chicken bones, and place them in the vinegar for twelve or more hours. The acid will dissolve the calcium and soften the bones. Softened bones can then be tied into a knot. This activity can lead into a discussion of diseases that result in bone softening or brittleness.

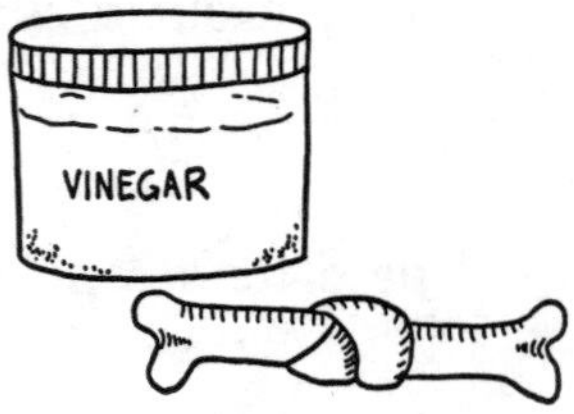

Activity 38. Butcher Best Foot Forward (Examine a Bone)

Concept/Description: It will be easier for students to comprehend the skeletal system if they know what the parts look like.

Objective: Students will visually and physically examine the parts of a bone.

Materials:

Bones obtained from a butcher shop

Directions:

Examine and discuss bone marrow, cartilage, ligaments, periosteum, etc.

THE MUSCULAR SYSTEM

Activity 39. Millie Muscular (Cut and Paste)

Concept/Description: Many different muscles make up the muscular system.

Objective: Students will recognize and know the location of several muscles.

Materials:

Millie Muscular Worksheet dittos (See 9-22)
Millie's Muscles dittos (See 9-23)
Construction paper
Scissors
Crayons or markers
Glue or paste

Directions:

Have students—

1. Color in the muscles and cut them out.
2. Paste the muscles onto the "Millie" worksheet in their proper position.
3. Label all parts neatly.
4. Mount the worksheet on construction paper.
5. Display

Activity 40. Make a Muscle (Showing Muscular Action)

Concept/Description: Muscles work in pairs. One works while the other rests.

Objective: Students will understand how muscles work to flex and extend a bone.

Materials:

3 Cardboard paper-towel tubes per group
2 Long balloons per group
Hole punch
Flexible wire
Strong tape

Directions:

1. Have students construct an arm as follows: place the 3 tubes together as shown in Figure 9-9. The tubes correspond to the three bones in the arm (radius, ulna, humerus).
2. To add the biceps and triceps muscles, blow a small amount of air into the two long balloons, and tie a knot at both ends. Tape the balloons onto the "arm" as shown in Figure 9-10.
3. Demonstrate and discuss how the biceps bends the arm at the elbow (flexion) while the triceps is resting, and then how the triceps extends the arm (extension) while the biceps rests.

Name ____________________ Date ____________ (9-22)

Millie Muscular

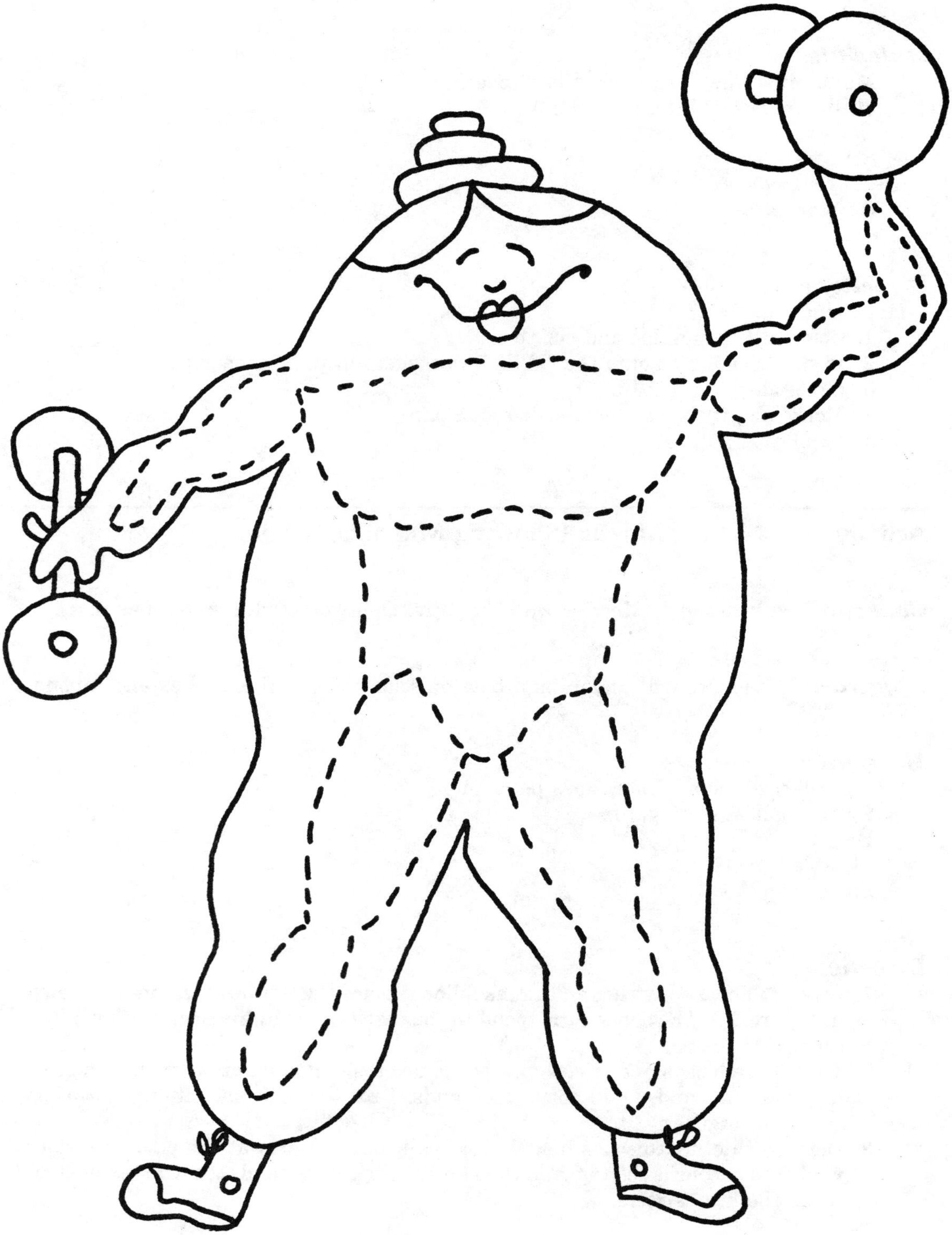

Millie's Muscles

DIRECTIONS: Color in the muscles below, cut them out, and paste them in the appropriate spots on Millie. Label all parts neatly.

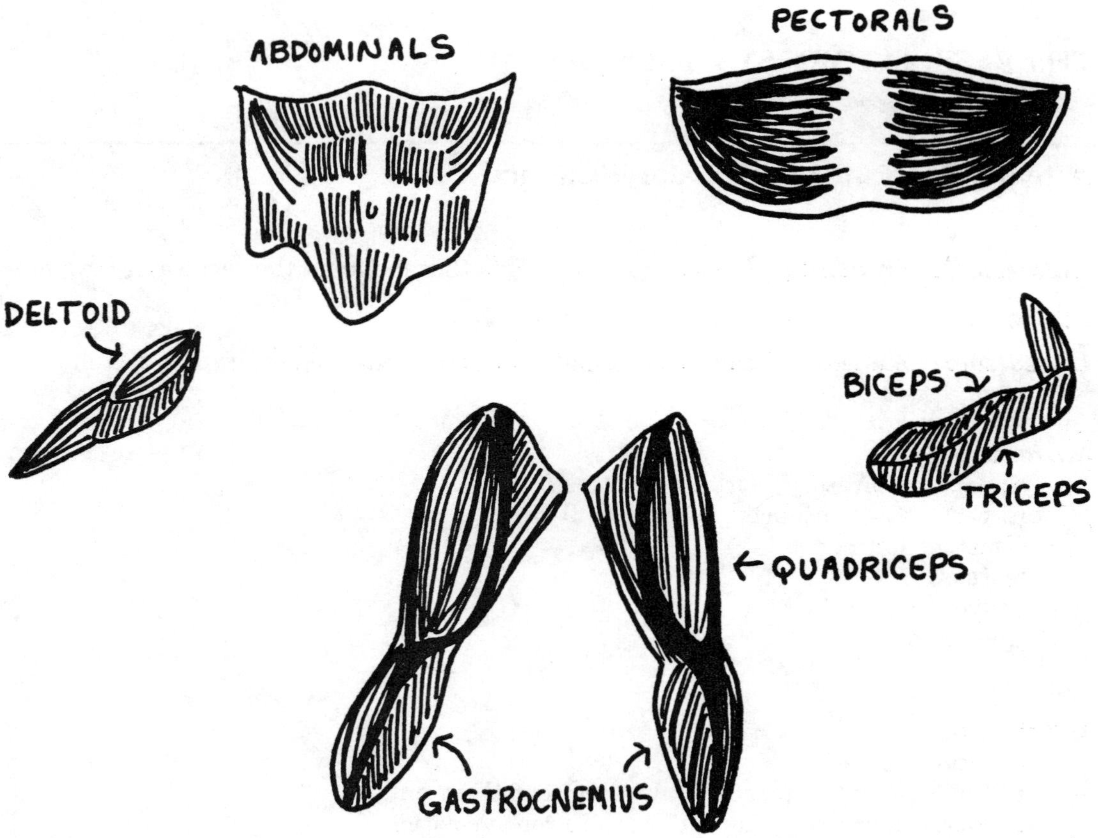

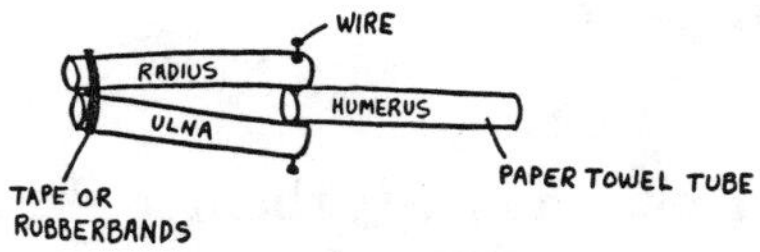

Fig. 9-9. Model of arm bones.

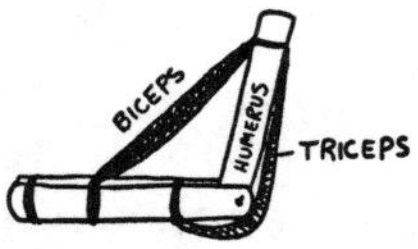

Fig. 9-10. Model of arm with muscles.

THE RESPIRATORY SYSTEM

Activity 41. Rupert Respiratory (Cut and Paste)

Concept/Description: There are many parts that make up the respiratory system.

Objective: Students will be able to make a paste-up of the respiratory system.

Materials:
- Rupert Respiratory Worksheet dittos (See 9-24)
- Rupert's System (parts) dittos (See 9-25)
- Construction paper
- Scissors
- Crayons or markers
- Glue or paste

Directions:
Have students—
1. Color in the respiratory parts and cut them out.
2. Paste them onto "Rupert" in the proper position.
3. Label all parts neatly.
4. Mount on construction paper.
5. Display.

Activity 42. Airing It Out (Making a Model Lung)

Concept/Description: The lungs expand and contract as air is exchanged through the circulatory system.

Objective: The concept of breathing can be demonstrated with simple objects found at home.

Name ______________________ Date ______________ (9-24)

Rupert Respiratory

Rupert's Respiratory System

DIRECTIONS: Color in the respiratory parts below, cut them out, and attach them to Rupert Respiratory in the proper positions. Label each neatly.

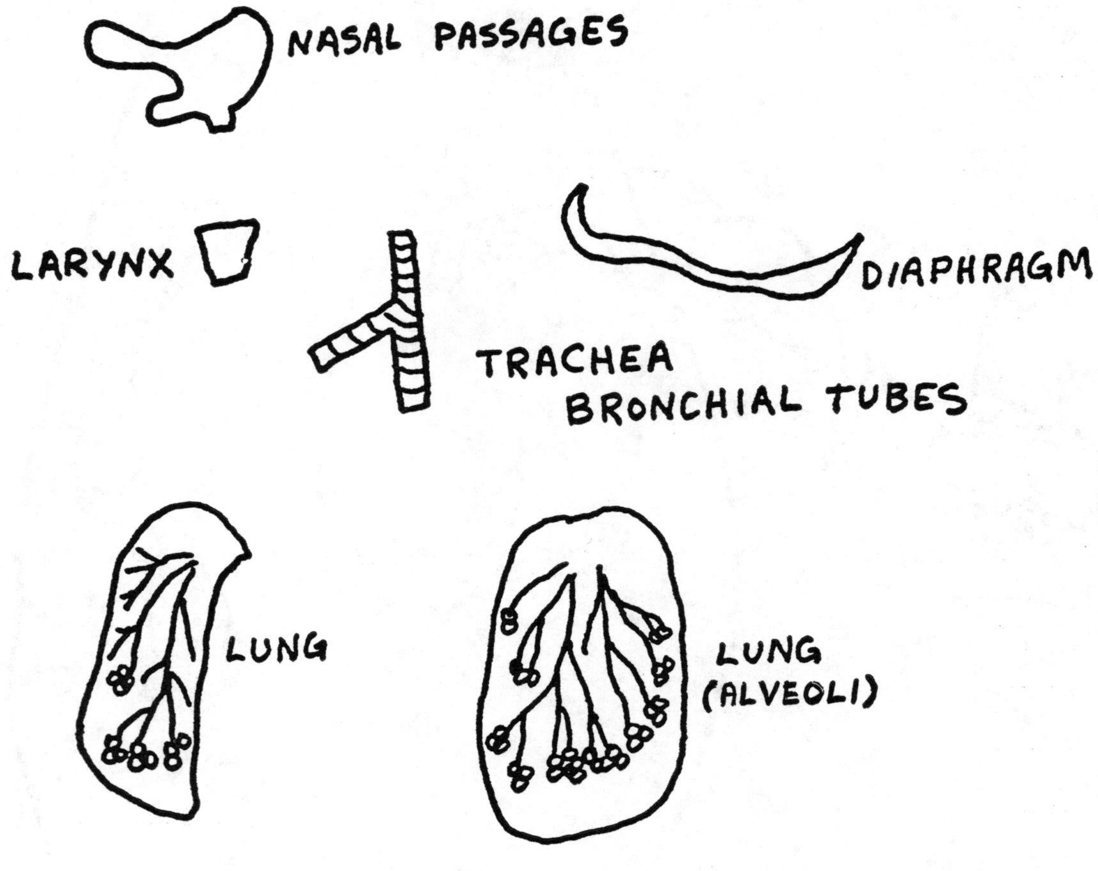

Materials:

- Clear plastic soda bottle with cap
- Clay or playdough
- Plastic straw
- 1 Round balloon cut open into a circle
- 2 rubber bands
- Scissors or a utility knife
- 1 Round balloon intact

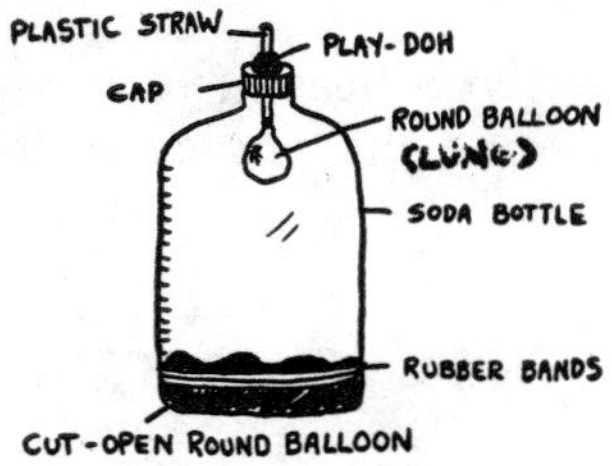

Fig. 9-11. Model lung.

Directions:

You can construct a model lung for use in your classroom by doing the following:

1. Cut the hard plastic bottom off a clear plastic soda bottle, using a utility knife or scissors.
2. Punch a hole in the bottle top, and place the plastic straw through the hole. Make an airtight seal, using the clay or play-dough.
3. Place the "intact" balloon on the straw, and secure it with a rubber band.
4. Stretch the rubber circle (cut-open balloon) *tightly* around the base of the bottle, and secure it with the other rubber band. (This is the diaphragm.)
5. To demonstrate, push up on the "diaphragm" and release. The air will rush in and out through the windpipe, and the "lung" will expand and contract.
6. Explain the relationship of the diaphragm muscle to the act of breathing.

Variation:

Use two balloons for the two lungs if you can obtain a piece of rubber tubing in a "Y" shape.

Activity 43. A Special Bulletin (Board, That Is)

Concept/Description: There are many environmental factors that can cause respiratory problems.

Objective: Students will develop a collage that will depict causes of respiratory problems.

Materials:

- Magazines
- Construction paper
- Scissors
- Paste or glue
- Stapler

Directions:
Make a bulletin board (collage or mobile) showing things that can cause respiratory problems (air pollution, cigarettes, ragweed, etc.).

THE ENDOCRINE SYSTEM

Activity 44. Edith Endocrine (Cut and Paste)

Concept/Description: There are several glands that make up the endocrine system.

Objective: Students will know the different glands that compose the endocrine system and know their approximate location in the human body.

Materials:
Edith Endocrine Worksheet dittos (See 9-26)
Construction paper
Scissors
Crayons or markers
Glue or paste

Directions:
Have students—
1. Color in the various glands and cut them out.
2. Paste them onto "Edith" in the proper position.
NOTE: Remind students that, since "Edith" is a female, she will have ovaries. A male would have testes.
3. Label all parts neatly.
4. Mount on construction paper.
5. Display.

Activity 45. And Now Reporting . . . (Reports on Hypo- and Hyper-Glands)

Concept/Description: There are many physical problems caused by malfunctioning endocrine glands.

Objective: Students will have basic information about several physical problems caused by over or under activity of endocrine glands.

Name ______________________ Date ______________ (9-26)

Edith Endocrine

DIRECTIONS: Color in the glands below, cut them out, and paste them onto Edith in the proper positions. Label all parts neatly.

Materials:

Encyclopedia
Reference books
Anatomy texts

Directions:

1. Assign various groups brief reports on the over activity and under activity of the endocrine glands.
2. Include topics such as dwarfism, Simmond's disease, gigantism, acromegaly, diabetes, insipidus, colloid goiter, Grave's disease, cretinism, myxedema, tetany, Addison's disease, Cushing's syndrome, diabetes mellitus, hypoglycemia, etc.
3. Have student groups give brief descriptions to the class.

Activity 46. What a Match! (Match the Gland to Its Function)

Concept/Description: Each endocrine gland has an important function.

Objective: Students will know the function of seven endocrine glands.

Materials:

Endocrine Match-Up Worksheet dittos (Answers are given below.) (See 9-27)
Pens or pencils

Directions:

Have students or groups try to match the gland to its function.

Answers:

1=F; 2=G; 3=E; 4=B; 5=D; 6=A; 7=C.

THE EXCRETORY SYSTEM

Activity 47. Englebert Excretory (Cut and Paste)

Concept/Description: The excretory system consists of different parts.

Objective: Students will recognize the different parts of the excretory system and know the approximate location of each.
(Continued on p. 240)

Name ______________________ Date ______________

Endocrine Match-Up

DIRECTIONS: Place the correct letter in the blank to match the endocrine gland with its function.

____ 1. Pituitary Gland	A. Produces testosterone for development of the male secondary sex characteristics.
____ 2. Thyroid Gland	B. Produces adrenalin and helps us respond to stress.
____ 3. Parathyroid Gland	C. Produces estrogen and progesterone for development of female secondary sex characteristics.
____ 4. Adrenal Glands	D. Produces insulin and regulates the blood-sugar level.
____ 5. Islet Cells of Pancreas	E. Maintains blood calcium and phosphorus levels.
____ 6. Testes	F. Growth of bones and other organs. Signals puberty to begin.
____ 7. Ovaries	G. Metabolic rate and growth and development.

Materials:

Englebert Excretory Worksheet dittos (See 9-28)
Englebert's Excretory System (parts) dittos (See 9-29)
Construction paper
Scissors
Crayons or markers
Glue or paste

Directions:

Have students—

1. Color in the excretory parts and cut them out.
2. Paste the parts onto "Englebert" ditto in the proper position
3. Label all parts neatly.
4. Mount on construction paper.
5. Display.

Activity 48. Danger Ahead (Researching Kidney Disorders)

Concept/Description: The kidney is an important organ because it functions to clear wastes from the body and to maintain fluid balance.

Objective: Students will understand the importance of the kidneys and be aware of signs that may indicate problems with the kidneys.

Materials:

Reference books
Encyclopedia
Anatomy texts

Directions:

1. Have students do research in order to find some of the signs of kidney problems (such as frequent urination, pale color of urine, swelling of body tissue, decrease or stoppage of urine production, failure to excrete urea.)
2. Discuss how we can live with one kidney, but cannot lose both.
3. Research and discuss dialysis and the profound effect it can have on a life.

Name ______________________________ Date ________________ (9-28)

Englebert Excretory

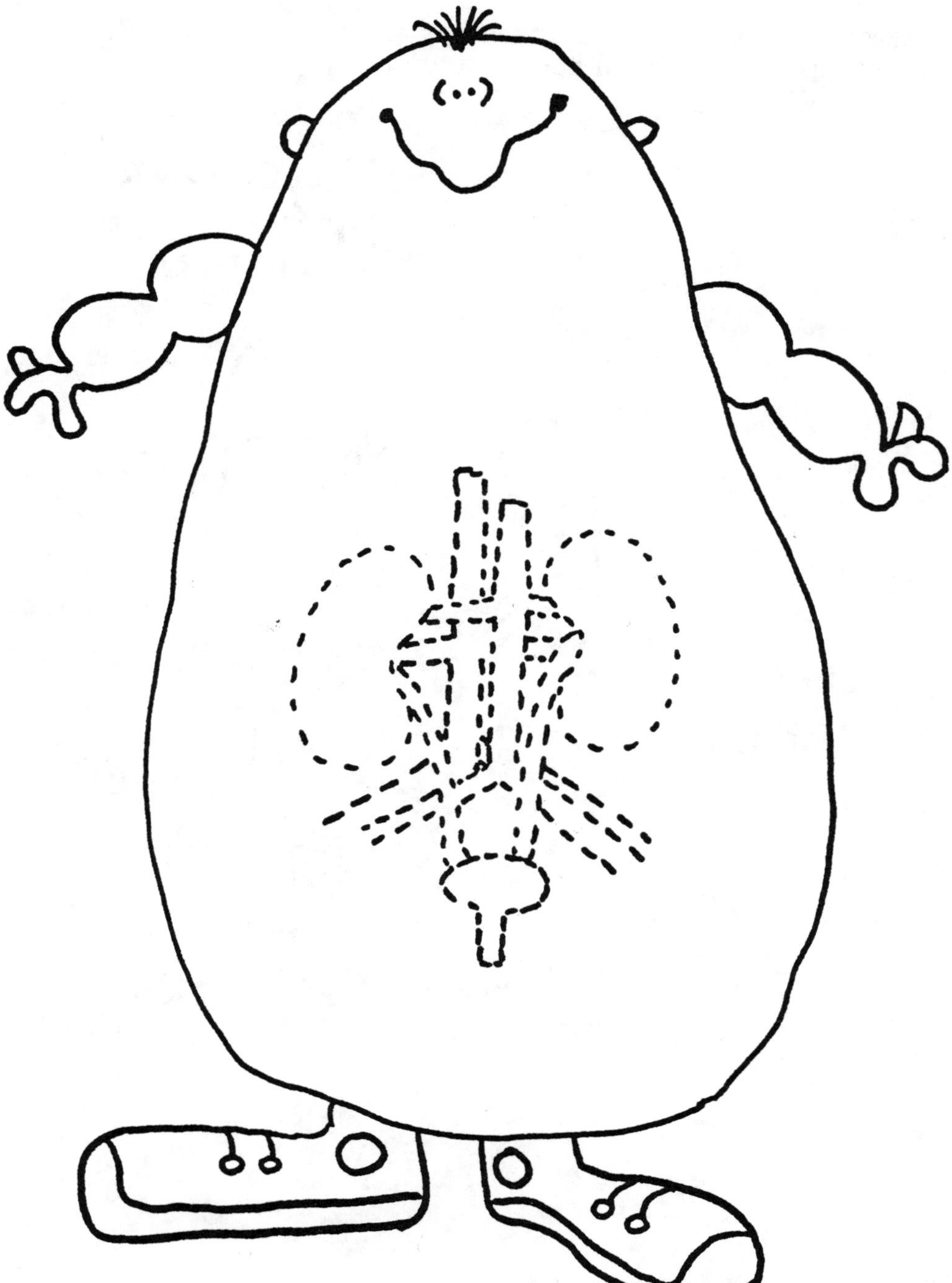

Englebert's Excretory System

DIRECTIONS: Color in the parts below, cut them out, and paste them onto Englebert in the proper positions. Then label all parts neatly.

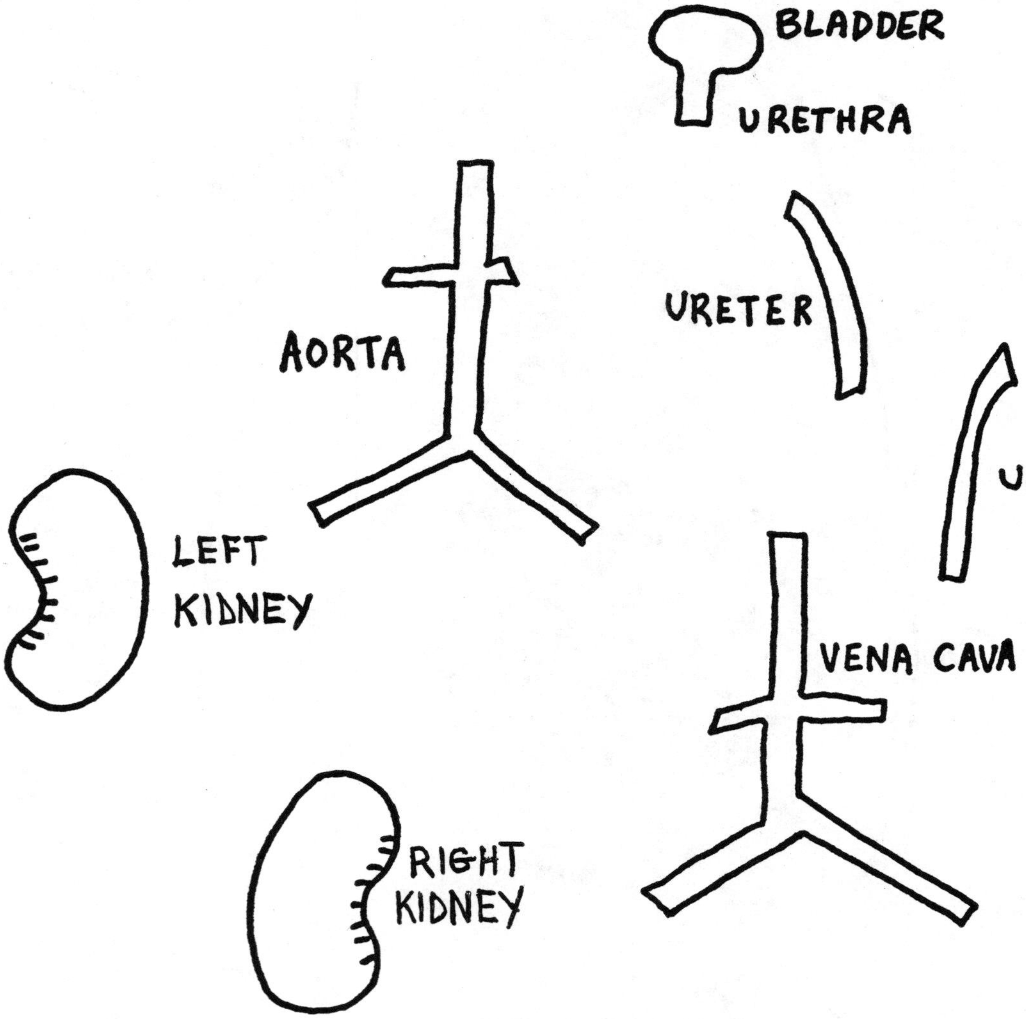

UNIT 10

AAA . . . CHOO!
Diseases and Disorders of the Past and Present

The ultimate goal of this unit is to help students choose a healthier life style. They will learn about steps they can take to reduce their exposure to disease and reduce the risk factors that lead to disease. They will also learn to view disease realistically, as something that is not just the concern of older people. Activities in this unit will help them make the connection between how they live now and diseases that may strike at any time or as they grow older.

Students will also gain an historical perspective on disease and the great strides medicine has made in eradicating diseases that once claimed millions of lives. You may also choose to use activities that focus on sexually transmitted diseases in general or A.I.D.S. in particular, if this fits in with your approved curriculum.

Activity 1. A Cause for Alarm (Causes of Disease)

Concept/Description: Diseases have different causes.

Objective: To discover and research some of the many kinds of diseases and categorize them according to cause.

Materials:

Reference books, encyclopedia
3 × 5 Index cards
Pens, pencils
Tape
Chalk, eraser
Chalkboard
List of Disease Causes (See p. 246)

Directions:

1. Divide the class into groups of four to six, and give each group several 3 × 5 index cards. Ask all groups to put a number or symbol in the corner of each card to represent their group.
2. On the board, write the seven categories and descriptions of disease causes that are listed below, leaving space under each category for students to write in corresponding diseases or disorders.
   NOTE: Some examples of corresponding diseases have been provided for your convenience. Do not write these on the board.

3. Give the groups time to look up diseases in the reference books.
   On one side of a 3 × 5 card, the group must write the name of a disease or disorder. A brief description of the disease should be written on the other side. When completed, a group member may come up to the chalkboard and tape the group's card in the correct category.
   For example, the Group #1 card might have "Hemophilia" written on the front of its card. On the back, it may say, "A disease where excessive bleeding occurs because the blood lacks the components necessary for clotting." The group would then tape its card under the heading "Heredity," since hemophilia is passed on genetically.
4. Each group receives one point for being the first to list a disease in the proper category. Once a disease is listed, it may not be listed by another group in the same category.
5. After a set time limit, the group with the most cards taped to the chalkboard (check numbers or symbols on the front of the cards to verify) is declared the winner.

Disease Causes:

1. *Heredity*—inherited from parents.
   (Examples: hemophilia, sickle cell anemia, Huntington's chorea)
2. *Diet*—too few vitamins, proteins, etc.; or too much food, cholesterol, fat, salt, etc., or too little food.
   (Examples: atherosclerosis, heart disease, malnutrition, rickets, scurvy)
3. *Smoking*—use of tobacco.
   (Examples: lung cancer, emphysema)
4. *Stress*—tension or strain
   (Examples: ulcers, colitis, some types of arthritis)
5. Environment—poor living conditions, heat, cold, chemicals, pollution, asbestos, etc.
   (Examples: emphysema, lung cancer)
6. *Age and/or Breakdown or Wearing Away of Body Systems*
   (Examples: cataracts, degenerative arthritis, some types of cancer)
7. *Infections*
   (a) *Bacteria*—one-celled organisms
   (Examples: tetanus, pyorrhea, tuberculosis, syphilis)
   (b) *Virus*—smallest form of life
   (Examples: A.I.D.S., mumps, smallpox)
   (c) *Fungus*—Spongy, abnormal growths (Examples: ringworm, athlete's foot)

Variation:

As a follow-up, assign groups or individuals to do research and report on the diseases listed by the class.

Activity 2. I've Got It! (How Disease Spreads)

Concept/Description: Communicable diseases are spread by other infected people, air, water, insects, or infected animals.

Objective: To show the possible consequences of having one or two contagious people in a group.

Materials:
(None)

Directions:

1. After some background discussion on the spread of disease, secretly write down the names of two students in your class and assign them a communicable disease such as measles, mumps, or chicken pox.
2. Ask each person in the class to walk around the room, shake hands with five other people, and remember with whom she/he shook hands. Then have all students return to their seats.
3. Announce that two students were infected with a disease and that anyone who came into contact with them, either directly or indirectly, is now infected. Announce the names of the two students (for example, Sue and Tim) and the diseases (mumps and measles). Ask for a show of hands of the people who came into direct contact with the disease carriers. (This will be the five students who shook Sue's hand and five who shook Tim's hand. Keep in mind that some may have shaken both Sue's and Tim's hand, thereby picking up two diseases. Also, Sue and Tim may have shaken each other's hands.)
4. Next, ask for a show of hands of anybody who shook hands with the people who came into direct contact with Sue and Tim, and so on. How many people were potentially infected? How many might have contracted one disease? Both diseases? Neither disease? Discuss.

Activity 3. The Doctor Is In (Some Common Diseases)

Concept/Description: Diseases have characteristics that may distinguish one disease from another.

Objective: To recognize disease characteristics.

Materials:

3 × 5 Index cards
Symptom Cards and Answer Key
(See 10-1 & 10-2)

Directions:

1. Before beginning the game, you may want to attach the Symptom Cards to sturdier 3 × 5 index cards.
2. Divide the class into two teams, and place the cards, face down, in the front of the room.
3. Have an "intern" from one team choose a card and read the symptoms aloud to his or her team. Give the group 30 seconds to decide on the diagnosis (in other words, guess the disease). The "intern" gives the group's answer and receives one point if correct. If incorrect, the card goes back into the pile.
4. Next, an "intern" from the opposing team chooses a card, gives an answer, and so on, until all cards have been used or until time is up.
5. The team with the most points is declared the winner.

Variation:

Give the team that guesses the disease one point for the correct diagnosis and a bonus point if it can recommend a specialist to treat the disease or disorder. For example, Team A may choose a card that says, "Mrs. Smith experiences excessive thirst, urinates frequently, has lost a lot of weight, and is weak and tired. She has indications of gangrene, especially on her feet." If Team A correctly guesses "Diabetes" and recommends an "endocrinologist," it thereby receives two points.

Activity 4. A Risk You Don't Have to Take (Controllable and Uncontrollable Risk Factors)

Concept/Description: There are certain risk factors we can and cannot control in our efforts to maintain optimum health.

Objective: To determine and illustrate which risk factors we can and cannot control in our lives.

Materials:

Magazines
Scissors
Paste or glue
Construction paper
Chalkboard, chalk

Directions:

1. Ask students to describe a life style that could cause a person serious health problems. Write their responses on the board. (Overweight; smoker; little or no exercise; under a lot of stress; eats a lot of salt, sugar, cholesterol, fat; drinks a lot of alcohol; uses drugs; uses a lot of products with caffeine, etc.)
2. Ask if people have control over these factors. (Yes)
3. Ask if they can think of any diseases or disorders that might be a result of this type of life style. (Cancer, heart disease, high blood pressure, emphysema, ulcers, cirrhosis of the liver, etc.)
4. Ask if they can think of any other reasons why a person might suffer from a disease or disorder. What risk factors might the person have no control over? (Age, heredity, sex, accidents)
   NOTE: In the case of some accidents, safety precautions (such as wearing a safety belt or crash helmet) could be taken.
5. What types of diseases or disorders would fit into the category of uncontrollable risk factors? (Degenerative arthritis, hemophilia, cataracts)
   NOTE: Be sure to mention that some inherited disorders can be controlled with conscious effort. For example, a person whose parents have high blood pressure could take extra precautions by limiting salt intake and having his or her blood pressure checked often.
6. After this discussion, divide the class in half. Have one half make collages, murals, or bulletin boards showing pictures that illustrate controllable risk factors (pictures of fatty foods, overweight people, salt shakers, etc.)
   (Continued on p. 252)

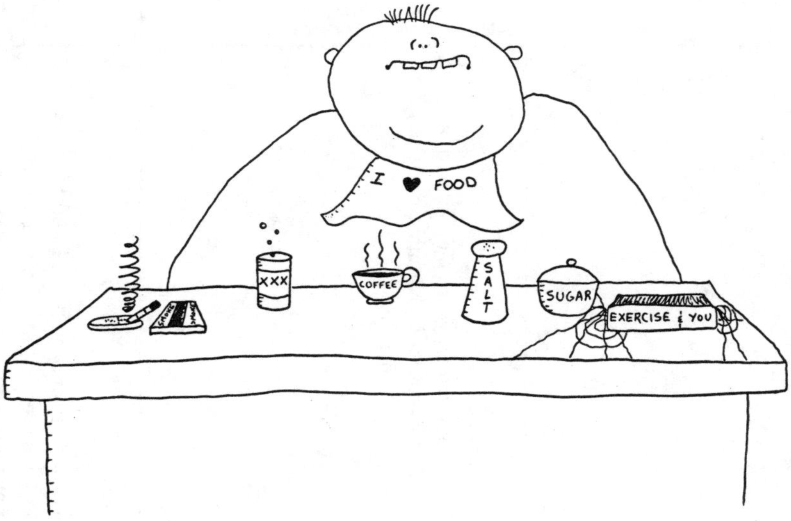

Symptom Cards

1. Mr. Salvatore is 65 years old. He has pain, swelling, stiffness, and deformity in his joints.	2. Five-year-old Ronnie has long coughing spells, both during the day and night. Sometimes she vomits. When she coughs, she makes a "whooping" sound.	3. Bill experiences frequent, difficult, and often painful urination.
4. Candace is thirteen years old. When playing field hockey, she often has trouble breathing and experiences "wheezing."	5. Mrs. Smith experiences excessive thirst, urinates frequently, has lost a lot of weight, and is weak and tired. She has indications of gangrene, especially on her feet.	6. Jennifer has rounded red patches covered with shiny dry scales on her skin. They are especially evident on her elbows, knees, lower back, and scalp. She has lost her hair in some affected areas.
7. Michelle is twenty years old and has severe pain in her lower abdomen, along with irregular menstruation and nausea.	8. Barry has severe nausea, vomiting, diarrhea, and abdominal cramps. He remembers eating some potato salad that tasted "bad."	9. John is a drug user who frequently injects heroin. Lately, he has no appetite, a high fever, and jaundice (yellowed skin and eyes).

Symptom Cards, cont.

10. Little Sandy has swollen glands, puffiness in the side of her face, difficulty opening her mouth and a mild fever.

11. Mr. Parker was working on his farm and punctured his foot on a piece of metal. The cut is now infected, and he is experiencing painful muscular spasms, fever, headache, and stiffening of the muscles of the neck and jaw.

12. Sarah has developed a fever, has general aches and pains, and now has severe headaches, vomiting, and intense pain.

13. Rob plays football for his high school team. Rob and some of his friends have noticed blistering, scaling and cracking of the skin between their toes. They have all used the shower stalls in the locker room.

14. Stefanie and her parents visited India recently. She is now experiencing increasing diarrhea, vomiting, loss of kidney function, and extreme thirst.

15. The blood vessels in Mrs. Thomas's eyes are dilated, and pus is evident around the eyes. Her eyelids are swollen, and it hurts for her to be out in sunlight.

16. Mr. Charles drinks a lot of coffee and loves to eat. Lately, he has gnawing stomach pains that awaken him in the night. It bothers him to eat.

ANSWER KEY—DIAGNOSIS AND REFERRAL

1. Arthritis/Orthopedist; 2. Whooping Cough/Pediatrician; 3. Bladder infection, prostate problem, or sexually transmitted disease/ Urologist; 4. Asthma/Allergist; 5. Diabetes/Endocrinologist; 6. Psoriasis/Dermatologist; 7. Infection of female reproductive system, endometriosis/Gynecologist; 8. Food poisoning or gastroenteritis/Gastroenterologist; 9. Hepatitis/General Practitioner; 10. Mumps/ Pediatrician; 11. Tetanus (lock jaw)/Neurologist; 12. Meningitis/Neurologist; 13. Athlete's Foot/ Dermatologist; 14. Cholera/Internist; 15. Conjunctivitis (pink eye)/Ophthalmologist; 16. Peptic Ulcer/ Internist

7. Have the other half of the class illustrate uncontrollable risk factors (pictures of boys and girls, pictures of elderly persons, pictures of parents with their children, pictures of accidents.)
8. Display.
9. Discuss precautions people could take to help them lessen their risk of contracting a serious ailment:
   (a) Safely losing weight
   (b) Getting regular checkups
   (c) Not smoking
   (d) Exercising
   (e) Managing stress
   (f) Watching intake of fat, cholesterol, salt, sugar, preservatives, caffeine
   (g) Limiting alcohol use
   (h) Not using drugs
   (i) Using safety measures, such as seat belts, bike helmets, etc.

Activity 5. Defend Yourself (The Body's Defenses)

Concept/Description: The body has natural defenses to ward off infection. Sometimes, these defenses are unable to work, but most often they keep us healthy.

Objective: To recognize that the body is constantly fighting off infection, often without us consciously realizing it.

Materials:

Body Defenses Worksheet dittos
Crayons or markers
Pens or pencils

Directions:

1. Ask students to refer to their worksheet and *label* the places designated by a pointer where the body is defending itself against infection.
2. Have students color the sheet, if desired.
3. Discuss which defenses might go unnoticed even as they are occurring. (Skin acting as a barrier; cilia sweeping away dust, dirt, and germs; saliva killing bacteria; white blood cells ingesting disease organisms; stomach acids destroying disease organisms in food or water)
4. Which defenses might you notice even if you did not recognize their function? (Tears washing away foreign substances; bleeding acting as "wash;" sweating to maintain normal body temperature; pain alerting you that there is infection or injury; and urine washing out some germs.)

Name ______________________ Date ______________ (10-3)

Body Defenses Worksheet

DIRECTIONS: Name each numbered body defense in the diagram below, and explain how that defense works.

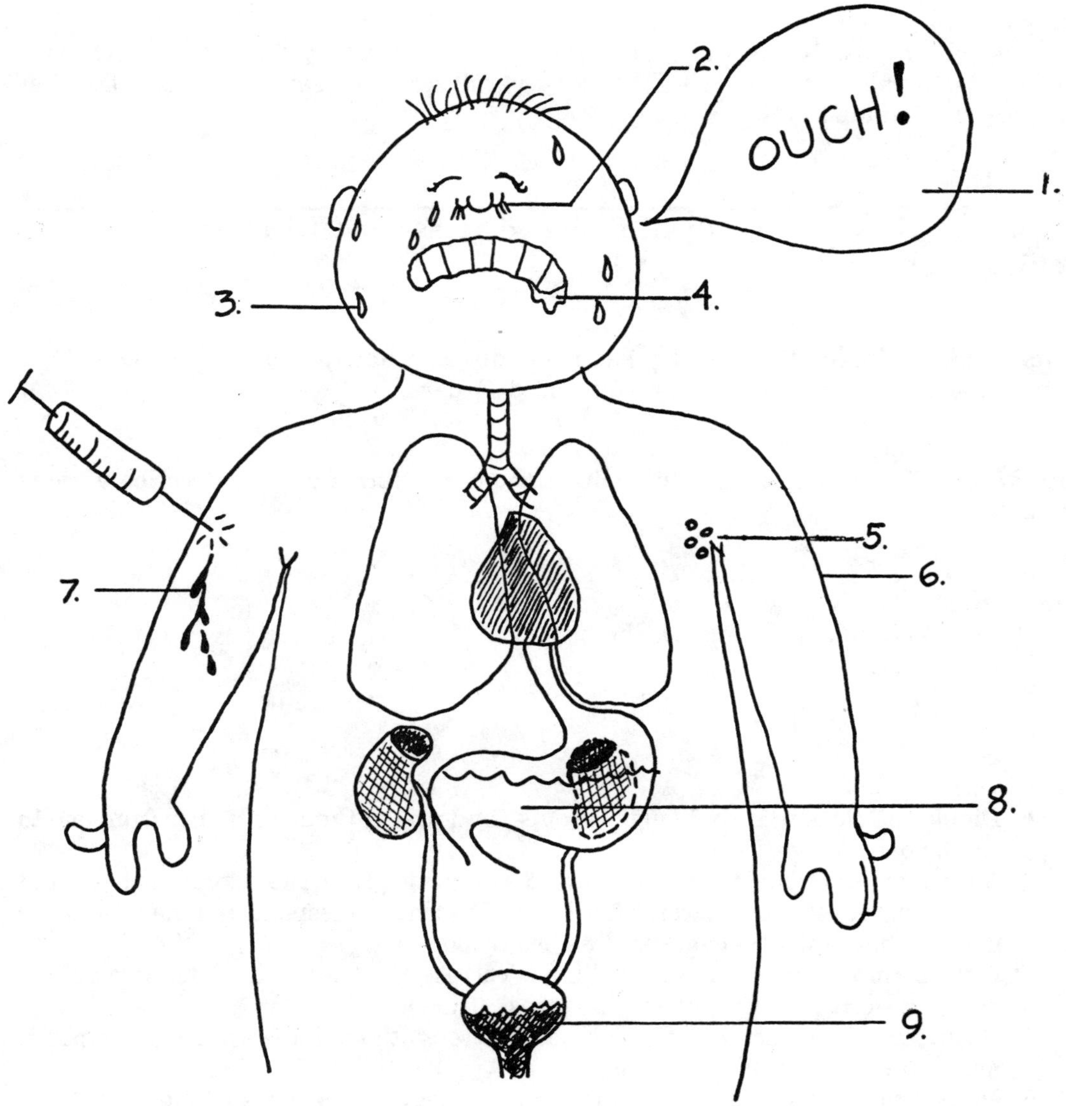

1. ______________________
2. ______________________
3. ______________________
4. ______________________
5 ______________________
6. ______________________
7. ______________________
8. ______________________
9. ______________________

Answers: 1. Pain—alerts victim; 2. Cilia—sweeps dust and dirt; 3. Sweat—helps maintain body temperature; 4. Saliva—kills germs; 5. White blood cells—ingest organisms; 6. Skin—protective barrier; 7. Bleeding—washes away germs; 8. Stomach acids—destroy bacteria in food and water; 9. Urine—washes out some germs

Variation:

Discuss situations that would hinder the body's ability to defend itself, such as a person's smoking causing the cilia to become paralyzed, or diseases, such as AIDS, that destroy the immune system.

Activity 6. How Do You Spell Relief? (Disease and Disorder Spelling Bee)

Concept/Description: The body has many diseases and disorders. It is possible to describe characteristics of these diseases and disorders.

Objective: To familiarize students with some of the terms used to describe various illnesses.

Materials:

Disease Vocabulary Reference Sheet
Pens or pencils
Scrap paper

Directions:

1. Divide the class into six to eight groups, and assign them a number from one to six, or one to eight.
2. Starting with Group #1 members, read a definition from the reference sheet, and ask them to *spell* the answer. They have 30 seconds to respond and may use scrap paper to jot down their guesses before responding.
3. If the term is correct and the spelling is correct, the team is awarded two points, and the word is no longer in play (cross it out).
4. If the term is correct, but the spelling is wrong, the team is awarded one point, and you can use the word in later play.
5. No points are awarded if the answer is incorrect, regardless of the spelling.
6. Continue reading definitions to each team (in numerical order) until all words are used up or until time is up.
7. The team with the most points is declared the winner.

Variation:

Have the students themselves come up with the terms and definitions to use for game play.

Disease Vocabulary Reference Sheet

1. Chronic—long-term ill health, such as emphysema.
2. Acute—short-term, severe illness, such as the flu.
3. Hypertension—another name for high blood pressure.
4. Diabetes—a disease where the body cannot make enough insulin.
5. Scoliosis—curvature of the spine.
6. Emphysema—lung disease where the alveoli (air sacs) lose their elasticity.
7. Arthritis—disease where the joints and surrounding tissues become deformed.
8. Atherosclerosis—hardening of the arteries.
9. Cirrhosis—liver disease, often a result of alcoholism.
10. Cancer—disease characterized by an uncontrolled growth of cells.
11. Carcinogen—cancer causing agent, such as asbestos.
12. Tumor—a lump or growth of cells with no purpose.
13. Benign—a non-cancerous tumor.
14. Malignant—a cancerous tumor.
15. Congenital—a defect that is present at birth.
16. Rheumatic—inflamed arteries of the heart muscle.
17. Stress—strain or tension
18. Cholesterol—a substance found in fatty foods and eggs.
19. Insulin—a hormone produced in the pancreas.
20. Cataracts—cloudiness of the lens of the eye, resulting in blindness.
21. Chemotherapy—treatment of a disease with large doses of drugs.
22. Communicable—any disease that is contagious.
23. Epidemic—a disease that affects a larger number of people in an area than it normally would.
24. Vaccination—introducing a live or dead infectious agent into the body to help to become immune to it.
25. Immunity—the ability to resist infection or disease.

Activity 7. An Ounce of Prevention (Controlling STD's)

Concept/Description: By recognizing the signs and symptoms of sexually transmitted diseases (STD's), using preventative measures, and seeking treatment for all involved, the spread of STD's can be controlled.

Objective: To discuss the importance of recognizing the signs of STD's, of getting prompt medical treatment, of telling partners about possible infection, and of using methods of prevention.

Materials:

Reference books, encyclopedias
Paper
Pens, pencils

Directions:

1. Divide the class into groups and have them research and/or discuss the following STD-related topics:
   (a) *Signs and Symptoms of STD's:*
   (Skin changes; burning urination; intense itching; genital discharge; severe pelvic pain.)
   (b) *What to Do If You Think You Have an STD:*
   (Get prompt medical care; follow your doctor's orders; tell your partner.)
   (c) *Reasons Why Someone with an STD Would Not Tell His/Her Partner or Go for Treatment:*
   (The person has no symptoms; is afraid; feels guilty; embarrassed; uninformed; has little or no money.)
   (d) *Why Is It Important to Tell Your Partner?*
   (So your partner can be treated; so you won't get reinfected.)
   (e) *Methods of Prevention That May Help:*
   (Abstinence; sex with only one partner who is not infected; use of a condom treated with nonoxynol-9; and the less effective methods, such as urinating and washing genitals after intercourse.)
   NOTE: Abstinence is the only 100% effective method of preventing most STD's.
2. Have groups report their findings and thoughts back to the class. Discuss.

Variations:

1. Have students discuss ways to let their partners know about possible STD infection. (Letter; phone call; in person; STD case worker, etc.)
2. Have students role-play a situation in which they must tell their partner that they have an STD. Discuss afterwards.

Activity 8. Ready for a Fight? (A Simplified Explanation of the Immune System and AIDS)

Concept/Description: The immune system is rendered ineffective by the AIDS virus.

Objective: To help students to understand the workings of the immune system, as well as its destruction by the AIDS virus.

Materials:

Objects or action figures to represent the components of the immune system. Some ideas and suggestions are provided.

NOTE: Children are usually very willing to bring in these objects (or to confiscate them from younger siblings).

Suggestions:

1. *White Blood Cells*—He-Man figures, GI Joe figures, Superman dolls.
2. *T-Cells*—Mr. T. dolls, tinker toys, magnetic letter T's.
3. *B-Cells*—Magnetic letter B's, blocks, bumble bee pictures.
4. *Antibodies*—Small cowboys and Indians, or toy soldiers.
5. *HIV*—play dough balls or silly putty balls.
6. *Virus* (or bacteria, fungus, protozoa)—toy skeleton or fuzzy object.
7. *Bloodstream*—Desk top, hoola hoop, red cardboard.

Directions:

Using the objects indicated, or others of your choice, explain the immune system as follows:

1. This "desk" represents your bloodstream. When a microbe such as a virus (pick up the fuzzy object and place it on the desk), enters your bloodstream, white blood cells survey the situation (place the GI Joe's next to the "virus"). They determine that the invader is a problem and chemically notify the helper T-Cells (place the Mr. T. dolls next to the "virus" and the "white blood cells").
2. The helper T-Cells reproduce themselves (add more Mr. T figures if possible). These cells, in turn, chemically signal the B-Cells (place letter B's on desk), which also reproduce themselves (add more letter B's).
3. These B cells produce antibodies that are specifically intended to destroy the microbe (place lots of toy soldiers around the "virus" and then remove both the "virus" and "antibodies" from the desk.)
4. Further explain that after the microbe has been defeated, the B-cells and helper T-cells return to their dormant state (lay the corresponding objects on their sides). This is how the immune system normally reacts to an "invader." Clear the desk.

Now explain the effect of the AIDS virus on the immune system:

1. When the invader is the HIV (human immunodeficiency virus), something different occurs (place a play-dough ball on the desk). The white blood cells survey the situation (add the G.I. Joe's) and chemically notify the helper T-Cells (add the Mr. T. dolls). Before the T-Cells can notify the B-Cells and antibodies, however, the HIV attaches itself to the T-Cell (stick the play-dough into the Mr. T. doll). This turns the T-Cell into an HIV-producing factory (add lots of play-dough balls.)

2. Explain that the T-Cells are now unable to stimulate the B-Cells so that they, in turn, cannot produce antibodies. Therefore, other infections that normally would not be a problem can now harm the body.

Activity 9. Oh, Rats!! (Some Major Diseases of the Past)

Concept/Description: Man has discovered ways to conquer some of the "killers" of the past, and there is hope to conquer the present-day "killers" through research.

Objective: To assist students in understanding how the medical profession has conquered and will continue to conquer diseases.

Materials:

Major Diseases of the Past Worksheet dittos
Reference books, encyclopedias
Pens or pencils

Directions:

1. Divide the class into eight groups, and assign each group a disease of the past to research and prepare for an oral report. Have the groups use posters, drawings, skits, etc., to "teach" the class about their disease. Ask the groups to find out the symptoms and the causes of each disease. You may also want them to discover when and where the disease was prevalent.

Name ______________________ Date ______________ (10-5)

Major Diseases of the Past

1. BUBONIC PLAGUE

   Symptoms: ______________________

   Cause: ______________________

2. YELLOW FEVER

   Symptoms: ______________________

   Cause: ______________________

3. CHOLERA

   Symptoms: ______________________

   Cause: ______________________

4. MALARIA

   Symptoms: ______________________

   Cause: ______________________

5. SCURVY

   Symptoms: ______________________

   Cause: ______________________

6. RICKETS

   Symptoms: ______________________

   Cause: ______________________

7. MALNUTRITION

   Symptoms: ______________________

   Cause: ______________________

8. BERI BERI

   Symptoms: ______________________

   Cause: ______________________

NOTE: Some of these diseases, especially malnutrition, malaria, and cholera, are still common in Third-World countries.

2. As each group presents its project, have class members fill in their worksheets.
3. Discuss the frustration physicians of the past must have experienced when trying to fight these diseases. Compare it to the frustration present-day scientists have in confronting diseases, such as cancer and AIDS.

Answers:

1. Bubonic Plague: Symptoms include internal bleeding, headache, swollen glands, boils, death. Cause was flea bites transmitting bacteria from infected rats.
2. Yellow Fever: Symptoms are high fever, yellow skin, hiccough, vomiting, death. Caused by bites from infected mosquitoes.
3. Cholera: Symptoms include vomiting, diarrhea, and death. Caused by bacteria in contaminated food and water.
4. Malaria: Symptoms include high fever and sometimes death, because it attacks the liver and red blood cells. Caused by bites from infected mosquitoes.
5. Scurvy: Symptoms include bleeding gums, hemorrhaging, death. Caused by a lack of vitamin C.
6. Rickets: Symptoms include softening of bones, crippling, pain, and deformity. Caused by lack of sunlight and vitamin D.
7. Malnutrition: Symptoms include swollen belly, rough skin, emaciation and death. Caused by a lack of protein.
8. Beri Beri: Symptoms include nerve damage leading to paralysis, heart failure, death. Caused by a lack of Vitamin B.

Activity 10. And Then What Happened? (A Time Line of Mankind's Fight against Disease)

Concept/Description: From earliest history, mankind has struggled to solve the mystery of diseases and illness.

Objective: To have students place some of the significant medical advances on a time line spanning prehistoric time up to the present.

Materials:

Butcher paper or brown paper
Markers or pens
Encyclopedias, reference books
Tape
Time Line Entries reference sheet (See 10-6)
Worksheet dittos

Directions:

1. Divide the class into research groups of six to eight students.
2. Give all groups a reference sheet and have them look up the information listed.

Ask them to write a brief description or definition where appropriate. Write down the time period for each item listed. (For example, they might write, "Robert Koch (1882) isolated the bacillus of tuberculosis.")

3. Have each group develop a time line, listing each item in chronological order on the worksheet.
4. Draw the line and information neatly on the butcher paper, and tape it to the wall. Add cartoons or drawings, if you wish.
5. Compare the time lines of the groups and discuss.

Name ______________________________ Date ________________ **(10-6)**

Time Line Entries

DIRECTIONS: Describe or define each item *briefly*, and then place it in chronological order on your group's time line.

1. William Harvey
2. Anton van Leeuwenhoek
3. Use of anesthesia
4. Louis Pasteur
5. Discovery of the X-ray
6. TB and Polio controlled
7. Hippocrates
8. Public sanitation (baths, sewers, aqueducts)
9. John Hunter
10. Florence Nightingale
11. Formation of WHO (World Health Organization)
12. Walter Reed
13. Medicine men treated patients
14. Robert Koch
15. Frederick Banting
16. Jonas Salk
17. Trephination
18. Leeches
19. Use of microscope
20. Edward Jenner
21. Joseph Lister
22. Pierre and Marie Curie
23. Use of vitamins, sulfa drugs, and antibiotics
24. Edward Trudeau
25. Karl Landsteiner
26. Alexander Fleming
27. AIDS becomes serious threat
28. Renee Laennec
29. Galen
30. Blood-letting
31. First heart transplant

UNIT 11

GIMME A BREAK!
Activities on Safety and Accident Prevention

In some areas of personal growth, a child can learn by experience. This can be disastrous when learning about accidents. It is, therefore, critical that children become safety-conscious from early childhood. The school can contribute by emphasizing safety procedures and accident prevention for all grade levels, including specialized coverage during health.

It seems that students are always faced with situations that are potentially dangerous. Part of this is because of the nature of children. They love to explore, to try new things, and they frequently do not comprehend that safety hazards can be present in an everyday activity. The activities in this chapter provide an opportunity for elementary students to confront accident situations in a simulated setting. This is more realistic than reading about accident prevention, but does not pose a danger to the students. Fire, weather conditions, poisoning, accident situations and traffic rules are some of the areas that are included in this chapter. Students will participate in activities that will help them follow acceptable safety procedures. The intent is to make all students safety-conscious. This applies to the five-year-old as well as the ten- or eleven-year-old.

Activity 1. Taste Makes Waste (Testing Your Poison IQ)

Concept/Description: It is difficult for adults to correctly distinguish poisons from candy or other dangerous substances from safe ones. Children are even more susceptible to poisoning.

Objective: To dramatize how difficult it is to differentiate between safe and dangerous items.

Materials:

Cleanser and flour in separate packets
Fruit punch and cough syrup in similar containers
Milk and white paint
Semi-sweet chocolate and a chocolate-flavored laxative
Various candies and over-the-counter drugs that can be dangerous to children, particularly if taken in large quantities
Cardboard and answer sheets

Directions:

1. Attach the items described above randomly to the cardboard, and number each item.

2. Have the students place a "D" (dangerous) or "S" (safe) on their answer sheets next to the corresponding number.
3. Ask students if they feel a young child could easily confuse the dangerous and safe items, and discuss possible complications.
4. After correcting their sheets, discuss why having even one wrong answer could be disastrous to a small child.
   (NOTE: Be extremely careful in keeping a record of all substances, and secure them in a safe place.)

Variation:

Since unsafe storage is responsible for thousands of poisonings each year, use this activity to emphasize the importance of safe storage. Select numerous items that are similar in appearance to other items. Put them in non-distinguishing containers, and mark each one with a number. Give the students an answer sheet, and see how many items they are able to correctly identify by sight alone. Share with the class the different answers that are given for each item. Discuss the implications for small children, who base their decision on what to put in their mouths largely on sight. NOTE: For safety reasons, *do not* allow students to open or smell the containers.

Activity 2. Show Me the Way . . . (Making an Escape Map)

Concept/Description: Children must be aware of escape routes from their homes in case of fire.

Objective: Students will draw a fire escape plan for their home and share it with their family.

Materials:

Paper (graph paper is good for this)
Pens or pencils

Directions:

1. Have pupils draw a diagram of their house and show two escape routes for each member of their family from his/her bedroom in case of fire.
2. Have students take the map home for their parents to review and make suggestions.

Variations:

1. Prior to making escape maps, have a visit from the Fire Marshall or some other fire-department or safety-commission official to explain about the importance of drawing an escape plan in case of fire.
2. Give extra credit if the family actually conducts a fire drill and practices the escape. Ask for a note from Mom or Dad verifying completion of the drill.

Activity 3. Only You Can Prevent . . . (Fire Prevention Week Activities)

Concept/Description: Fire prevention week helps students become more aware of the dangers of fire.

Objective: Students will participate in various activities relating to fire prevention and develop greater awareness of fire prevention techniques.

Materials:

Dependent on activity

Directions:

Set up several activities for the week:

1. Have pupils write a story telling why they think fire prevention week started.
2. Collect pictures and stories about fires. Have the class discuss possible reasons for the fires and ways the fire might have been prevented.
3. Have a local fire department official visit the class and discuss fire equipment, prevention, and general safety rules.
4. Take a field trip to a fire department.
5. Have a poster contest on some aspect of fire prevention, e.g., (a) in the home, (b) in the school, (c) while camping, (d) building construction.
6. Let your class propose a series of activities for your school to the principal for fire prevention week.
7. Invite parents whose professions involve fire prevention to come to speak to your class. They might be architects, store managers, workers in industrial plants, or mechanics.

Activity 4. Rain, Rain, Go Away (Weather Emergencies)

Concept/Description: Many deaths occur each year because people are unfamiliar with safety rules during weather emergencies.

Objective: Students will be able to say what steps should be taken in different kinds of weather emergencies.

Materials:

Detective Cards (See 11-1)
Detective Cards Answer Key (See 11-2)

Directions:

1. Give a Detective Card to each group of 5 or 6 students.
2. Have each group solve the mystery on its card.

3. Have one spokesperson from each group read the problem to the rest of the class and a reporter explain the group's conclusions. (It is best to have each group write out its conclusions.)
4. Have each group defend its findings when questioned by classmates.

Variations:

1. Have students make up the Detective Cards.
2. Make up similar cards for other types of emergencies.

Activity 5. Weather or Not? (Weather Emergency Scrapbook)

Concept/Description: Extreme weather conditions necessitate knowledge of appropriate safety procedures.

Objective: To make a scrapbook that will tell the story of different kinds of weather phenomena.

Materials:

Articles and pictures from magazines and newspapers
Scrapbook

Directions:

1. Have students collect pictures and articles about weather phenomena, such as floods, thunderstorms, heat waves, winter storms, and hurricanes.
2. Make a class scrapbook of different categories of natural disasters.
3. Have students research safety rules and preventive techniques and place this information in the appropriate locations in the scrapbook.

Variations:

1. Make a map of the U.S. Indicate on the map the locations of extreme weather phenomena that are reported and illustrated in newspapers and magazines. Determine weather patterns.
2. Do the same thing with a map of the world.

Activity 6. My Decision? Incision! (Visual Aids from Play-Dough)

Concept/Description: It is easier to recognize injuries when you are able to see the injury or a model of the injury.

Detective Cards

#1. During a hurricane, Mary was riding in her car. She thought about her situation and decided to get out of her car and hide in the nearby drainage ditch. What did she do wrong? What should she have done?	#4. After the shaking from the earthquake finally stopped, Pattie went downtown to look at the buildings. What is wrong with this?	#7. After the tornado, Mollie decided to check the damage to her small apartment. Finding the electricity was out, she took a candle and went to the basement to check for gas leaks. What should she have done?
#2. When his house caught on fire, Jeff opened all the windows to let the smoke out. What did he do wrong? What should he have done?	#5. Hearing a tornado warning, Robin closed the windows tightly and watched through her picture window to see if she could sight the funnel cloud approaching. What did she do wrong? What should she have done?	#8. During a thunderstorm, Barney decided he would keep calm. He couldn't find his deck of cards, so he plugged in his desk lamp to look around. The next day Barney was found dead. What caused his death? What should he have done?
#3. During a heavy thunderstorm, Barb got on the phone to alert her neighbors and then went upstairs to take a bath. What were her mistakes?	#6. After the flood, Kathy and Lorraine took their rubber rafts outside to float around in the flood waters on their street. Why was this dangerous?	#9. When a thunderstorm came up while Chris and Alex were golfing, they put down their clubs and went to stand under a tall tree. Why was this a bad idea? What should they have done?

Detective Cards Answer Key

#1. 1. Car could be overturned by high winds. 2. Find suitable shelter. 3. Drainage ditch can fill rapidly with water. 4. Leave area when severe hurricane warnings are given.	#4. 1. Stress from earthquake could cause buildings to collapse later. 2. There could be an aftershock.	#7. 1. An open flame might cause explosion, if gas is leaking. 2. Open some windows. 3. If gas leaks are suspected, leave the house immediately. 4. Call fire department and gas company from neighbor's house.
#2. 1. Oxygen feeds and spreads the fire. 2. Stay low to the floor, and crawl out *immediately*. 3. Call fire department from a neighbor's house.	#5. 1. Tightly closed windows increase pressure on house. 2. Picture window may shatter. 3. Tornado could easily tear down entire house in seconds. 4. Go immediately to the basement or sheltered interior hallway if there's no cellar.	#8. 1. He might have been electrocuted when plugging in lamp. 2. He should have had an emergency flashlight available.
#3. 1. Telephone lines may be struck by lightning. 2. Stay away from electrical appliances, metal, and water. 3. Stay away from windows.	#6. 1. Floodwater is often moving fast and is treacherous. 2. Floating or submerged debris could puncture or capsize raft. 3. Water is contaminated.	#9. 1. Lightning tends to strike tall objects, so standing under a tree is putting yourself at risk. 2. Find safe shelter inside.

Objective: Students will recognize the different types of wounds

Materials:

Play-dough or dough-art material

Directions:

1. Shape four pieces of play-dough into flat pancakes to illustrate the four major types of wounds.
2. Make a model of each type of wound. (Figure 11-1)
3. Have students number the models, identify each type of wound, and explain the potential complications (infection, bleeding, etc.) of each.

Variation:

Use play-dough to create models of first-, second-, and third-degree burns. (Apply charcoal, chalk, and paint to show various levels of damage to the underlying tissue.)

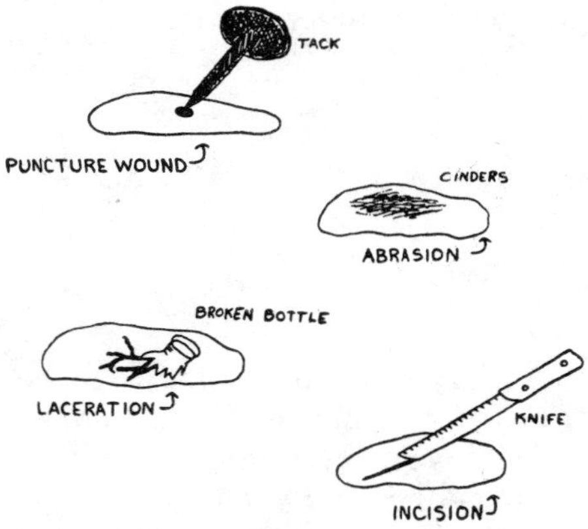

Fig. 11-1. Wound models.

Activity 7. Look Ma! No Hands! (Safety Booklet)

Concept/Description: There are many different safety areas about which students need to be knowledgeable.

Objective: To make a safety booklet.

Materials:

Materials for making a booklet, such as construction paper, paste, pens, crayons, glue, tape, picture.

Directions:

1. Make up a safety booklet for your class.
2. Let the class decide the safety areas that will be covered, and have different students work on each area. This booklet is appropriate for any age. Younger children can draw pictures to show safety procedures they should follow.
3. The booklet may include chapters on bicycle safety, gymnasium safety, home safety, walking to school, or any other aspect of the students' lives.
4. Distribute the booklet to the school population, if not too costly, or have copies available in the school's library.

Activity 8. Better Safe than Sorry (Safety Hazards)

Concept/Description: Safety must be considered in all plans and in different situations.

Objective: Students will recognize safety hazards.

Materials:

Pictures of scenes that would be familiar to students
Paper and pencils

Directions:

1. Draw or obtain pictures of typical scenes that would be familiar to the students in your class (family preparing dinner in the kitchen, students playing soccer on a playground, students riding in the family car, etc.)
2. Give all students two papers each. On one paper, have them write down all the safety practices they see in the picture. On the other paper, have them write down all the safety hazards they observe. (For example, in a soccer picture, there may be students without shin guards or mouthguards, or the benches may be too close to the field.)
3. Have the class discuss safety practices that should be followed to remove the safety hazards.

Variations:

1. Use a transparency on an overhead projector to show different scenes to the class.
2. Have students draw pictures with safety hazards and have a contest to see who can find the most hazards.
3. Use the Safety Scene worksheet provided and circle the safety hazards.

Name ______________________ Date ______________ (11-3)

A Safety Scene Worksheet

DIRECTIONS: In the cartoon below, you will find numerous examples of safe and unsafe behaviors. On a separate sheet, list these behaviors.

Activity 9. Skateboarding Isn't for Highways (Safety Practices)

Concept/Description: Students must learn and follow appropriate safety practices for a variety of situations.

Objective: Students will write safety practices that should be followed.

Materials:

Safety Chart Gameboard for each student (See 11-4)
Pencils
List of safety situations (see below)

Directions:

1. Pick an item from the safety situations list below, and read it to the class.
2. Students write on their Safety Chart Gameboard, beginning at *start*, as many safety practices as they can think of that apply to the safety situation you announced. For example, for *Bicycling*, they might come up with knowing traffic rules, riding in safe places, keeping bicycle in good condition, and so on. Have a time limit for each situation.
3. Keep reading out new situations until someone has reached *home* safely by filling in all the spaces. The first student home should yell, "Home!"
4. Continue the game with new charts until all the situations have been used.
5. At the end of the game, have students share the safety practices they wrote on their charts.

Safety situations:

sunburn	hurricane	home safety	preventing accidental falls
taking risks	shock	first aid	keeping small children safe
tornado	hiking	skateboarding	preparing for emergencies
storing poison	bicycling	house fire	emergency phone numbers
stranger in a car	babysitting	lightning	playing soccer

Activity 10. What Did You Do Yesterday? (Everyday Safety Hazards)

Concept/Description: We are constantly faced with situations that can be dangerous to us.

Objective: To make the students aware of common safety hazards that they confront in their daily activities.

Name ______________________ Date ______________ (11-4)

Safety Chart Gameboard

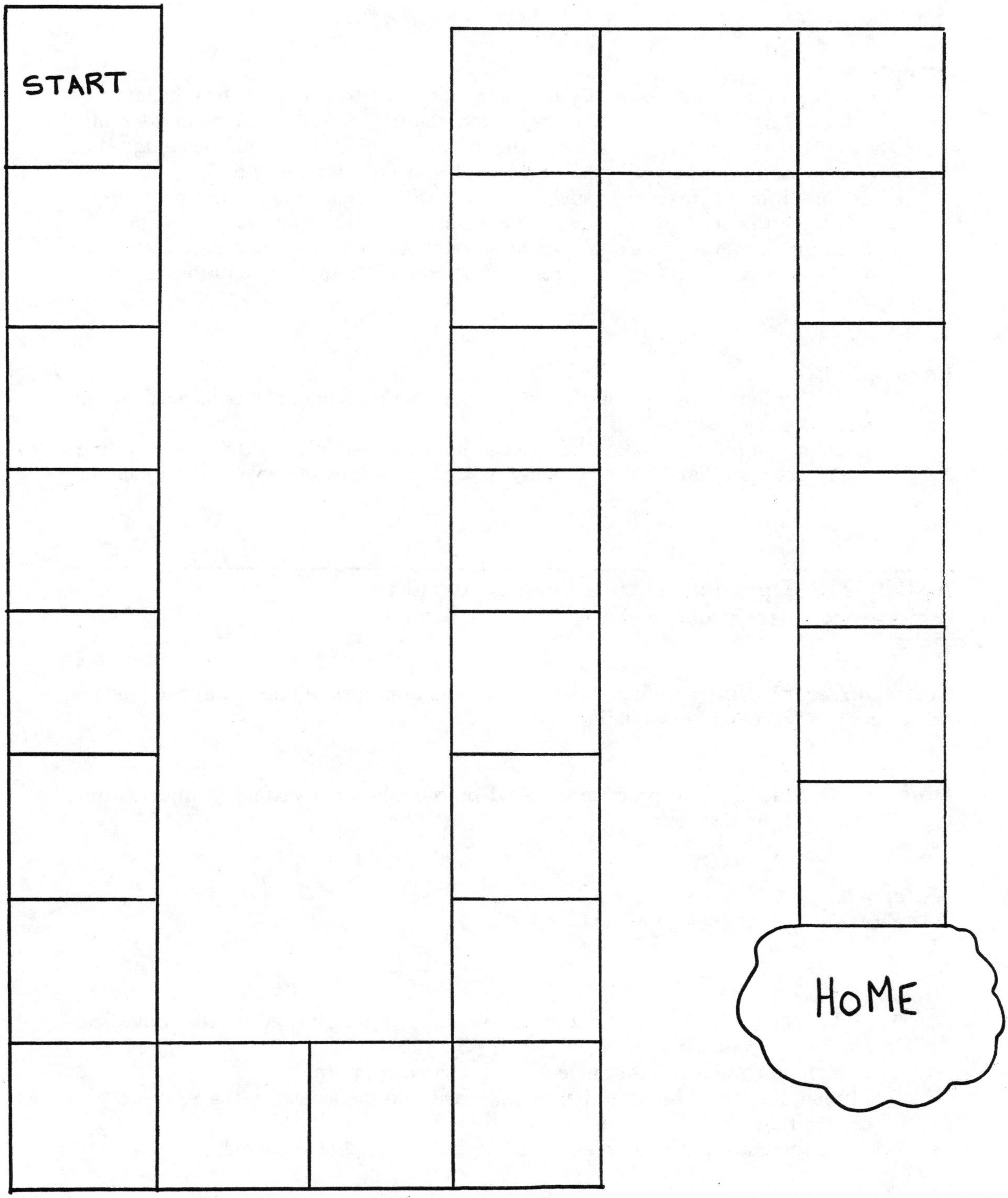

Materials:

Paper
Pens or pencils

Directions:

1. Give all students a sheet of paper and ask them to list ten safety hazards or potential safety hazards that they faced the day before, such as accidentally leaving the rake facing up after raking leaves, an electrical appliance plugged in near water, a game with small pieces left out on the floor, etc.
2. Set up different categories, such as home safety, school safety, and play safety, and have the students list their safety hazards in the appropriate category.
3. Use the information as a basis for the students to participate in a class discussion on the importance of being aware of situations that could pose a problem to their safety.

Variations:

1. Make a bulletin board display of safety hazards that students face as part of their normal daily activities.
2. Write a pamphlet on safety hazards at home, school, play and while traveling.
3. Carry out a similar survey of safety hazards that they observe in their community.

Activity 11. Operator, There's Been an Accident! (Emergency Care Situations)

Concept/Description: Being able to react in an appropriate manner at the scene of an accident may save a person's life.

Objective: Students will practice first aid procedures for a variety of injuries that typically result from accidents.

Materials:

Situation Cards (See 11-5)

Directions:

1. Make up situation cards that cover emergency first aid situations that have been studied in your class.
2. Group your students, and give one card to each group.
3. Students act out the situation on the card and demonstrate the first aid procedure that should be followed.
4. Have the class critique and correct any mistakes that occurred.

Situation Cards

#1 After a fast-paced game of basketball, your friend says that he feels dizzy. His face is pale and dry.	#4 Your six-year-old brother comes in the house crying. Upon questioning, you find he has stepped on a nail protruding from a board, and the nail has penetrated deeply into his foot.	#7 You jump out of a tree house and feel a sharp pain in your ankle when you land. You can't put any weight on your ankle, and it is starting to swell and throb.
#2 You and your friend witness an auto accident in which a young girl is thrown from a car. She is bleeding severely from a gash on her hand and is moaning that her head hurts.	#5 You are eating chicken at a family picnic when suddenly your 45-year-old uncle starts to choke and then turns blue, finding it impossible to take a breath.	#8 A friend of yours is riding a skateboard and suddenly loses his or her balance, falls, and slides along the pavement. There are severe abrasions on both legs, and blood is streaming from one knee.
#3 You are visiting in your friend's home. When you go into the kitchen, you find your friend's three-year-old brother drinking from a bottle of cleaning fluid that is marked poison.	#6 Your neighbor cuts his arm severely with his power saw, and the blood is spurting from his arm as he comes running outside calling for help.	#9 You helped to mow the lawn, but when putting the lawn mower away, you touch the muffler and severely burn your forearm.

Variation:

1. Have one group act out the situation on its card and another group apply the proper first aid. Set a time limit.
2. Have one team or one student critique the first aid procedures that were used.

Activity 12. No Turn on Red (Traffic Regulations)

Concept/Description: Students must know traffic rules and regulations.

Objective: Pupils will follow traffic rules

Materials:

Traffic course (Figure 11-2) that includes traffic signs, such as "Stop," "No left turn," and "yield." (Simulated traffic lights can be made by attaching red, yellow, and green circles to a pole that is turned by one of the students. One of the parents may be able to design a traffic standard with red, yellow, and green bulbs that can be manually operated.)

Bicycles, big wheels, or vehicle boxes (Figure 11-3)

Fig. 11-2. Traffic course.

THIS COULD LOOK LIKE A CAR, TRUCK, BUS, ETC.

Fig. 11-3. Vehicle box.

Directions:

1. Have the students design a traffic course using cones to designate roads, if appropriate lines are not on the playground.
2. Several students will ride their bikes around the course at the same time. They must all obey traffic safety rules that have been established and obey the signs on the course.
3. Give traffic assignments to other members of the class. Some can direct traffic, others can regulate the stop lights, and some can operate emergency vehicles.
4. Critique bicyclists when they finish their turns.

Variations:

1. Have the students walk rather than ride a bicycle. You can have the students simulate different vehicles by having them paint the outside of boxes to represent trucks, cars, etc.
2. Set up smaller traffic courses in the gymnasium to teach safety principles.

UNIT 12

WATER, WATER, EVERYWHERE, BUT NOT A DROP TO DRINK

Activities about Environmental Health

The Environment is a topic of concern to everyone. Drastic alterations in our environment are causing problems that are becoming more alarming each year. Students of all ages must be taught to respect the environment and to work toward alleviating problems that have been brought about by modern technology and misuse of natural resources.

The activities in this chapter are designed to assist the teacher in making environmental issues meaningful to the students. Activities and games will do more than make students aware of problems. This teaching method has the potential to develop a deeper understanding of the underlying factors that impact on our quality of life. Even more importantly, the students are able to grasp the consequences of their involvement in activities that have negative environmental repercussions.

The activities in this chapter are structured to encourage progressive attitudes towards taking the necessary steps to attack varied forms of pollution. Involving students at all grade levels in environmental issues creates a much better chance of a world citizenry that will strive to clean up the environment.

Activity 1. The Sight of Blight (Environmental Blight)

Concept/Description: Environmental blight is present in different degrees in every community.

Objective: Students will recognize different kinds of blight.

Materials: Newspapers and magazines

Directions:

1. With your students, go over characteristics that make an area blighted.
2. Have class members search newspapers and magazines for illustrations that depict examples of blight.
3. Divide the class into groups, and have each group use its illustrations to make a bulletin board display showing blighted areas.
4. Have each group compare the similarities and differences of the blighted areas.

Variations:

1. Take the students to a blighted area, and have them make drawings of the environmental blight that they observe.

2. Have students take pictures of environmental problems that they see in their community. Share with class members. (For older students.)

Examples of Blight Characteristics:

- Houses in need of repair
- Dirty streets
- Garbage in evidence near homes and in empty lots
- Decaying debris
- Lots overgrown with vegetation
- Piles of old tires
- Abandoned cars
- Scarcity of recreational areas
- Excessive traffic
- Unpleasant odors
- Disturbing levels of noise

Activity 2. Save Our Nest! (Ecology Principles)

Concept/Description: Mutual relationships of organisms with each other and with the environment form the basis for ecological balance.

Objective: The students will understand the interrelationship of animals and plants.

Materials:
Materials to construct a model.

Directions:

1. Have students research examples of how humans have destroyed the ecological balance. (For younger children, teachers can provide examples: destroying habitats of various animals; importing animals that do not have predators; killing natural predators (like wolves); killing birds through use of pesticides; and deforestation.
2. Have the class design an ecology model which visually shows the effect that disruption of the ecological balance can have on a person or a community. Examples:
   (a) Painting or making clay models of before-and-after scenes showing the effects of deforestation: soil being washed away; animals dying because of lack of food; and people losing the opportunity to use hiking as a recreational activity.
   (b) Diorama showing the effects of use of pesticides on birds.

Activity 3. Clean-Up Time (Beautify Your Community)

Concept/Description: It is possible for even a few people to have a positive effect on the environment.

Objective: Students will clean up an unsightly area in the community.

Materials:

Sacks to pick up debris
Use of a community truck or waste disposal bin

Directions:

1. Make arrangements with the appropriate person or organization in your community to involve your class in a clean-up day. (Mayor, Environmental Commission, Council member, etc.)
2. Have your students clean up a specific area. This could be a stretch of a roadside or another area that needs to be cleaned up.
3. Have some students keep a record of the types and numbers of each item that were found. (Use categories such as bottles, cans, etc.)
4. Take a picture of all the debris that was collected.
5. Take a picture of the area before and after clean-up.
6. Get maximum amount of publicity from the community media and in the school publications.
7. Have the students write a booklet summarizing their clean-up activity. Distribute to school officials, parents, and selected community officials.

Activity 4. What Am I Drinking? (Combatting Water Pollution)

Concept/Description: Water pollution is an environmental problem that affects everyone on a daily basis.

Objective: Students will understand that much of our water supply is polluted and will be aware of steps that can be taken to alleviate the problem.

Materials:

(None)

Directions:

1. Visit the water treatment plant in your community.
2. Obtain information which shows the harmful substances that are in the water before treatment.

3. Review the process that purifies the water.
4. Have the students write a summary explaining why harmful substances are present in the water. Explain why it was possible for the first settlers to drink water directly from rivers and streams.
5. Investigate what cities, states, and countries are doing to reduce water pollution.
6. Have the class design a model plan that could be followed worldwide to lessen water pollution.

Variation:

A person from the water treatment plant could come to your class, provide information about water treatment, and serve as a resource person.

Activity 5. I Wanna Swim (Testing Pool Water)

Concept/Description: Water purity cannot be determined by visual scanning and must be treated using chemicals.

Objective: Students will understand that differences in water quality cannot be determined by looking at the water.

Materials:

Swimming pool testing kit
Samples of swimming pool water

Directions:

1. Invite someone who is experienced in testing swimming pools to come to your class and demonstrate testing procedures.
2. Have members of the class look at different swimming pool samples and write down any differences they can observe.
3. Have guest demonstrate testing procedures and explain how differences in water quality cannot be observed with the naked eye.

Variation:

Have students bring to the class samples of water from different sources (lakes, streams, run-off after a rain, etc.) Send several samples to a bacteriology laboratory for testing. Compare quality of the various samples when the reports are returned. Make a chart of the different kinds of bacteria that were present, and determine what constitutes a dangerous level of each.

Activity 6. Let Me Breathe (Anti-Air Pollution Techniques)

Concept/Description: It is possible to reduce air pollution.

Objective: To familiarize pupils with techniques and procedures that will reduce air pollution.

Materials:

Tic-Tac-Toe Sheets (See 12-1)

Directions:

1. Each student will make Tic-Tac-Toe cards and write, on the cards, different anti-pollution techniques or procedures. (The number of cards can depend on the age and background of the students. A minimum of five cards are needed to play.)
2. Students will pair up.
3. One student will make an "X" at the bottom of his/her cards, and the other student will place an "O."
4. The winner will be the first student to get Tic-Tac-Toe.

Anti-Air Pollution Techniques:

- Emission control standards
- Planting of trees
- Smoking cessation program
- Smoke-free buildings
- E.P.A. action shutting down polluters
- Clean air legislation
- Concerned citizens group
- Construction of "cleaner" factories
- Walking instead of driving

Variations:

1. Have the Tic-Tac-Toe board filled in with anti-pollution procedures.
   (a) Have nine cards that correspond with the anti-pollution procedures listed on the board.
   (b) Mix the cards, and lay them face down.
   (c) Players alternate drawing the cards and placing an "X" or "O," in pencil, on the corresponding name of the board.
   (d) The winner is the first player to get Tic-Tac-Toe.

Name ______________________________ Date ________________ (12-1)

Tic-Tac-Toe

Your playing board:

Blank cards (fill them in as your teacher directs):

2. Write anti-pollution procedures in the spaces on a game board or ditto sheet with an even number of spaces.
   (a) Give a point value to each anti-pollution procedure on the board.
   (b) Write, on cards, anti-pollution procedures that correspond to the procedures listed on the board.
   (c) Have students alternate drawing cards and placing them on the corresponding space on the board.
   (d) Have students keep a tally of the point value of each space they cover.
   (e) The winner will be the person who ends up with the most points.

Activity 7. Clean-Up Your Act! (Solid-Waste Disposal)

Concept/Description: Solid-waste disposal is a major problem throughout the world.

Objective: Students will understand the different techniques that are being used to dispose of solid waste.

Materials:
Depends on students' activity designs.

Directions:
1. Divide the class into two groups, and have them design an activity that will compare different methods of disposing of solid wastes.
2. Have them compare land fills, incineration, ocean-dumping, recycling, and underground disposal.
3. Have a debate on which method is safest, best, most cost-effective, etc.

Activity 8. What a Mess! (Types of Solid Waste)

Concept/Description: There are many different types of solid waste that contribute to waste disposal problems.

Objective: Students will be able to list several examples of generating sources of different types of solid waste.

Materials:
Pencil and paper for each team

Directions:

1. Divide the class into teams of 4 or 5.
2. The teacher will give each team an example of a type of solid waste and allow the teams a designated amount of time to write down as many examples of that type of waste as they know.
3. The winning team will be determined by the total number of examples that they have.

Examples of Solid-Waste Categories:

1. Municipal waste
2. Food processing industry
3. Commercial waste
4. Residential waste
5. Recreational waste
6. Agricultural waste
7. Paper and plastic waste
8. Packaging materials
9. Hospital waste
10. Industrial waste
11. Chemical waste

Variation:

Assign one type of solid waste each class period, and let the students find examples to bring to the next class.

Activity 9. Give Me Clean Air, Land, and Water (Environmental Pollution)

Concept/Description: There are many types of pollution that affect every person.

Objective: Students will become aware of the different kinds of pollution that impact on them each day.

Materials:

One die for each group.
Pollution board for each group (See 12-2)
Marker for each student (cardboard tabs, coins, leggo pieces, etc.)

Directions:

1. Divide the class into groups of 3 to 6.
2. Players alternate throwing die and moving designated number of spaces.
3. Students follow directions indicated in the space on which they land.

(Continued on p. 292)

Pollution Game Board

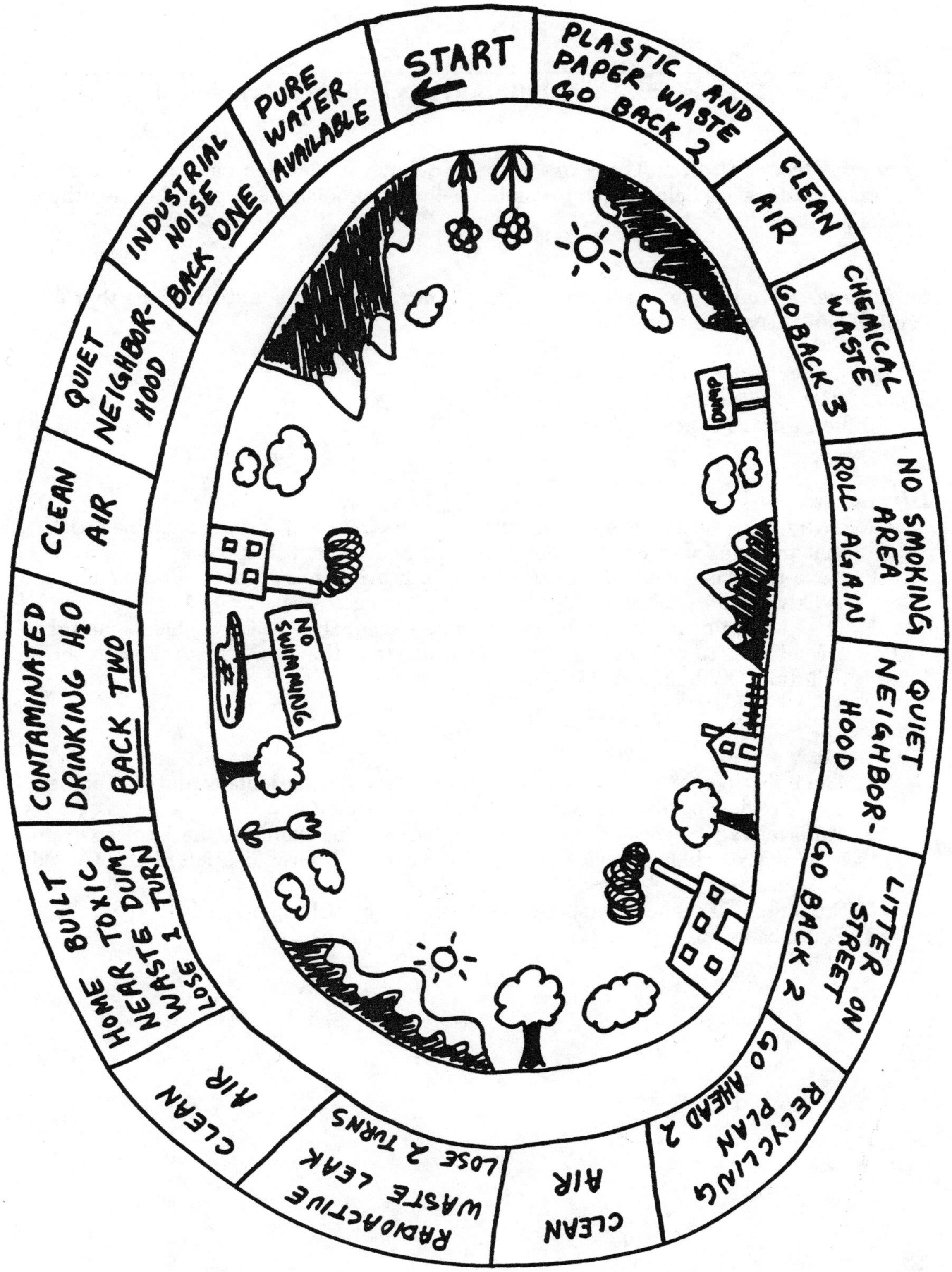

4. Winner is the person who has gone the farthest distance after a predetermined number of rounds or during designated time. (Each player records the number of times he or she passes *start*.)

Activity 10. Let's Work This Out! (Solving Pollution Problems)

Concept/Description: There are many air, land, and water pollution problems. Fortunately, steps are being taken to combat pollution problems and provide a healthier environment.

Objective: Students will become aware of current problems and the steps that are being taken to overcome environmental difficulties.

Materials:

Bulletin board space.

Directions:

1. On a weekly basis, have students bring to class newspaper and magazine articles that provide information about land, air, and water pollution.
2. Have the class members make a bulletin board display which will be changed weekly. (Different groups can be responsible each week.)
3. The bulletin board should have two parts—one part to cover problems, and the second part to provide information about steps that are being taken to solve pollution problems.

Variations:

1. The bulletin board can cover local issues one week, national examples another, and a review of international pollution issues another.
2. Material can be requested from other sources, for example, the local environmental protection agencies and the World Health Organization of the United Nations.
3. Students can make a puppet show covering the pollution issues.
4. Skits, based on collected materials, can be presented.

UNIT 13

PERSONALLY, I'M GOING TO BE AN OTORHINOLARYNGOLOGIST

Activities Teaching about Health-Related Careers

One of the fastest growing employment areas is the medical health field. New jobs are being created daily as technological advances are made and the scope of the health care industry increases. Students are aware of physicians, dentists, and nurses, but these three careers form only a small percentage of all the careers related to health. This unit has activities that will help students to become aware of the wide variety of careers available in the health field.

Students need to know that there are careers in health to suit differing individual interests, talents, and skills. Satisfaction can also be obtained, regardless of age, through volunteer work, which is plentiful throughout the health industry. A goal of this chapter is to interest students in helping others through a health career or by volunteering to use personal skills to support a health service.

Students will become aware of all the people whose work forms the support network required by health professions. These spin-off careers should also be considered by students.

Activity 1. It's a Match (Matching Career Descriptions to Career Names)

Concept/Description: There are specific job responsibilities for health careers.

Objective: Students will be able to recognize the work involved in selected health professions.

Materials:

Health Career List (See p. 296)
3 × 5 Cards
Answer sheets numbered 1–10

Directions:

1. Divide the class into teams of five to seven.
2. Provide each team with the names of ten health careers numbered from one to ten.
3. Each team takes ten 3 × 5 cards that are numbered to correspond with the names of the ten health careers that were given to them. Team members then write a brief description, on each card, of the responsibilities of a person in the career that is designated by the number on the card. (For example, for a physical therapist, a student might write, "Someone who uses exercises in treating or

rehabilitating an injured person." The sophistication of the descriptions will vary with the age of the students using this activity. It may be appropriate to let students use encyclopedias or other resources to get their definitions.

4. Each team will take the cards of another team and write on its team's answer sheet the health career names that it thinks are being described on each card.
5. If time permits, teams can follow the same procedure with another team or team's descriptions and keep a cumulative score.
6. The winning team is the team with the most correct answers at the end of the game.

Health Careers:

Acupuncturist
Alcohol counselor
Allergist
Anesthetist
Audiologist
Biomedical engineer
Candy striper
Cardiologist
Chiropractor
Clinical lab technician
Coroner
Cytological technician
Data processing—health
Dental assistant
Dental hygienist
Dental lab technician
Dentist
Dermatologist
Dietician
Drug control officer
Endodontist
Food and drug inspector
Food and drug protection
Food technologist
Gastro-enterologist
Gynecologist
Health care inspector
Health communication/information
Hematologist
Hospital administrator
Industrial hygienist
Inhalation therapist
Internal physician (internist)
Laryngologist
Medical assistant
Medical record librarian
Medical social worker
Medical technologist
Midwife
Mortician
Naturopathic consultant
Neurological surgeon
Nurse, licensed practical
Nurse, registered
Nurse's aide
Nutritionist
Occupational therapist
Ophthalmologist
Optician
Optometrist
Oral surgeon
Orderlies
Orthodontist
Orthopedic surgeon
Orthotist
Otologist
Pediatrician
Pedodontist
Periodontist
Pharmacist
Physical therapist
Physician
Plastic surgeon
Podiatrist
Prosthetist
Prosthodontist
Psychiatric social worker
Psychiatrist
Psychologist
Psychometrist
Public health administrator
Public health dentist
Public health educator
Pulmonologist
Quality control coordinator
Radioisotope technician
Radiologist
Rhinologist
Sanitation technician
Speech pathologist
Surgeon (general)
Thoracic surgeon
Urologist
Venereal disease control officer
Veterinarian
Vocational rehabilitationist
X-ray technician

Variation:

1. Have the student draw pictures depicting careers and match pictures with the appropriate description.

Activity 2. That Seems Fair! (Health Career Information Fair)

Concept/Description: There are many different health career choices.

Objective: Students will know several different health career possibilities.

Materials:

Display tables

Directions:

1. Set aside an evening to have a Health Fair at your school.
2. Invite organizations from varied health fields to bring materials to display.
3. Ask the exhibitors to develop their displays around the theme of careers in health.
4. Have the pupils invite their parents to attend the Health Fair with them.
5. Class project to follow the fair:
   Hand out a list of all the exhibitors at the Health Fair. Have the students write down all the careers they can think of in each organization. (Students should be encouraged to take notes at the Health Fair.)

Activity 3. Act On It! (Acting Out the Role of Health Professionals)

Concept/Description: A career can be understood better if one knows what is required to be successful in that career.

Objective: Students will learn about a health career in depth in order to demonstrate the work that is required.

Materials:

(Items selected by students to include in their skit).

Directions:

1. Divide the students into groups of three or four.
2. Each group will select a health career to demonstrate to the rest of the class.
3. Set up a stage in your classroom or use the school auditorium if it is available.
4. Have each group present a skit which demonstrates a health career. Encourage the students to use props to support their acting.

Variations:

1. Present the skits to another class.
2. Videotape the performance so that the students can see themselves performing.

Activity 4. Now I Get It! (Peer-Teaching)

Concept/Description: Teaching others is one of the best ways to learn.

Objective: Students will incorporate what they have learned about health careers in a class project.

Materials:

(Determined by the project selected by the students.)

Directions:

1. Have your class design a project that they could present to younger children to help them understand the many different health careers that are possible. (This would be done only after your students have neared the completion of their unit on health careers.)
2. Let the students use their ingenuity to come up with innovative ways that they can describe different health careers to younger children.
3. Schedule a time for your class to make their presentation to another class or classes.

Activity 5. My Mom, The Dentist (Parents with Careers in a Health Field)

Concept/Description: Some parents of children in a typical classroom will have a health career.

Objective: To find out how many parents have careers in health or have careers that relate to a health profession.

Parent's Name ______Mrs. Smith______

Occupation or Profession ______Library Aide______

Is it a Health Career? Yes _____ No __X__ If yes, explain.

____

____

____

If not a career in a health field, give examples of how this career might relate to people who are in health careers.

I can provide statistical information for our township's health department.

____

Fig. 13-1. Sample parent survey.

Materials:
Survey for each parent

Directions:
1. Have students survey each parent or guardian (see sample survey above).
2. Make a diagram in class showing how many health careers are represented by parents or guardians.
3. Discuss ways that non-health careers included in the survey relate to health professions.

Activity 6. A Community Affair (Surveying Health Careers)

Concept/Description: Communities have many health careers represented.

Objective: Students will realize that their community has people from a wide variety of health fields.

Materials:
Telephone directories

Directions:
1. Have pupils survey the community telephone directory and list all the businesses, professions, and organizations that they think would include careers in

health. Tally the number of health-related businesses in your community, the number of health-related professions, and the number of health organizations.

2. Have the students form teams of three or four.
3. Distribute the names of businesses, professions, and organizations among the teams. Select only one of each type of business, profession, or organization. (The number given to each team will depend on the age of the students and the time that is available.)
4. Have all team members write down all the health careers that they think would be available in each business, profession, and organization on their list.
5. Make transparencies showing the many different health careers in your community.

Variations:

1. Make a bulletin board display of health careers available in your community.
2. Write a booklet showing the types of careers that are found in different businesses, professions, and organizations.
3. Search for pictures or draw pictures of people working in the different health fields.

Activity 7. To Whom It May Concern (Writing For Information)

Concept/Description: Information about health careers is available from many organizations.

Objective: Students will learn how to write and obtain information about different health careers.

Materials:

Addresses of health organizations (given below)

Directions:

1. Supply the students with a list of health organizations. (See pp. 301-302)
2. Have each student write to one or two organizations requesting information and asking about the different health careers that are available.
3. Have the students share the answers they receive with all members of the class.

Variation:

Make up a chart with the information that is received.

Health Organizations

American Academy of Orthopedic Surgeons
222 S. Prospect Ave., Park Ridge, IL 60068

American Association of Medical Assistants
20 N. Wacker Dr., Suite 1575, Chicago, IL 60606

American Association of Pathologists and Bacteriologists
9650 Rockville Pike, Bethesda, MD 20814

American College of Sports Medicine
P.O. Box 1440, Indianapolis, IN 46206

American Dental Association
211 E. Chicago Ave., Chicago, IL 60611

American Dietetic Association
216 W. Jackson Blvd., Suite 800, Chicago, IL 60606

American Hospital Association
840 N. Lake Shore Drive, Chicago, IL 60611

American Medical Association
535 N. Dearborn Street, Chicago, IL 60610

American Medical Record Association
John Hancock Center, Suite 1850,
875 N. Michigan Ave., Chicago, IL 60611

American Nurses Association
2420 Pershing Road, Kansas City, MO 64108

American Nursing Home Association
1201 L. St., N.W., Washington, D.C. 20005

American Occupational Therapy Association
1383 Piccard Dr., Suite 301, Rockville, MD 20850

American Optometric Association
243 N. Lindberg Blvd., St. Louis, MO 63141

American Orthotics and Prosthetics Association
717 Pendleton St., Alexandria, VA 22314

American Pharmaceutical Association
2215 Consitution Ave., N.W., Washington, D.C. 20037

American Physical Therapy Association
1111 N. Fairfax St., Alexandria, VA 22314

American Society for Hospital Pharmacists
4630 Montgomery Ave., Bethesda, MD 20814

American Society of Radiological Technologists
1500 Central Ave., S.E., Albuquerque, NM 87123

Environmental Management Association
1019 Highland Ave., Largo, FL 34640

Food and Drug Administration
Parklawn Building, 5600 Fishers Lane, Rockville, MD 20850

Hospital Financial Management Association
2 Westbrook Corporate Ctr., Suite 700, Westchester, IL 60154

National Association for Practical Nurse Education & Service
1400 Spring St., Suite 310, Silver Spring, MD 20910

National Institute of Health
900 Rockville Pike, Bethesda, MD 20892

National Institute of Mental Health
Parklawn Building, 5600 Fishers Lane, Rockville, MD 20850

National League for Nursing
10 Columbus Circle, New York, NY 10019

National Recreation and Parks Association
3101 Park Center Dr., 12th Floor, Alexandria, VA 22302

Activity 8. When I Grow Up (Health Career Possibilities)

Concept/Description: Students can find out about health careers by attending a health fair.

Objective: Students will be exposed to many different health careers.

Materials:
(None)

Directions:
1. Make arrangements for your class to attend a health fair sponsored by a local university, hospital, or civic organization.
2. Have all students select one exhibitor each to "interview" and from whom to obtain career information to share with the class when they return.

Variation:
Collect information to display on classroom bulletin boards.

Activity 9. I Have the Pleasure of Introducing . . . (Guest Speakers)

Concept/Description: Guest speakers can serve as excellent resources to obtain information about health careers.

Objective: Students will get firsthand information about several health careers.

Materials:
(None)

Directions:

1. Set up a series of guest speakers on health careers.
2. Ask children's parents who are health professionals or in a health-related occupation to be among the guest speakers. (Use the parental survey—Activity 5—to obtain needed information.)
3. Give students responsibility for welcoming and introducing the guest speakers and writing thank-you notes.
4. Provide time for asking questions.

Variation:

Have the students write a newspaper covering the information they received from each guest speaker. Students can be assigned to write about the different speakers. The newspaper can be expanded to cover additional health careers.

Activity 10. Let Me Help You (Volunteer Opportunities)

Concept/Description: Working in a health organization is a valuable learning experience.

Objective: Students will have an opportunity to do volunteer work with a health professional.

Materials:
(None)

Directions:

1. Arrange for students to spend a half day or a full day as a volunteer with a health organization or a health professional. (School board approval will be needed.)
2. It might work best if two or three students go together (depends on age).
3. Have students make up a list of places where they would like to be a volunteer. (Don't forget to use parents as resources for this project.)

4. Match students with available locations. Possibilities include hospitals, dietician offices, dental offices, American Heart Association office, medical record offices, nursing homes, rehabilitation centers, and city health offices.
5. When the students return to class, have them write a description of the type of work that is involved at the location where they served as a volunteer.
6. Have the students share their experiences with other members of the class.

Activity 11. It's a Two-Way Street (Cooperation Among Health Professionals)

Concept/Description: Optimum health care is dependent on the cooperation of different health providers.

Objective: Students will find out how quality of medical care received by an injured person is dependent on the cooperation of ambulance squad, hospital, and physician.

Materials:

Paper
Marking pens or other writing utensils

Directions:

1. Invite a local ambulance squad to bring an ambulance to your school.
2. Have your students write questions that they can ask about the work of the ambulance squad.
3. Have the squad members demonstrate the equipment they use.
4. Ask the squad members to explain how their responsibilities are related to the functioning of hospitals and physicians when they receive an emergency call.
5. As a class assignment, have the students present, through drawings or diagrams, the cooperation that is required between emergency health vehicles and other providers of care to an injured person.

Variation:

Have the students develop a project which shows the value of good communications in providing emergency health care. (Example: A skit showing a person calling an ambulance; the ambulance squad picking up a person with a heart attack; the communications that take place between the ambulance, the hospital, and the physician while the heart attack victim is being transported to the hospital.)

Activity 12. People Who Need People (Health-Care Support Staff)

Concept/Description: Many careers are generated by health professions and occupations.

Objective: Students will be aware of the people who are needed to support suppliers of health care.

Materials:

A large sheet of paper for each student
Pencils, crayons, marking pens, or paints and brushes.

Directions:

1. Put the title of a health-career position (neurologist, medical technologist, FDA inspector, etc.) on a 3 × 5 card. Have one card for each student in the class.
2. Have each student select a card.
3. The students will write the health title that is on their card at the top of a large sheet of paper. They then have the task of drawing pictures of people who are involved in a health-related career because they provide support for the health profession or occupation that appeared on the card they selected.
4. The students complete their project by explaining to their class what each drawing represents. They should also explain how the people in the drawing contribute to the health profession that is represented. For example, an FDA inspector sheet may have drawings representing a store manager, refrigeration expert, lab researcher, publisher, law maker, and farmer.

Variation:

Make a list of all the people whose careers support another health profession or occupation.